The Desert Flowers – Willow

Judith Keim

BOOKS BY JUDITH KEIM

THE HARTWELL WOMEN SERIES:

The Talking Tree – 1
Sweet Talk – 2
Straight Talk – 3
Baby Talk – 4
The Hartwell Women – Boxed Set

THE BEACH HOUSE HOTEL SERIES:

Breakfast at The Beach House Hotel – 1
Lunch at The Beach House Hotel – 2
Dinner at The Beach House Hotel – 3
Christmas at The Beach House Hotel – 4
Margaritas at The Beach House Hotel – 5
Dessert at The Beach House Hotel – 6
Coffee at The Beach House Hotel – 7
High Tea at The Beach House Hotel – 8 (2024)

THE FAT FRIDAYS GROUP:

Fat Fridays – 1
Sassy Saturdays – 2
Secret Sundays – 3

THE SALTY KEY INN SERIES:

Finding Me – 1
Finding My Way – 2
Finding Love – 3
Finding Family – 4
The Salty Key Inn Series . Boxed Set

THE CHANDLER HILL INN SERIES:

Going Home – 1
Coming Home – 2
Home at Last – 3
The Chandler Hill Inn Series – Boxed Set

SEASHELL COTTAGE BOOKS:

A Christmas Star
Change of Heart
A Summer of Surprises
A Road Trip to Remember
The Beach Babes

THE DESERT SAGE INN SERIES:

The Desert Flowers – Rose – 1
The Desert Flowers – Lily – 2
The Desert Flowers – Willow – 3
The Desert Flowers – Mistletoe and Holly – 4

SOUL SISTERS AT CEDAR MOUNTAIN LODGE:

Christmas Sisters – Anthology
Christmas Kisses
Christmas Castles
Christmas Stories – Soul Sisters Anthology
Christmas Joy

THE SANDERLING COVE INN SERIES:

Waves of Hope – 1
Sandy Wishes – 2
Salty Kisses – 3

THE LILAC LAKE INN SERIES

Love by Design – 1
Love Between the Lines – 2 (2024)
Love Under the Stars – 3 (2024)

OTHER BOOKS:

The ABC's of Living With a Dachshund
Once Upon a Friendship – Anthology
Winning BIG – a little love story for all ages
Holiday Hopes
The Winning Tickets (2023)

PRAISE FOR JUDITH KEIM'S NOVELS

THE BEACH HOUSE HOTEL SERIES

"Love the characters in this series. This series was my first introduction to Judith Keim. She is now one of my favorites. Looking forward to reading more of her books."

BREAKFAST AT THE BEACH HOUSE HOTEL is an easy, delightful read that offers romance, family relationships, and strong women learning to be stronger. Real life situations filter through the pages. Enjoy!"

LUNCH AT THE BEACH HOUSE HOTEL – "This series is such a joy to read. You feel you are actually living with them. Can't wait to read the latest one."

DINNER AT THE BEACH HOUSE HOTEL – "A Terrific Read! As usual, Judith Keim did it again. Enjoyed immensely. Continue writing such pleasantly reading books for all of us readers."

CHRISTMAS AT THE BEACH HOUSE HOTEL – "Not Just Another Christmas Novel. This is book number four in the series and my introduction to Judith Keim's writing. I wasn't disappointed. The characters are dimensional and engaging. The plot is well crafted and advances at a pleasing pace. The Florida location is interesting and warming. It was a delight to read a romance novel with mature female protagonists. Ann and Rhoda have life experiences that enrich the story. It's a clever book about friends and extended family. Buy copies for your book group pals and enjoy this seasonal read."

MARGARITAS AT THE BEACH HOUSE HOTEL – "What a wonderful series. I absolutely loved this book and can't wait for the next book to come out. There was even suspense in it. Thanks Judith for the great stories."

"Overall, Margaritas at the Beach House Hotel is another wonderful addition to the series. Judith Keim takes the reader on a journey told through the voices of these amazing characters we have all come to love through the years! I truly cannot stress enough how good this book is, and I hope you enjoy it as much as I have!"

THE HARTWELL WOMEN SERIES:

"This was an EXCELLENT series. When I discovered Judith Keim, I read all of her books back to back. I thoroughly enjoyed the women Keim has written about. They are believable and you want to just jump into their lives and be their friends! I can't wait for any upcoming books!"

"I fell into Judith Keim's Hartwell Women series and have read & enjoyed all of her books in every series. Each centers around a strong & interesting woman character and their family interaction. Good reads that leave you wanting more."

THE FAT FRIDAYS GROUP :

"Excellent story line for each character, and an insightful representation of situations which deal with some of the contemporary issues women are faced with today."

"I love this author's books. Her characters and their lives are realistic. The power of women's friendships is a common and beautiful theme that is threaded throughout this story."

THE SALTY KEY INN SERIES

FINDING ME – *"I thoroughly enjoyed the first book in this series and cannot wait for the others! The characters are endearing with the same struggles we all encounter. The setting makes me feel like I am a guest at The Salty Key Inn...relaxed, happy & light-hearted! The men are yummy and the women strong. You can't get better than that!*

FINDING MY WAY- "Loved the family dynamics as well as uncertain emotions of dating and falling in love. Appreciated the morals and strength of parenting throughout. Just couldn't put this book down."

FINDING LOVE – "I waited for this book because the first two was such good reads. This one didn't disappoint.... Judith Keim always puts substance into her books. This book was no different, I learned about PTSD, accepting oneself, there is always going to be problems but stick it out and make it work. Just the way life is. In some ways a lot like my life. Judith is right, it needs another book and I will definitely be reading it. Hope you choose to read this series, you will get so much out of it."

FINDING FAMILY – "Completing this series is like eating the last chip. Love Judith's writing, and her female characters are always smart, strong, vulnerable to life and love experiences."

"This was a refreshing book. Bringing the heart and soul of the family to us."

THE CHANDLER HILL INN SERIES

GOING HOME – "I absolutely could not put this book down. Started at night and read late into the middle of the night. As a child of the '60s, the Vietnam war was front and center so this resonated with me. All the characters in the book were so well developed that the reader felt like they were friends of the family."

"I was completely immersed in this book, with the beautiful descriptive writing, and the authors' way of bringing her characters to life. I felt like I was right inside her story."

COMING HOME – "Coming Home is a winner. The

characters are well-developed, nuanced and likable. Enjoyed the vineyard setting, learning about wine growing and seeing the challenges Cami faces in running and growing a business. I look forward to the next book in this series!"

"Coming Home was such a wonderful story. The author has a gift for getting the reader right to the heart of things."

HOME AT LAST – *"In this wonderful conclusion, to a heartfelt and emotional trilogy set in Oregon's stunning wine country, Judith Keim has tied up the Chandler Hill series with the perfect bow."*

"Overall, this is truly a wonderful addition to the Chandler Hill Inn series. Judith Keim definitely knows how to perfectly weave together a beautiful and heartfelt story."

"The storyline has some beautiful scenes along with family drama. Judith Keim has created characters with interactions that are believable and some of the subjects the story deals with are poignant."

SEASHELL COTTAGE BOOKS

A CHRISTMAS STAR – *"Love, laughter, sadness, great food, and hope for the future, all in one book. It doesn't get any better than this stunning read."*

"A Christmas Star is a heartwarming Christmas story featuring endearing characters. So many Christmas books are set in snowbound places...it was a nice change to read a Christmas story that takes place on a warm sandy beach!" Susan Peterson

CHANGE OF HEART – *"CHANGE OF HEART is the summer read we've all been waiting for. Judith Keim is a master at creating fascinating characters that are simply irresistible. Her stories leave you with a big smile on your*

face and a heart bursting with love."

Kellie Coates Gilbert, author of the popular Sun Valley Series

A SUMMER OF SURPRISES – *"The story is filled with a roller coaster of emotions and self-discovery. Finding love again and rebuilding family relationships."*

"Ms. Keim uses this book as an amazing platform to show that with hard emotional work, belief in yourself and love, the scars of abuse can be conquered. It in no way preaches, it's a lovely story with a happy ending."

"The character development was excellent. I felt I knew these people my whole life. The story development was very well thought out I was drawn [in] from the beginning."

THE DESERT SAGE INN SERIES:

THE DESERT FLOWERS – ROSE – *"The Desert Flowers - Rose, is the first book in the new series by Judith Keim. I always look forward to new books by Judith Keim, and this one is definitely a wonderful way to begin The Desert Sage Inn Series!"*

"In this first of a series, we see each woman come into her own and view new beginnings even as they must take this tearful journey as they slowly lose a dear friend. This is a very well written book with well-developed and likable main characters. It was interesting and enlightening as the first portion of this saga unfolded. I very much enjoyed this book and I do recommend it"

"Judith Keim is one of those authors that you can always depend on to give you a great story with fantastic characters. I'm excited to know that she is writing a new series and after reading book 1 in the series, I can't wait to read the rest of the books."!

THE DESERT FLOWERS – LILY – *"The second book in*

the Desert Flowers series is just as wonderful as the first. Judith Keim is a brilliant storyteller. Her characters are truly lovely and people that you want to be friends with as soon as you start reading. Judith Keim is not afraid to weave real life conflict and loss into her stories. I loved reading Lily's story and can't wait for Willow's!

"The Desert Flowers-Lily is the second book in The Desert Sage Inn Series by author Judith Keim. When I read the first book in the series, The Desert Flowers-Rose, I knew this series would exceed all of my expectations and then some. Judith Keim is an amazing author, and this series is a testament to her writing skills and her ability to completely draw a reader into the world of her characters."

<u>THE DESERT FLOWERS – WILLOW –</u> *"The feelings of love, joy, happiness, friendship, family and the pain of loss are deeply felt by Willow Sanchez and her two cohorts Rose and Lily. The Desert Flowers met because of their deep feelings for Alec Thurston, a man who touched their lives in different ways.*

Once again, Judith Keim has written the story of a strong, competent, confident and independent woman. Willow, like Rose and Lily can handle tough situations. All the characters are written so that the reader gets to know them but not all the characters will give the reader warm and fuzzy feelings.

The story is well written and from the start you will be pulled in. There is enough backstory that a reader can start here but I assure you, you'll want to learn more. There is an ocean of emotions that will make you smile, cringe, tear up or outright cry. I loved this book as I loved books one and two. I am thrilled that the Desert Flowers story will continue. I highly recommend this book to anyone who enjoys books with strong women."

The Desert Flowers - Willow

The Desert Sage Inn Series
Book - 3

Judith Keim

Wild Quail Publishing

The Desert Flowers - Willow is a work of fiction. Names, characters, places, public or private institutions, corporations, towns, and incidents are the product of the author's imagination or are used fictitiously. Any resemblance to actual events, locales, or persons, living or dead, is coincidental.

wildquail.pub@gmail.com

www.judithkeim.com

Wild Quail Publishing
PO Box 171332
Boise, ID 83717-1332

ISBN 978-1-962452-23-6

Dedication

For my writer friends in my Wednesday morning coffee group:
Cate, Lynn, Mel, Nikki, and Peggy
Thanks for your support!

CHAPTER ONE

WILLOW

Willow Sanchez had a lot to think about as she grabbed a bottle of water and tiptoed outside in the quiet, early-morning hours on this late April day; her life had completely changed. She'd been happy to upend her teaching career in Boston and return home to help Alec Thurston, a man who was like a father to her and who was dying of cancer. He wanted her and two other women to oversee the sale of his hotel, the Desert Sage Inn, to The Blaise Hotel Group.

Alec called her, Rose Macklin, and Lily Weaver, his Desert Flowers, similar to Charley's Angels on an old television series. They'd each played a special part in his life and had talents that could help him preserve the image and reputation of his hotel with the transition to new ownership.

Restless, Willow breathed in the cool, clean air of the desert well aware the day would be a hot one. She decided to take advantage of the coolness and hike up to Alec's cabin, which was actually a casita in the foothills above the inn with no running water, just a bed, table and chairs, and a fantastic view to relieve anyone's stress.

As she walked along the path by the inn's golf course, she admired the desert flowers, various shrubs, and palm trees against the backdrop of the adjacent foothills that added dimension to the green carpet of the fairways and putting greens. She noticed a bird pecking at a branch of a cactus and heard the whirring of wings before a brightly colored hummingbird darted at her pink T-shirt, hovered, and then took off looking for something better.

"'Bye, little hummer," she said playfully, perked up as always by these tiny birds.

She loved the desert, hadn't realized how much she missed it at Boston University where she taught business accounting in the School of Hospitality Administration. She'd lived in Palm Desert since she was a child while her parents, Juanita and Pedro Sanchez, worked at the inn and then directly for Alec in his home. Alec was the person who'd taught her to love the hospitality business. As her mentor, he'd helped her get into the School of Hotel Administration at Cornell University. She'd always hoped eventually to work at the inn with him, but now, with his illness, that wasn't going to happen. But after returning to her hometown a few months ago, she'd decided to stay in Palm Desert and seek work at other hotels if she didn't get the job she wanted at the Desert Sage Inn.

Thinking of her uncertain status, Willow began climbing on a trail up the foothills at the edge of the inn's property. Maybe the clear view would help settle her thoughts. Work and living arrangements weren't her only concerns. Dan McMillan, the sexy guy in charge of the fitness program at the Inn, had asked her out again. He'd attracted her from the beginning when Alec had hired him to conduct a teambuilding program for the three women before they started their work for him. But now she sometimes felt as if Dan thought of her as a sister, someone to have fun with, more than a woman he wanted in a lasting relationship.

Before returning to the desert, she'd had her heart shattered. The man with whom she thought she had a future had introduced her to his parents, who'd rudely rejected her because of her immigrant parents and her working-class background. Unlike her ex, Dan wasn't prejudiced, but he didn't seem that serious about the future—with her or anyone else.

"Why would I set myself up for disappointment?" she asked a king snake she saw sunning itself on a rock about five feet off the trail.

The snake slithered into the rocks and brush away from the path, leaving behind an answer she knew was right. She'd go out with Dan, but she'd be careful about getting too close too fast. Still, she longed to find a man who was ready to commit to something long-term—someone who'd not only love her as she was but also understand her need to grow her career as an homage to Alec and to respect her independence.

Willow reached the casita and sat down on a bench outside it, grateful for the rest. She gulped a long swallow of water and slowly recovered her breath. The climb wasn't an easy one. But when she looked out at the scene below to the resort and then lifted her gaze to study the snowcapped mountains in the distance to the north and northwest, she was glad she'd made the effort. The textured, blue-gray mountains always gave her a sense of peace, often a sense of purpose. Willow sat for several minutes while she contemplated the view, enjoyed the fresh breeze and the warmth from the sun, and sorted her thoughts.

As she descended the trail, fresh resolve filled her.

She was competing with the two sons of the owners of the Blaise Group to become manager of the Desert Sage Inn. While Brent Armstrong was a spoiled brat, his cousin, Trace Armstrong, appeared to be the opposite—kind, thoughtful, and smart. Still, both were determined to take over the management of the inn after the sale went through. Willow knew she was as capable as they, but that her chances of getting the job were next to none because it was, after all, a family business. Still, she'd do her best to protect the inn's reputation as Alec wished. She knew more about running it, its history and cachet than they'd ever know.

She thought of the women who were her colleagues. They made an interesting trio. Rose was the eldest of the three at fifty-two, recently engaged to Hank Bowers with whom she'd been assigned to work, and was, more or less, the leader. Lily Weaver and Brian Walden, the head of the Blaise Group transition team, had quickly married following a personal crisis for each of them, including the unexpected care of two children. Lily recently announced she was pregnant, leaving Willow, at thirty-one, the only unattached woman of the group.

Maybe, thought Willow, that was the reason she was feeling so unsettled.

When Willow arrived back at Alec's house, she walked through it and out to the patio and pool in the back. Rose had just climbed out of the pool and was drying herself off with a towel. Tall and thin, with red hair and green eyes, she was a striking woman.

"Hey, girl! You're up early!" said Rose. "Where've you been?"

"I hiked up to Alec's cabin. I needed to get a fresh perspective on things before my meeting this morning with John Rodriguez, Trace, and Brent."

Rose immediately gave her a look of concern. "Is everything all right?"

Willow shrugged and sat down in one of the poolside chairs. "I just needed to think about the future. The closing of the sale of the inn is approaching, and I'm going to need to find another job here in the valley. I don't want to leave."

"You've done a fabulous job of heading the assistant team for the transition, I shouldn't think you'd have any trouble finding a good job in management." Rose came over to her and gave her a quick hug. "I'm happy to give you as many references as you want."

"Thanks. I'm not sure whether I'm going to rent or buy a place here, but that's something I'll think about after I get another job."

"Hank and I are still pondering living choices here. We're thinking of buying a house and then getting something smaller in Atlanta where his daughters live."

"You're still waiting to get married until after Alec leaves us?" Willow knew how Rose, like Lily, had thought at one time that Alec would marry her. But she and others in the valley had heard the story of how Alec's young wife, Willow's cousin Conchita, and unborn daughter had died in a house fire for which he blamed himself. He had, Rose confessed, told her he'd never marry again, that his conscience wouldn't allow him to do that. Twisted a bit, perhaps, but true, thought Willow.

"Yes, I wouldn't feel right about moving out while Alec is still alive. I've promised to stay with him until the end. You know?" Rose said, sitting in a chair next to her. "Poor Lily had no choice, but I'm content to wait." She winked at Willow. "That'll give you a chance to catch up."

Willow chuckled and shook her head. "It might be a long time. Dan has asked me out, but I'm not sure it's going anywhere."

They looked up as Lily joined them. "Good morning, you two! What's up?"

Lily was small and blond, almost waif-like until you knew the strength behind her.

"Nice to see you," said Rose to Lily. "Willow is thinking about her future, wondering where she's going to work, and ..." Rose paused for effect "... how her date with Dan will go."

Willow elbowed Rose playfully. “It’s much more than worry about a date. I’m concerned about where I’m going to work after our job for Alec is done.”

“But she’s staying here in Palm Desert,” said Rose. “I’m not going to let her leave.”

“Me either,” said Lily. “And, Willow, as far as dating, you don’t need to rush into anything. You’ll know when the right man comes along.”

Willow smiled her appreciation. “Thanks.”

“How’s Alec today? Anyone know?” Lily asked with a frown.

“I haven’t spoken to any of the new nurses yet.” Rose sighed. “After all this time of knowing what’s going to happen, I still can’t bear the thought of him dying.”

“It’s not time yet, is it? The nurses arrived to help Juanita, not because it’s the very end for him. Right?” Lily’s voice trembled with emotion.

“Yes,” said Willow. “When it’s time, Hospice will be brought in. My mother said he’s trying his best to hang on until the sale of the hotel goes through.”

“The three of us originally wanted to stay here for the duration of our job and as long as he lived. My situation has changed because of Brian and the kids, but as much as possible I want to be here for Alec,” said Lily.

“How are things going with Izzy and Ollie?” Willow asked. At three, Izzy, Lily’s niece and now her child, was adorable. And Ollie was a darling eight-year-old boy who’d unexpectedly entered Brian Walden’s life as the child Brian never knew he had. After the trauma of his mother introducing him to his father and then dying of cancer, Ollie was now settling in with them.

“Each day is better,” said Lily. “Ollie still has some bad days, but Izzy adores him, which helps them both.”

"You and Brian are very admirable," said Rose. "I love Hank's granddaughter, Leah, but I imagine it would be difficult to go from single and childless to married with children."

Lily let out a breath and shook her head. "I often wake up and wonder who I am. It all happened so quickly. But even though my sister's death was horrific, I'm in a good place. I have a man who loves me, the family I've always wanted, two wonderful friends, and a fulfilling career."

Willow and Rose squeezed her hands.

"The emotional abuse Jeremy put my sister through was awful," said Lily, unable to hide her pain. "I still wonder if I could've done something to get Monica away from him sooner and, perhaps, prevent her death. Maybe if ..."

Rose held up her hand. "Unh, unh. We're not going to let you go there. Right, Willow?"

"Right," she said firmly. "It's not worth the trip. Now, who wants coffee?"

They moved into the kitchen, and as on many mornings, continued their conversation over a cup of java.

Later, as Willow entered the hotel to attend her meeting, she took a moment to gaze around the lobby. The understated color scheme of desert-sand brown worked with pops of purple and turquoise accents, giving a sophisticated, pleasant feel to the area. The Desert Sage Inn was all about the quality of guests' surroundings and the excellent service they could expect. Like Alec himself, you knew what you were going to get—an honest representation of what he offered.

She waved to her friend Sarah Jensen, a part-time assistant manager. She was a pretty, vivacious, brown-haired young mother who'd returned to her parents' home with a two-year-old son while her husband was doing his last stint in the army in Korea. They often sipped cups of coffee at work together and on some evenings, went out for a glass of wine.

Willow laughed when Sarah gave her a thumbs-up signal. She and everyone else knew how difficult working with Brent Armstrong could be.

In the past Willow had wondered why Brent was the way he was. He came from a privileged background, had every opportunity handed to him, and yet was nasty, bossy, and ready to lash out at anyone who disagreed with him. After she met his father, Duncan, the younger of the two brothers who owned The Blaise Hotel Group, Willow understood. With a smaller share of the company than his brother, Duncan was aggressive, constantly trying to outdo Mitchell. He pushed Brent into thinking he was better than anyone else and that he, not Trace, should end up with a larger portion of the company. Unrealistic, but a continual squabble nevertheless. The fact that Brent bought into it didn't help.

Before going to John Rodriguez's office, Willow grabbed a cup of coffee from the guest hospitality coffee service in the corner of the lobby. She'd need all the caffeine she could get to keep on her toes with Brent around. He'd once copied her notes on a presentation she'd put together and tried to pass them off as his own.

When she got to the office, Brent and Trace were already there with John. "Good morning!" she said cheerfully and sat in the empty chair in front of John's desk.

"You're late," said Brent.

"Good morning," John said, giving her a smile. "We were just chatting about the weather and sales figures. Though we're not a big conference center, some of our business comes from small group sales, and when bad weather comes into play across the country, it definitely is a factor."

"I've been working on an idea about coordinating sales

from one Corona property to another through cross-promotions. I'm not quite ready to present it, but it could be a lot of fun for our guests," said Willow.

"Fun? Is it profitable for the Blaise hotels?" Brent said, scowling.

Willow rolled her eyes.

"I'm sure Willow has all three of the hotels in mind when she's talking about the Corona Collection," said John in measured tones.

Trace glanced at her and shook his head, apparently as tired of Brent as the rest of the staff at the hotel.

The meeting proceeded at a brisk pace. Willow was busy typing notes, starring a few of them for further investigation, when John stood.

"I have another meeting. We have only a few weeks before the transition of the hotel to the Corona Collection is to take place. I ask that each of you make a list of questions and suggestions you have about the timing that day so we can discuss them. A smooth transition is what we've all been working toward. Let's make it happen."

After he left the room, Brent said, "Wonder why he's so uptight?"

"Maybe because every time he spoke, you had to add something," Willow replied.

"Yeah, Brent, just cool it," said Trace. "It's annoying."

Brent stood and shrugged. "It's my job." He turned to Trace. "Want to grab a cup of coffee before we head to the links?"

Trace shook his head. "No, go ahead. I'll meet up with you later."

"Why?" Brent looked at Willow and then turned to Trace. "You're going to ask her? Don't bother. If she won't go out with me, she won't go out with you."

Willow watched Trace's cheeks color and felt sorry for him. "What did you want to ask me?"

Trace glanced at Brent and let out a sigh of irritation before facing her. "I'd like to take you to dinner tonight," he said quietly. "Are you free?"

Willow shook her head. "Not tonight, but I am tomorrow." She almost laughed at the look of surprise on Brent's face, and smiled sweetly at Trace. *How dare Brent make such a decision for her!*

Trace winked at her. "Okay, then, I'll be in touch. Thanks, Willow."

Brent was still frowning as the two of them left the room.

Willow left John's office to print off the notes she'd been working on, wondering if she'd done the right thing. Trace was nice, good-looking, and ambitious, but he was part of a situation that was unsettling. She'd already been treated badly by one set of wealthy parents; why would she put herself into another vulnerable position? But it was too late now. She wouldn't go back on her word.

In the meantime, she had a date with Dan.

CHAPTER TWO

WILLOW

That night, Willow tried to tell herself it was just another friendly date with Dan. But she spent extra time with her long black hair, brushing it until it shone. She'd learned that plain, classic clothes suited her best. The short khaki skirt and turquoise sleeveless blouse she'd chosen to wear showed off her trim body nicely. Her high-heeled tan sandals made her legs seem longer.

She went to the living room to wait for Dan. Sitting in Alec's house, she felt like a school girl waiting for a date to pick her up. She was used to living on her own. But she didn't mind staying here at Alec's house as part of the Flowers' plan to remain with him as long as they could. His time on earth was coming to an end, and she, like Lily and Rose, wanted to show her love and support for him in every way she could.

At the sound of the knock at the door, Willow rose to answer it. She opened it. Dressed in jeans and a black knit shirt, his brown hair groomed and with bright-blue eyes sparkling at her, Dan was definitely hot. His muscular body, the friendly smile that came easily to him, and his pleasant features were a magnet to every female hotel guest who used the fitness center. She'd seen how women at the center threw themselves at him. Dan said he played along only to be polite, that it was part of his job, but Willow wondered if he'd ever tire of it.

Dan stepped inside and gave her a kiss on the cheek. "Wow! You look great!"

A flush of pleasure went through her. “Thanks. So, do you.”

“Guess it’s going to be a good evening,” Dan replied with an inviting grin.

“It should be,” she said, unwilling to do anything foolish. Though she was attracted to him, she couldn’t afford to let anything interfere with her plans for eventually managing one of the hotels in the area.

Dan led her to his car, a low-slung, black convertible that suited him. He held the door for her, hurried around the car, and slid behind the wheel. “Hope you don’t mind that I have the top down.”

She shook her head. “Not a problem. It’s a lovely evening.”

“We’re going only as far as El Paseo for dinner. Thought it might be fun to eat outside. Hope you’re hungry for seafood.”

“Sounds delicious. Thank you.”

He turned to her with a smile. “I’m glad we have tonight to get to know one another better. A real date.”

She quirked an eyebrow. “Is that what this is? A real date?”

He grinned but kept his eyes on the road ahead. “I like you, Willow.”

“I like you, too,” she said, deciding to relax and enjoy the evening. They’d always gotten along.

Dan found a parking spot along the street, and they walked to the restaurant. The outdoor scene was alive with visitors and locals who liked the convenience of an assortment of restaurants mixed in with high-end shopping.

They were seated on the patio of a restaurant on the second floor of an outdoor mall and had a nice view over El Paseo of the mountains to the north and west.

“Good choice, huh?’ Dan said as the hostess walked away.

“Yes. We should be able to see the sunset from here, too.” She studied him. He was a good-looking man who enjoyed people and was well known in the area. She wondered how long it would be before someone he knew stopped at their table.

As if her thoughts had conjured her up, an older, blond woman approached. "Hi, Dan! Have you missed me? I was away for a couple of weeks at a friend's wedding, but I couldn't wait to see you again at the Desert Sage Inn. It's nice that locals have the chance to sign up for classes there."

Dan stood. "Hello, Marjorie. Of course, I missed you. When are you coming to the spin class again?"

"Don't worry. I'll be there this week." She patted her almost-concave stomach. "Can't put on any pounds, you know." Willow told herself not to roll her eyes. The woman was skin and bones.

"Okay, see you then." Dan lowered himself into his chair as the woman blew him a kiss and then walked away.

"Sorry. One of my admirers," he said, shaking his head. "I promised Alec I'd always be a gentleman, but sometimes it's difficult. All part of the promo for the hotel."

"I imagine it gets tiresome," she said, commiserating with him. "How long has this been going on?"

"I've been at the inn for close to four years. During that time, a lot of people have come and gone. Me? I love it here. In the summer when it's hot, I take my vacation and head to a cooler spot such as the Sawtooth Mountains in central Idaho for a while, but the rest of the year, it's great. With my job, I get to play golf at the hotel and have the chance to meet some interesting people."

"Like the Armstrongs?" Willow said, unable to resist offering the bait for a lively discussion.

Dan laughed. "Some of us at the hotel have a bet going as to when you're going to blow your stack at Brent. So far, I'm winning, but I'm worried about how long you can put up with him."

Willow laughed. "We'll see."

The waitress approached for their drink orders.

Dan looked at Willow. "Beer or the chardonnay you like?"

Pleased he'd remembered from other outings with the hotel group, she said, "The Carneros Chardonnay, please."

"And I'll have a light lager,"said Dan.

As soon as the order was settled, the waitress walked away leaving them alone again.

Dan reached across the table and took hold of her hand. "I'm glad we have this time together. I know how busy you are at the hotel."

"Same," she said. "But I have to start thinking of the time when Alec won't be around. Like you, I love it here. I want to stay here in the Coachella Valley in some sort of hotel management position."

"You should be able to get a good job right at the inn. That's what everyone on the management team wants, isn't it?"

"I don't think the new owners of the hotel are going to give that position to someone outside their company. Brent would do anything to get me out of the way."

"What about Trace? He seems like a fair guy."

"He's not only much nicer; he's very capable. Between Trace and Brent, Trace is the one who should get the job."

Dan frowned. "Doesn't seem fair. You're every bit as capable as they are."

"Yes, I know. But I have to be realistic. I've got a few other ideas in mind and plan to take it one day at a time. Is your job secure with new ownership?"

He smiled and nodded. "I've been told that not only do they want me to stay, they're going to give me a greater stake in the sales of clothing and equipment."

Willow returned his smile but wasn't aware of any such plans, which made her wonder what else didn't she know about the future of the inn.

Their drinks came.

They continued to talk about their pasts as they sipped and enjoyed the warm evening.

And later, after Willow finished her sea scallops, making sure to get the last of the *beurre blanc* sauce, she let out a sigh of contentment. The meal and the company had been delightful.

When Dan suggested they go back to his place after dinner, Willow agreed, wondering how their date would end.

Dan led her inside a comfortable condo, not too different from the one she hoped to rent and perhaps buy. With things being unsettled until the hotel was sold, she was patiently waiting to see if her plans would work. In the meantime, of course, she was staying at Alec's house.

"Very nice," Willow said, following Dan to the balcony on the second floor of the three-story building. She had a view of the neighborhood clubhouse and swimming pool in the distance, and directly opposite them, she could see a well-landscaped green on a neighboring golf course.

"Yeah, I was lucky to get this condo. One of the ladies at the gym told me about it." He put his arm around her. "Want a cold beer? Ice water? Anything?"

"Ice water sounds perfect," she responded.

"Okay, be right back," he said. "First, I'll take care of the music."

As he hurried back inside, Willow wondered if he had a regular routine, including special music, for all his dates. The caution she'd brushed aside came back to cling to her with a hug of worry.

He returned carrying a glass of ice water for her and a cold beer for himself. He handed her water to her. "I've had a really nice time, Willow."

"Me, too. It's different—us not being part of a group. I've enjoyed it."

He wrapped an arm around her shoulder. "Maybe we can go out for a drink later this week."

"That sounds good." She liked that he was not rushing into anything.

They stood at the railing on the balcony and began talking about their past, what they hoped for the future.

"What's going to happen to your parents after Alec is gone?" Dan said at one point. "They've worked for him for years."

"They'll continue living here. It's where family and their friends are. It's one reason I want to stay here. To make sure they're all right. Alec has assured me money won't be an issue but losing Alec will be hard for them. Conchita, Alec's wife, was my mother's cousin. So, they feel very close to one another."

"And that's why he's been so good to you," said Dan.

"Yes. The thought of him dying is sad," Willow commented, feeling a tug of sorrow inside.

Dan pulled her closer and kissed the top of her head. "Alec is a great guy. I'm sorry." He checked his watch. "I hate to end a special evening like this, but I have to get up early to meet a client."

Willow stepped away. "Of course, me too."

"I didn't realize it was this late." He studied her before pulling her into his strong arms. "But I can't let any more time go by without kissing you. I've wanted to do that all evening."

His lips came down on hers—soft but sure.

She responded, loving the gentle way he held her. It felt nice simply to relax in his embrace.

CHAPTER THREE

ROSE

Rose got up for her early morning swim, walked out to the patio, and stopped in surprise. Alec was lying on a lounge chair. When he saw her, he lifted a hand and waved. From a distance, he looked like a mere shadow of the vibrant man he'd once been. At one time, with his thick, gray hair, tall body, and rangy motion he could've been a Sam Elliott look-alike.

Tears stung her eyes as Rose walked toward him. It was anyone's guess how long he'd live. Determination was a factor. He'd taken over the ownership of the Desert Sage Inn after his business partner died when Alec was a young man. Then, after the tragic death of his wife and unborn child, Alec had poured his energy, hopes, and dreams into the property, making it the outstanding inn it was today. He wasn't about to let anyone else undo what he'd carefully crafted. Rose and the other two Desert Flowers were doing all they could to make sure that didn't happen. Alec, stubborn man that he was, would fight his disease to the end to ensure their success.

Rose bent over and kissed his cheek. "Good morning! What brings you out here this early?"

"I couldn't sleep. Thought the cool air might help." He shook his head. "The nurse Juanita insisted upon hiring isn't happy with me, but as long as I can move on my own, I'll go where I damn well please."

This was more like the Alec of old. "Sounds like you've got it under control. Want to take a dip in the pool?"

He shook his head. "No, I'll watch you instead. You always were a beautiful swimmer, Rose."

They smiled at one another as memories played in their minds. Rose had dearly loved Alec, had stayed with him for six years before he broke it off, telling her he was never getting married to her or anyone else, that he couldn't because of the guilt he felt over his wife. Still, she'd always be grateful to him for believing in her ability to do anything she set her mind to doing. That, and proving to her that she was lovable after being raised to believe she wasn't.

She sat beside him, lifted his hand, and kissed it. "I was such an insecure woman when we first met. I don't know where I'd be today if I hadn't come to the Desert Sage Inn and worked for you."

"You were beautiful and a lovely person then and you are now. Hank Bowers is a lucky man. I'm happy you've found each other. You're too special to go on living alone."

Rose grinned at him. "I still think you've played a part in all these romances. Me and Hank Bowers. Lily and Brian Walden. What about Willow?"

"What about me?" Willow joined them.

"How was your date with Dan McMillan last night?" Rose asked, winking at Alec.

Willow's lips curved. "Okay. We're going to try to get together later this week."

"Nice," said Rose. "A good match."

Willow lifted her hands in protest. "Now, Rose, don't go pushing me into anything because you and Lily broke all records on getting engaged and married."

Rose stood and gave her a hug. "I love you, sweetie, and want you to be happy."

"I'll be happy once I don't have to deal with Brent Armstrong ever again."

"I'll agree to that. Race you into the pool?"

Willow tossed down her towel and dove into the water.

Rose took off after her.

CHAPTER FOUR

WILLOW

After racing Rose in the pool, Willow climbed out of the water to find Alec had gone. She grabbed her towel and began drying herself off, thinking of how much she'd miss him and the guidance he'd provided to all of them.

Rose joined her. "I knew you were an excellent golfer, but I didn't realize you're such a strong, competitive swimmer. You gave me a real workout."

Willow wrapped the towel around her waist. "When I was growing up, Alec treated me like his own child, and urged me to excel in everything I did."

Lily walked out onto the pool deck, joining them in the early hours before her children demanded her attention. "Anyone want coffee? I can bring it out to you."

"I'd love a cup! You know how I like it, just a bit of milk," said Willow.

"And I take mine black. Thanks," said Rose.

Willow and Rose took seats at the table and let out similar sighs of contentment.

"Love these morning hours," said Rose. "It'll be better when I'm living full-time with Hank. But I want to be here with Alec as often as I can, like we planned."

"Yes, me, too," said Willow.

Lily joined them carrying a tray holding three coffee mugs and a plate of Juanita's blueberry muffins. She handed out the coffee mugs and set the tray down on the table before pulling up a chair for herself. After taking a sip of coffee, she faced them with a smile. “Okay, what did I miss?”

“Nothing new for me, but Willow had a date with Dan last night,” said Rose.

“How did it go?” asked Lily. “Is he as hot as I’ve always thought?”

Willow drew a breath. “He’s very ... nice. He had to cut the evening short because he had to meet with a client early this morning.”

Rose sat up straighter. “Whoa. Did you kiss?”

“Of course,” said Willow.

“And how was it?” Lily said, studying her.

Willow thought back to how she’d felt in Dan’s arms. “It was okay. Very nice.”

Rose and Lily exchanged meaningful glances, and then both looked at Willow with concern.

“What?” said Willow, unable to hid her dismay. “Why are you looking at me like that?”

Rose clasped Willow’s hand. “Are you willing to settle for okay? For nice?”

Willow puffed out a breath and sat back in her chair, her thoughts whirling. Was “okay” enough? Had she become so used to being on edge at work that just “nice” was a choice she really wanted?

“Oh, hon,” said Lily. “We don’t mean to upset you. We just want you happy.”

“Not just an ordinary happy, but a kiss that says a ‘wow-it-was-magic’ kind of thing,” said Rose. “You know what I mean?”

Willow nodded thoughtfully. “Just give me time to see where it’s going. I owe myself that.”

“Indeed, you do,” Rose readily agreed. She turned to Lily. “Where are the kids?”

“At home with Anna. I want them to get used to having her

appear in the morning so when I work my days at the law office, they're comfortable about having her there taking over for me. She's wonderful with both Izzy and Ollie." Lily smiled. "By the way, both of you are coming to the party next week, aren't you?"

"Absolutely," said Willow. "I can't wait to celebrate your wedding with you and Brian."

"I wouldn't miss it for the world," Rose said.

"I understand the hotel is going all out for the two of you," said Willow. "John told me the chef and his staff are delighted to be part of it."

"It's going to be a small group," said Lily, "but you know Brian. He wants everything to be exceptional for his mother, a few friends, and others in the hospitality business. Ollie's aunt, Susannah Graham, and her husband, Bill, have promised to come. I'm a little nervous to meet them."

"You have nothing to worry about, Lily. They'll love you just like Ollie does," said Willow. "It's been fun to see how close you've become."

"He's a darling little boy," said Rose. "I can't wait for Leah to meet both him and Izzy. I think they'll be friends in no time at all."

After chatting a little while longer, Willow rose. "Guess I'd better get ready for work."

"Before you go, I want to set up a girls' night out soon," said Lily. "Are you interested?"

Willow grinned. "Sounds great. The three of us and who else?"

"Sarah," said Lily. "I figure just the four of us."

"Sounds good. I'm free most nights." Willow was glad Lily hadn't asked about meeting this evening. She didn't want either Lily or Rose to know she was going on a date with Trace. She could well imagine what kind of teasing that would bring.

Back in her bedroom, Willow plopped onto her bed and stared into space. Rose and Lily talked about magic kisses and hot dates. She was attracted to Dan, had fun with him, but there were no fireworks. He, not she, was the one to call it a night. That was a clue so big she'd missed it. Theirs was always going to be a friendship. Nothing more.

At work, she sat with Brent and Trace in the office at the hotel that had been assigned to the three of them. She, Brent, and Trace were analyzing the cost impact of totally revamping the bidding and purchasing procedures for most products the three hotels bought. This involved a detailed review of all bid specifications, purchase orders, vendor qualifications, delivery requirements, and receiving procedures at each hotel. Also, they had to review each hotel's physical layouts in the receiving areas, storerooms, and kitchens to ensure that supplies could be accessed easily and quickly as needed while still maintaining control over inventories. They were also evaluating a centralized purchasing department for all three properties.

Once, feeling as if someone was staring, she looked up to find Trace gazing at her.

He quickly turned away, but she'd seen the interest on his face and felt a stirring of excitement that she quickly suppressed. She wasn't a flighty young teen crushing on one and then another guy. But being attracted to someone and feeling a sizzle were two different things.

Willow was looking at the comparative costs of in-house laundries at each hotel and using commercial laundry services when she felt a presence behind her. She turned to find Brent standing at her shoulder.

"What do you want?" she asked, covering her paperwork and quickly closing her laptop. He'd already once tried to steal her work and claim it as his own.

"If you go out with Trace tonight, you at least owe me one date." He winked at her. "Just to play fair."

"I'm not playing with anyone," she answered, offended by the implication. "We're co-workers going out. That's all."

"Hey, Brent, it's none of your business what either Willow or I do outside of the hotel," said Trace quietly but firmly. "Have you finished your section of our report for John?"

"Not yet, but I will," said Brent, sulking like a schoolboy as he walked back to his desk.

A short while later, Willow rose from her chair. "I'm done. I've emailed my report to John. See you later."

Trace walked over to her. "I'll pick you up at six. Dress casual."

"Okay, see you then," she said, surprised. She'd thought he'd choose someplace fancy for dinner, more in keeping with the status of his background.

When she arrived at Alec's house, her mother was in the kitchen, fixing homemade chicken noodle soup for Alec.

Juanita welcomed her with a smile. "You're home early. What's up?"

"I'm going on a date with Trace. I talked myself into it because Brent told Trace I'd never go out with him." Willow sat at the kitchen table and gave her mother a gloomy look. "I don't know what I'm doing. I thought I was interested in Dan, but as Rose and Lily pointed out, there's not much magic there. Oh, he's nice enough, but not electrifying, you know."

Her mother came over to the kitchen table and sat down beside her. Taking Willow's hand in her own, she said, "When you find someone that you think you might like to share your life with, many qualifications come to mind, but none more important than the seeds of lasting love. You know them—

kindness, consideration, encouragement, and generosity are just a few. But for a love to survive through years of disappointment, illness, or other challenges, there must be a bit of magic between the two of you, the glue that holds you together."

"So, you and *Papi*?"

Her mother's cheeks turned pink. "I knew he was right for me from the beginning. Not that I'd let him know. Your dad had to prove that he was right for me."

"You and *Papi* still kiss all the time and hold hands. I want something like that," said Willow and stopped herself.

Her mother smiled at her. "I wish for more than 'nice' for you, my sweet girl. Your father and me ..." She stopped as her cheeks turned pink.

"TMI," said Willow laughing and holding out her hands for her mother to stop. "Too much information."

Smiling, her mother got to her feet and kissed Willow's cheeks. "Go, have a good time. You'll know when the right one comes along."

Watching her mother walk away, Willow swore there was a sway to her step that hadn't been there moments ago.

Sighing, Willow headed to her bedroom. She had time to relax and read for a while before getting ready for her date.

Later, though Trace had said dress was casual, Willow soaked in the tub, fussed with her hair, and applied a light touch of makeup before going to her closet to choose clothes. Flipping through hangars, she decided on a V-neck, lime-green tunic in a swishy fabric and white jeans. Her turquoise and silver necklace and earrings added a perfect touch to the ensemble.

The memory of Brent taunting her back in college filled her with a sudden panic. *What in hell am I doing going out with Trace? He's part of the same family.*

"Willow? Your date is here," said her mother, opening the door to her bedroom a crack.

"Okay, I'll be right there." Too late to back out now. Besides, she was Willow Sanchez, daughter of Juanita and Pedro, a graduate of Cornell, and an accomplished woman. Straightening her shoulders, she lifted her purse from the chair next to her desk and headed out to greet Trace.

Standing by the front door, he looked handsome as ever in a pair of khaki shorts and a blue polo shirt that brought out the color in his eyes.

He grinned at her. "You look beautiful! Ready to go?"

She followed him out to the car he was renting—a small, white Lexus. Nothing outrageous, but classy just the same.

He held the car door for her, and as she moved past him onto the seat, he said, "M-m-m, you smell good."

"Thanks." Her favorite perfume was Gucci Bloom and she loved it too..

He went around the car and slid behind the wheel. "I hope you don't mind, but I thought we'd have a low-key evening. I want the chance to get to know you better. I'm fixing dinner at the house my parents recently bought."

Willow couldn't stop herself from asking, "Does Brent live there too?"

"No, he's bought his own condo, thinking he's going to need it in the future," said Trace, annoyance creeping into his voice. "I know you don't care for him, and after hearing stories and seeing how he's acted toward you in the past, I understand your feelings. Even though he's my cousin, I don't like him much either."

"He's not a very nice person," said Willow, thinking he was much less than that. A self-centered creep. Two years ahead of her in the hotel school at Cornell, Brent had been with an elitist group who'd made fun of her, calling her "Enchilada."

That kind of bullying was one reason she was determined to outshine both Brent and Trace, who were vying with her for the job she badly wanted.

Trace glanced at her. "I hope you're going to give me a fair chance, Willow. I'm not at all like Brent."

"I know," she replied. "Why do your relatives put up with him?"

"It's a long story." He sighed. "A battle between two brothers that will never end. If it's any consolation, my parents are opposed to Brent representing the company. But they will honor the agreements set out at the formation of the company." He reached over and covered her hand with his. "Let's not make this about the Armstrongs. It's an evening for the two of us alone."

"You're right," she said, wondering if it was going to work. Families always counted.

Trace pulled up in front of a lovely, sprawling house atop a steep slope that met the foothills close to the Indian Wells border. It was not too far from the Premio Inn, a small, upscale resort where Willow hoped to work one day if, as she worried, she didn't get the job at the Desert Sage Inn.

"How beautiful!" Willow exclaimed. It was every bit as attractive as Alec's house.

"Yeah, my mother's pretty excited about it. She can't wait to decorate it the way she wants. Right now, it's furnished with a lot of pieces that came with the house. C'mon, let's go inside."

He climbed out of the car, hurried around the back, and got to her just as she stepped onto the pavement of the front circle.

He took hold of her hand and stood gazing at her for a moment. "I'm glad you agreed to spend this time with me."

Willow allowed her heart to slow. For a moment, she'd

thought he was going to kiss her.

He opened the large, carved-wood front door and led her inside to a marble-floored entry. From there, she faced the living room and beyond it, the pool and manicured stone garden.

"We'll be back in the kitchen. That's a bit less intimidating," said Trace.

She followed him to the right, through a formal dining room to the kitchen. As she'd expected, it was beautifully equipped with stainless steel appliances, gray-marble countertops, and white, raised-panel wooden cupboards.

"This is beautiful. Does your mother like to cook?"

Trace smiled at her. "Actually, she does. So do I."

"Me, too. My mother is a fabulous cook, but I like to experiment on my own."

He grinned. "I always end up in the hotel kitchen talking to staff there to get new ideas."

Willow set down her purse on the countertop. "You said you were going to cook dinner. Do you want help?"

Trace handed her an apron. "You bet! It's more fun that way."

He reached into a drawer, pulled out another apron, and put it on. He handed her an iPad. "Here's the recipe. Take a look at it, and we can get started. I thought we'd make this Lemon Chicken Casserole, a tossed green salad, and a carrot, onion, and thyme dish I've already prepared to put in the oven. I wanted to keep it simple and give us time to sit and talk before dinner."

Willow looked over the recipe. It had received rave reviews. Better yet, there was nothing difficult about making it. While she waited for Trace to gather the ingredients, she gazed around the kitchen. She especially liked the built-in chopping block next to the sink in the center island. Another sink sat beneath a window that overlooked the back lawn. A warming oven, along with double-ovens, a microwave, and a multi-functional toaster oven were among the appliances.

"A little over the top, but this kitchen has everything any cook would need, including a Viking commercial gas range," said Trace with a note of excitement.

Willow returned his grin, sensing how much he enjoyed cooking. Every chef liked a great kitchen.

"How about a glass of wine as we cook?" Trace held up two bottles. "White or red?"

"Red, please."

"A nice Oregon pinot noir it is," said Trace, setting the bottle down on the counter and putting the other bottle in a wine cooler tucked underneath the counter.

After opening the bottle and pouring small amounts into two wine glasses, he handed one to her and lifted up the other. "Good color and legs on the glass. Let's see what it tastes like."

Willow lifted the glass to her face and inhaled. "Lovely bouquet." She took a sip, letting it roll around inside her mouth, and swallowed. "Nice and smooth!"

"Yeah, it's from the Chandler Hill Winery outside McMinnville, Oregon. The owner, Cami, and her sister, Lulu, are great people and great hostesses, if you ever want to make the trip," said Trace.

"I've heard good things about them and their wine," said Willow. "Now I know why. This is superb."

Willow and Trace sipped in silence, and then Trace said, "Okay, let's cook."

He seasoned the chicken and sautéed it while Willow assembled the sauce ingredients and sliced lemons thinly to place on top of the chicken as it baked.

Willow was pleasantly surprised when Trace began to join in to a song on his iPhone.

"Hey, you can sing!" she said.

He shook his head. "Not very good, but I can't help doing it."

They put the casserole together, and Trace slid it into the oven. "Okay, we have a half-hour to sit and talk. Let's go out by the pool."

The pool was rectangular and long enough for doing laps. Willow thought of Rose. She'd love the pool for her morning workouts. The patio and pool deck were spacious and well-furnished. Willow walked over to one of the wicker couches and sat down facing the foothills nearby.

Trace settled beside her and placed his bare feet on the coffee table in front of the couch. "This is a great place to relax."

"Yes, it's lovely. I get the same view at Alec's house."

Trace turned to her. "What is it with you and Alec? He's your mentor?"

"And much more," she said. "He's like a second father to me. I've known him since I was a little girl. He's the one who got me interested in the hotel business. I was going to help run the inn with him one day, but, obviously, that's not happening now." She blinked rapidly to stem the sting of tears. "He's a wonderful man."

Trace studied her. "My father admires him and likes what he's done."

"He worked hard to build the inn into the property it is today. That's why we Desert Flowers are devoted to helping him. That, and the special friendship he has with each of the three of us."

"I have to admit he couldn't have better representatives. You three are talented. To have that, combined with loyalty, is a winning combination." He took another sip of wine and studied her. "What are you going to do next, if you don't get the job at the Desert Sage Inn?"

"I'm going to stay here in the area. I'll find something else, even if it's only temporary."

"Ah," he said. "Would you be willing to move?"

Willow shook her head. She'd thought a lot about it lately and had decided to follow her heart and stay where she was surrounded by people who loved her—her parents, her extended family, and her new friends, Rose and Willow.

"Really?" A look of disappointment crossed his face and disappeared.

"Yes, I'm staying here in the desert," she said, confirming her answer.

He sat back against the cushions and stared into space. "Everyone thinks I'm lucky to have a background like mine, ensuring me of a good job. But sometimes I feel trapped. After all my parents have done for me, I don't have a choice. I have to stay in the business. Someday, I'll take over for my father."

"Why don't you leave it up to Brent? He's dying to do that," teased Willow. She laughed when she saw Trace make a face.

"You know I can't do that," he said, laughing with her. "It's so hard. You can choose your friends, but you can't choose your family."

"I'm lucky I've got mine," Willow said, with a new respect for Trace. She smiled at him.

He leaned toward her. "May I?"

His lips met hers. She reacted to the surge of energy between them and reached for him. This was not a Dan-like kiss; it was much more. When they pulled apart, Willow understood what Rose and Lily had been trying to tell her.

Trace grinned. "Thanks. I knew it could be like that."

Just then, Brent appeared. "Hey! Am I in time for dinner?"

Willow swallowed a groan.

Trace jumped to his feet and turned to face Brent. "What

are you doing here?"

"Aw, I couldn't resist. You and Willow? I don't know why she's being nice to you, but I wouldn't trust her. She wants our job."

Willow noticed the way Trace clenched his hands into fists and stood. "I'm sure there's enough food for us all," she said to break the tension.

Trace flashed her an angry look and then said, "Willow's being super nice. But, Brent, this is the last time you pull a stunt like this. Understand?"

"We'll see," said Brent, winking at her.

Willow pressed her lips together to keep from saying the words that popped into her head. No way was she going to stoop to Brent's level. Better yet, this gave her a clear understanding of how a relationship with Trace would go. The thought of having Brent in their lives made her sick to her stomach.

She managed to get through the meal, but it was apparent that neither Trace nor she was happy with the situation. For Willow, it went deeper than an evening gone wrong. Trace's kiss had proved to her what she was missing with Dan, but she realized she couldn't pursue a relationship with Trace, not with Brent part of the deal.

CHAPTER FIVE

WILLOW

Trace was quiet as he drove her back to Alec's house, but she sensed his anger and disappointment.

"I'm sorry about the evening," Willow said, "but maybe it's for the best that we don't date. There's an old saying—don't fish off the company pier. As long as we're working together, we shouldn't be dating. I think both your father and Alec would agree with that."

He pulled the car to a stop in front of the house and turned to her. "I like you, Willow, and I'm mad as hell at the way the evening turned out. Maybe, after this project with Alec is over, you'll reconsider."

"The problem isn't you, Trace. It's your circumstances. Anything long-term would never work out between us."

Trace glared at her. "Let me get this straight. You're judging me by my family? Isn't that what you hated about Brent's treatment of you in college?"

Willow clapped a hand to her mouth. That's exactly what she was doing. "Brent's problem was my race. I'm sorry, Trace. The rule about dating while we're working together still stands. If at the end of the project, we still want to date, then we'll be free to do so."

"Okay. We don't have too many more weeks left before the hotel should be sold. By then we'll know who's won the management opportunity at the Desert Sage Inn." He covered her hand with his and drew her closer.

Willow closed her eyes and allowed him to kiss her, to see

if the earlier connection was real. As before, heat radiated through her at the touch of his lips.

She pulled away and let out a troubled sigh. If the timing was right and everything else was settled, she'd think about dating Trace. But as she thought it, she knew it was not going to be easy.

Trace walked her to the door. "Thanks for the evening."

"Talk to you later," Willow said, glad he was a gentleman.

She opened the door and stepped inside. She stood a moment, letting her eyes adjust to the dim light, and startled when she noticed a figure sitting on the couch.

"Alec! What are you doing up?"

He waved her over. "I couldn't sleep. I sometimes think a part of me is afraid of getting too much sleep and missing out on something during the last days I have."

She sat beside him on the couch and took hold of his hand. "Is it getting much worse?"

"Today made me realize there's no going back, that the disease is winning, and I just have to ride it out. But I won't let go until I know the hotel is safe."

"Rose, Lily, and I are doing everything we can to do that for you within the Blaise Group."

"I'm grateful to you. Now, tell me where you've been."

"I went out with Trace. He and I cooked dinner at his parents' new house. It was a nice, relaxing evening until Brent crashed the party." She sighed. "Trace is a nice guy. I like him a lot."

"But?"

"But I realize I shouldn't date him or let a relationship between us grow because of his situation. Brent and his father aren't nice. They'd always be part of any life I might have with Trace."

"Is your relationship with Trace serious? I had no idea you

were dating him."

Willow shook her head. "We've had only this date, but I like him a lot. Yet, I see trouble ahead because of his family."

"Has Trace or his father ever said or done anything to disrespect you?" asked Alec, giving her a worried look.

"No, not at all," said Willow. "In fact, I know Mitchell likes the work I do."

"Well, then, see how things unfold. Sometimes, it's best to step away and allow time to take care of a situation."

"Yes, I suppose you're right, though I sometimes feel as if my life is already on hold."

Alec gave her hand a squeeze. "It'll all play out soon. Now, how about walking me back to my rooms."

Willow helped Alec to his feet and walked slowly beside him, shocked at the change in the man who'd always seemed like a god of sorts to her with his energy and strength. Hiding her tears, she led him to the far end of the house where his private rooms were located.

They were met by a nurse, who clucked her tongue at Alec. "Sneaking out again, are we?"

"It's his house," Willow softly reminded her.

The nurse, an older woman with a plump body and a kind heart said gently, "Come, then, Alec, let's get you settled."

Willow walked away feeling as if things would never be right with him gone.

The next morning when Willow walked into the kitchen, her mother looked up at her from where she was putting the last touches onto a tray for Alec. "So, how did it go?"

Willow shrugged and went over to the coffee maker. She hadn't slept well, and a cup of coffee was just what she needed.

Her mother approached. "I take it things did not turn out the way you wanted."

Willow took a sip of coffee and let out a sigh. "I like Trace a lot but his relatives worry me. We've decided not to date until the hotel is sold and things are settled. But I'm not sure I want to do it even then."

"Then don't," her mother said. "This is a difficult, emotional time for all of us. Don't worry about meeting a man. Rose and Lily's experiences shouldn't dictate yours. Be sensible."

Each of her mother's words felt as if they'd been hammered inside her head though they'd been spoken softly. She headed out to the patio with her cup of coffee.

Rose was in the pool doing her morning laps.

Willow took a seat at the table and watched her, comforted by the continuity of each day's routine.

When Rose stopped swimming and climbed out of the pool, she gave Willow a little wave. "Good morning. Where were you last night? Hank flew back to Atlanta, and I thought we might have our girls' night out."

"I was on a date with Trace," said Willow, waiting for the reaction she was sure would come.

"Trace Armstrong? You're kidding. How'd it go?" Rose wrapped a towel around her torso and sat at the table.

Willow sighed and filled Rose in on the evening's events.

"Did you kiss him? Is that why the sad face?" Rose asked, giving her a steady look.

"Yes, and I might as well tell you that it was nothing like Dan's kiss. Better. Much better."

Rose grinned and gave her a quick hug. "The evening wasn't all lost if that's what you discovered. Don't worry. Things will fall in place for you soon. You're beautiful, smart, and savvy."

"Not so savvy I know my own mind. I've decided the best thing for me is to focus on my job. Then, after we all recover from losing Alec, I'll be ready to think about a future and the possibility of having a relationship with someone I feel very connected to."

"Good idea," said Rose. "Until then, we Flowers will stick together. Lily wants to set up a girls' night out. Let's talk to her, and if she is free tonight, we'll make it happen."

"Thanks," Willow said, feeling better already. She wouldn't let Rose and Lily and their romances affect her personal goals. She had success at her fingertips and would fight for the job she, Trace, and Brent all wanted. Working long-term at the Desert Sage Inn was something she'd planned with Alec a long time ago. She would do her best to make it happen without worrying about her love life.

CHAPTER SIX

LILY

Bleary-eyed, Lily sipped her coffee. Izzy had awakened in the middle of the night with a bad dream, and it had taken her hours to settle her back down. Now, Izzy was happy as could be as she cheerfully lifted her cereal bowl to her mouth and sipped the last of the milk from it, spilling half of it on her nightgown. Across the table from Izzy, Ollie quietly ate his scrambled egg, while Jake, faithful dog, sat nearby and gazed hopefully at his owner. Brian was in the shower, getting ready for a meeting at the hotel. A meeting she'd not been invited to join.

Lily pushed fatigue and resentment away, telling herself that though this one was unexpected, a family was something she'd always wanted. And with her pregnancy recently confirmed, she knew she'd better get used to it. So far, morning sickness wasn't an issue.

Her cell phone on the counter chirped. She picked it up, checked Caller ID. *Rose.*

"Hey, there!" Lily said, feeling more a part of this familiar scene.

"Hi! Did I catch you at a bad time? I hear crying," said Rose.

"No, it's all right. Izzy is fussing because she spilled milk on herself. Hang on a minute while I take off her wet nightgown. It's time for her to get dressed for the day anyway." Lily set the phone down, helped Izzy out of her nightgown and gave her a comforting kiss.

"Okay, where were we?" said Lily.

Rose laughed. "We were at 'Hello.'"

"Oh, yeah, Right. How are you, Rose?"

"Good," Rose said. "Willow and I are ready for a girls' night out. How about you? Do you think you can get away tonight to join us for drinks at Jasper's?

"I'll make it happen," said Lily, smiling at Brian as he walked into the room, moving easily with the prosthesis he wore on his left leg.

He returned her smile. "Make what happen?"

"Girls' night out tonight. Will you take the kids?"

He gazed at her, glanced over at the mess at the kitchen table and said, "Okay. I'll come home early."

"Yes!" Lily cried into the phone. "You're on! I'll meet you there at six." She clicked off the call. "Thanks, Bri. I need this. Besides, tonight I'm going to tell them about the baby."

"I guess you better go then," said Brian, grinning at her as he picked up a clean plate off the floor. Jake looked up at Brian with big brown eyes and wagged his tail, hoping for more. Ollie had disappeared, along with Izzy.

"I need to go check on the kids," Lily said, giving Brian a kiss. "Coffee is made, cereal and fruit on the counter."

"Okay, but I want to say good morning to you the right way," he said, wrapping his arms around her and lowering his lips to hers.

Lily felt the mess in the room evaporate as he kissed her. Nothing mattered at that moment but the two of them. She melted in his arms ... until a cold nose brought her back to reality with a jolt. She stared down at Jake and pulled away from Brian.

"Love you, but I better go."

He chuckled. "On your way, Mom."

She left him and went into Izzy's room. Wearing a new pink sundress, Izzy was sitting on the floor trying to get her white sandals on.

"Here, let me help," she offered.

"No, I want to do it," said Izzy. As Lily watched, Izzy changed shoes to the correct feet and closed the Velcro straps.

"Good job! Anna will be here a bit later. Why don't you pick out a few books for her to read to you?"

"Okay." Izzy got to her feet and threw her arms around Lily's waist.

Fighting tears, Lily picked her up and hugged her tight. Just when Lily was exhausted from the care of her, Izzy did something unexpected like this.

She left Izzy looking at books in her room and went to check on Ollie. He was sprawled on his bed reading. "Are you all set for the day?" she asked, coming over to sit beside him. He was a quiet child, still getting used to all the changes that had taken place in his life—his mother's illness and death, being introduced to a father he'd never known, a move to a new state, and a stepmother and sibling. Lily was careful not to push him too fast to settle in his new situation.

"Look, Lily! There's a lizard like Leo."

She forced a smile as she studied it. Though she was afraid of the lizard, she did her best to act interested because she'd do anything for the little boy she already loved.

CHAPTER SEVEN

WILLOW

Willow entered the office she shared with Brent and Trace determined not to show her new awkwardness around them. She'd kissed Trace and had liked it. Brent now knew this and would use it against both of them if they allowed it to show.

Fortunately, John Rodriguez, the resident manager of the Desert Sage Inn and the man for whom they were working, didn't know anything about it. She intended to keep it that way.

Shortly after she was seated behind her computer, John appeared.

"Good job, everyone, on the purchasing department analysis for the Corona Collection. This should greatly simplify the entire purchasing process, standardize uniforms, linens, towels, and other commonly needed items between the hotels, reinforce the image of the Corona Collection, and eventually save the hotels significant money. There are a few areas that need refinement and clarification, so there's some more work to do.

"Duh," muttered Brent.

Willow gritted her teeth but managed a smile for John.

"We'll get right to it," said Trace to John, ignoring both her and Brent.

"Okay, that's how we'll play it," said Willow to herself. She took the sheet of information John handed her and went to work.

###

At the end of the day, Willow was exhausted from the research she'd done in an atmosphere that pulsed with tension. She didn't know whether to say anything to Trace about their evening together and the resolution they'd made or to keep on ignoring the elephant in the room.

Brent approached her. "How about that date with me? I've got tickets to a show in Palm Springs."

She shook her head. "No, thanks."

"You're kidding! Do you know how many women would be glad to go out with me?"

Willow remained quiet. The fact that he'd ask her after she'd made it clear to him that she never wanted to date him, made her angry. But she knew the minute she showed it, he'd pounce. He was that kind of person. Someone she never wanted in her life after the project they were working on was concluded.

Ignoring Brent's angry stare, she left the hotel and headed back to Alec's house using the golf cart she'd been given to get around the hotel property. As she made her way along the paved path, she breathed in the aroma of blooming flowers, watched hummingbirds hover above their brightness, listened to the sibilant rustling of palm fronds in the breeze, and felt tension leave her.

Approaching Alec's house, she thought of the condo Brian had left. He'd offered to have her sublease it in the hopes of buying it when the lease was up. It was something she was definitely interested in doing, but with Lily gone from Alec's house on a permanent basis and Rose living there only half-time, she felt committed to staying there as support for him.

She parked the cart in the designated spot inside the four-car garage and headed indoors, happy to feel at home here.

Her mother was in the kitchen preparing a meal for Alec

when Willow walked in. "How was your day, darling?" her mother asked, giving her a loving look.

Willow walked over to her and kissed her on the cheek. "Let's just say I'm glad it's a girls' night out kind of evening. Rose said Lily sounded desperate for it. I am too."

"Ah, it's lovely that you three have become close. Women need other women to help them through tough times and celebrate victories." She placed her hands on her hips. "And no one is going to get away with making you unhappy as long as I'm around to protect you."

Willow grinned and squeezed her mother in a quick hug. "*Mami*, I'm over thirty years old, not a baby you can protect. But I love you for the thought."

"You'll see. A mother never stops being a mother to her children."

"Well, what I need right now is someone to go out drinking with." As Willow said the words, she was grateful for her mother's support. When she'd been working away from home for a number of years teaching in Boston, she'd sometimes felt alone. Being back home felt very good.

Willow went to her room and decided a refreshing shower was what she needed before she went out. Something to erase the strain of the day.

Standing under a stream of water, she felt her body relax as warm water struck her skin and slid over it in caressing strokes. Sighing with satisfaction, she reminded herself to forget about Brent and Trace and concentrate on the job. Her work for Alec was too important to let it slip, and though she kept from mentioning it to the other Flowers, she desperately wanted the job of managing the inn. If she got it, all Alec had done to help her would prove to be right.

She wondered what other people saw when they looked at her. Rose had called her beautiful, but she didn't consider herself that. Her figure was curvy and her nose was, in her opinion, a tad too strong. While her image would never grace magazine covers, she was happy with what she saw. She was herself and that was good enough.

She pulled a short, tropical-print wrap skirt of many colors out of the closet and selected a bright orange linen shell to wear with it. She'd be colorful, even if she had to work on her attitude. Thinking of Rose, Lily, and her friend, Sarah, she knew she'd be in good company.

A short while later, Willow walked into Jasper's, a cute little bar on El Paseo that was a favorite. The patio outside the bar was packed. Mostly tourists, she suspected, because the locals tended to stay inside at the back of the place.

She noticed Rose waving to her and hurried to the high-top table where Rose, Lily, and Sarah already sat. "How is everyone?" she asked, sliding onto the tall, empty chair they'd saved for her.

"Ready for some fun," said Sarah. "I've had a tough two-year-old type of day. I swear I can't wait until my son turns three and gets past the stage he's in."

A waitress came to the table for their orders. Willow placed her order for red wine. Rose quickly chose a mojito and Sara, a margarita. They waited for Lily to order. She hesitated, then said, "I'll have a club soda and lime."

After the waitress left, Willow and the others quietly studied Lily.

Lily beamed at them. "I was waiting to tell you until I had my physical, but I'm pregnant."

"Pregnant? Oh, my! How thrilling!" said Rose, jumping to her feet to hug Lily.

"Wow!" said Willow. "I'm so surprised! But that's great news!" She reached over and gave Lily an affectionate squeeze.

"How's Brian taking it?" asked Sarah, giving Lily a bright smile.

Lily chuckled. "Like a rooster in a hen house."

The women laughed together.

"I'm hoping for another baby as soon as Eric gets back from his deployment," said Sarah. "As much as Henry is a challenge at the moment, I don't want him to grow up an only child."

"I was an only child in unhappy circumstances," said Rose. "How often I wished for a brother or a sister."

"I'm an only child, but there were a lot of cousins my age growing up," said Willow, realizing how lucky she'd been to have them. Though many, like she, had moved away, she still had one or two she kept up with.

"I still can't believe I'm actually having a baby," said Lily. "But the doctor assures me that though I'm in my early forties, everything will be fine. Right now, I'm too busy to worry. The good thing is I don't have morning sickness. I feel pretty good."

"How are the plans for the party coming along?" Rose asked.

"Brian has everything under control," said Lily. "I'm letting him take care of it. He did such a good job planning the wedding."

"I'm very happy for you," said Sarah giving Lily's hand a squeeze.

Willow sat and listened to everyone talk, feeling out of place. She let her thoughts drift to the arrangement she had with Trace to reconsider their relationship once the project was over. It probably was a stalling tactic for both of them, but she wouldn't do anything more about it.

She was jolted back to the present by Lily's voice calling out, "Hi, Craig! C'mon over and say hello to my friends."

A tall, broad-shouldered man with caramel hair strolled toward them wearing a smile that sent a sparkle to his green eyes.

Willow couldn't help staring. The man was drop-dead gorgeous.

Lily beamed at him as she explained, "This is Craig Kincaid, one of the lawyers in the office where I work."

"Hi, everyone! Lily said she was going to meet her friends at Jasper's. Thought I'd stop in. I usually end up meeting a friend or two here." His lips curved, showing off his white teeth and sent a crinkle of pleasure to the outside corners of his incredible eyes.

All four women at the table inhaled and let out breaths that sounded like soft sighs.

A young blonde approached, breaking the spell. "Hey, Craig. I'm saving a space for you next to me at the bar." She batted her eyes at him.

"Okay." He waved to them and walked away with her.

Willow watched them as several other women rushed over to Craig, clinging to his arms, gazing up at him as they flirted outrageously with him. He appeared to be enjoying all the attention he was being given. Disgusted, she shook her head. *Another player*.

"Isn't he something," gushed Lily. "The first time I met him and heard his name, I imagined him wearing a kilt and actually sighed at the thought. He's got the looks and the build to be on the cover of one of those historical romance books about Scottish heroes."

"It's a good thing Eric is coming home soon," said Sarah, fanning herself playfully. "He's hot."

"Yep, a kilt would look great on him," Rose said. "Or off."

They turned to Willow.

Willow waved their interest away. "Don't look at me. He's

not my type."

"He's every woman's type," Sarah countered.

"What are we doing?" said Rose. "We don't need to spend time looking at any guy. This is girls' night out. Let's just have fun."

"Yes," said Willow, smiling at her. "*Girls*' night out. So, tell me, who wants to go to the discount mall with me tomorrow? The stores are having sales."

Willow relaxed as they began to discuss clothing, the best deals, and the coolest clothes to wear in the heat.

By the time she returned to Alec's house, Willow was happy to let go of all thoughts about her love life. But, later, as she climbed into bed, she knew she'd have to talk to Dan.

After working the next morning and shopping in the afternoon, Willow headed to the fitness center ready to decompress with a little exercise. It would also give her time to speak to Dan.

When she arrived at the center, Dan was acting as personal trainer to an older woman. She listened to him give the woman encouragement and thought once more that he was a nice guy. And that was the problem. As Rose and Lily had indicated to her, she deserved more than nice; she wanted magic too.

She changed into her workout clothes, hopped on the treadmill, and turned on her headphones to listen to music. She was lost in the lively sounds of rock when she felt a tap on her shoulder.

Dan was smiling at her.

She whipped off her headphones and turned to him.

"Have a minute?" he said, at the same time she said, "We need to talk."

They laughed together.

"Come on over to my office," Dan said. "We'll have privacy there."

Willow followed him and took a seat in front of his desk. He closed the door behind him.

"About the other night," he began.

Willow lifted a hand to stop him. "I know what you're going to say and I feel the same way. We're meant to be friends. That's all."

"Yeah. That's how it is for me too," said Dan. "I like you a lot, Willow, and want to continue to be friends."

"Same. I need a friend like you for a guy's perspective on things. It's hard to date at the moment. Things are coming to a close with the project. Then, I can think about that part of my life."

"I get it. I really do." He bent down and kissed her cheek. "You're someone special, Willow. I mean it."

She smiled up at him, relieved at how things had gone. As great a guy as he was, when the time came, she wanted more.

CHAPTER EIGHT

ROSE

Rose left Jasper's feeling lucky she had such good friends. Of all ages, their small group had come together nicely. She felt safe talking about anything with the other women. They truly supported one another. Willow had been pretty quiet most of the evening. Rose understood the dilemma Willow faced, of wanting something magical with a man she was serious about. She also needed some time to figure out where she was going with her professional life. One did not equal the other.

Her thoughts flew to Hank. Talk about magic! She'd never known the kind of love they shared. She glanced down at her engagement ring. It sparkled at her as if it knew what went on between Hank and her when the blinds were drawn. Being engaged was a new experience for her, and she was enjoying the fact that, after the hotel was sold, she and Hank could begin planning their wedding. He'd been understanding when she'd told him she wanted to wait, but she knew he was growing impatient for the official ceremony.

When she got back to Alec's house, she checked the time. It was much too late to call Hank in Atlanta. She texted him instead. *Miss you. Love you. Hope you're having a good time with the girls.*

She got ready for bed, anticipating his return.

CHAPTER NINE

LILY

The intimate wedding reception Brian had worked on with the chef at the hotel was as elegant as Lily had hoped. She stood in the private dining room admiring the tables dressed with soft-pink linen tablecloths which matched the roses in crystal stem vases in the center of each of the two tables, flanked by flickering candles. Crystal wine glasses sparkled, and silverware gleamed at each place. At one end of the room a bar had been set up. Friends were chatting happily with one another, filling the room with a pleasant hum. When Izzy and Ollie, all dressed up, made an appearance with Anna, Lily couldn't hold back the tears of joy she'd fought all evening. Her new family and friends meant everything to her.

Holding Izzy in her arms, Lily greeted some members of the hotel staff they'd invited and then spent time talking with Trace.

When dinner was about to be announced, she walked Izzy and Ollie to the front door of the hotel with Anna, kissed the children good night, thanked Anna, and waited for the hotel van to take off with them.

Brian greeted her at the door to the private dining room where they were about to eat.

"Everything okay with the kids?"

"Anna is wonderful with them. I don't worry; they love her, and so do I."

He grinned. "Good. Now let's enjoy the meal."

Two tables of eight were set up in the room. Rose, Hank, Willow, Juanita, and Pedro were joined by two hotel staff members, along with John Rodriquez, Trace, and Brent. Lily gave a little wave to Loretta and her husband, sitting next to Bennett Williams and his wife. A perfect number for a small, intimate party.

The meal started with a simple bouillon soup with fresh sliced mushrooms. A filet of beef tenderloin accompanied by sweet, buttery lobster was served with a vegetable mélange, followed by a crisp green salad with a simple oil and balsamic vinegar dressing. For dessert, Lily had opted not to have a wedding cake, but chose to have individual moist lemon cakes with a buttercream frosting, topped with raspberries served to each guest.

After dessert was distributed, Brian stood. "Thank you, everyone, for coming here tonight to help Lily and me celebrate our marriage. There have been a lot of surprises along the way, but we treasure the steadfast support you've given us. Here's to us all!"

Among the cheers that followed, Brian sat, and facing her, kissed her long and hard.

Everyone clapped, bringing a flush to Lily's cheeks when they pulled apart.

Brian chuckled. "You're beautiful, you know."

Lily gazed into his eyes, not at all sure that was true. But it didn't matter because, with him, she felt that way.

The next morning, Lily walked into the law offices of Williams and Kincaid, grateful for the chance to be able to work part-time. Being with adults for part of the day gave her the energy to be with her kids the other parts of the day. She hadn't realized what a stay-at-home mom had to endure in terms of lack of time for herself and the loss of conversation on an adult level. She'd been caught in the trap of thinking those mothers had it easier than most. Thankfully, she had the best of both worlds. At least for the time being. The addition of a new baby would mean another adjustment.

She'd just tucked her purse into her desk when Craig approached her. "Hey, Lily, good to see you at Jasper's the other night. Who's the dark-haired beauty who was sitting with you?"

"No one who's interested in you," she responded, feeling a fierce need to protect Willow.

"Give me a break. I'm serious. I want to know who she is," said Craig.

Lily sighed. "She's Willow Sanchez, one of the Desert Flowers, and I'm telling you she has no interest in dating you. We're all trying to concentrate on Alec's project. Once that's over, you might have a chance, but I doubt it. We all saw the women in the bar swarming all over you."

He grinned. "Can I help it if I'm adorable?"

She frowned.

"Aw, I'm just kidding. I like to have fun."

"That may be your problem. Willow isn't looking to be one of the many women in a man's life. Loretta told me she's waiting for you to find a nice girl and settle down with her." *Good lord, has motherhood changed me? I sound more like a grandmother than a woman my age.*

Craig shook his head. "Ever since she's taken over for my mother, Loretta's been on my back. But I love her for it because she and my mother were best friends."

Loretta approached them. "Did I hear my name?"

A short, plumpish woman with gray hair pulled back into a bun behind her head, Loretta was, as Bennett Williams put it, the boss of the entire office. Her dark eyes sparkled as she studied them.

"I was just telling Lily what a nag you've become," said Craig, grinning at her.

Lily and Loretta looked at one another and laughed. Craig could be an adorable tease.

"Well, this nag says it's time for you to get back to work so that you can leave to take Bennett's place in his weekly golf game. He just called to ask me to set it up for him."

"Okay. The same crew? Your Ricardo and my dad and who else?"

Loretta shook her head. "That, I don't know. With Alec unable to play, they have to find someone else."

Craig left, and Lily turned to Loretta. "He's interested in my friend Willow. I told him she wasn't interested in him."

"Willow Sanchez?" Loretta gave her a thoughtful look. "I'm friends with Juanita and Pedro. They know what a playboy Craig is, and I don't think they'd approve. I love that young man like my own. Ever since his mother died, he's become a real party guy."

"You have to admit he's one of the most handsome men around."

"Yes, he is," said Loretta. "And that's the problem."

CHAPTER TEN

WILLOW

When Willow got out of Alec's pool, she was surprised to see her mother standing by. Her heart thudded with alarm. "What is it? Is Alec okay?"

Juanita smiled at her. "He has a favor to ask of you. He's wondering if you can take his place at his weekly golf game. His usual substitute is unable to make it."

"Who would I play with?"

"Ricardo Morales, Ken Kincaid, and Bennett Williams."

"I guess so. I haven't played much recently so I probably won't be my best."

"*Cariña,* your worst is better than most," her mother said, affection coating her words.

Willow loved the encouragement her parents and Alec always gave her. Whenever she was down, one of them would speak up. It's what had helped her through challenging times.

"Okay. Tell Alec not to worry. I'll take his place and win for him." Ricardo was once a golf pro and had taught her a lot of what she knew about the game. He was still very good. Ken and Bennett were beatable.

Willow went into her room glad for a day away from work. As the time was drawing to a close for the hotel sale to take place, things were in good shape for a transition. It was a matter of following through to see the changes were ready to be implemented seamlessly. Most of that task fell to Brian.

###

The May morning indicated a hot day ahead as Willow got onto her cart loaded with her clubs and headed down the hill to the hotel. At one time she'd been a high school state champion golfer. Living in the northeast, she'd had fewer opportunities to play and she'd lost interest. Now that she was back in the desert, she had intended to pick it up again but had only hit balls on the range. Today would be a challenge she'd welcome.

When she arrived at the golf pro shop, she parked her cart and went inside to find the others.

The place was busy, so she headed into the café and bar to see who else in the foursome had arrived. Ricardo Morales, Loretta's husband, waved her over. A good-looking man still in excellent physical shape, he and her father were close. She recognized Ken Kincaid, a friend of Alec's and gave him a warm smile.

"Hi, there!" said Ricardo. "It's been a while since I've seen you. I heard you were working for Alec. No time for golf?"

"Not for a while." She felt someone approach and turned around.

The guy everyone wanted to see in a kilt grinned at her.

Ken spoke up. "Willow, do you remember my son, Craig? As children, you met once or twice. He's filling in today for Bennett."

"I do. As a matter of fact, we saw one another at Jasper's the other night."

"For just a moment. We haven't really met as adults," Craig said, holding out his hand.

Forced to shake it or be considered rude, Willow took it. A stream of electric shock traveled up her arm, rolled down her back, and swept through her body.

Stunned by the energy between them, Willow dropped her hand and forced a smile, praying no one else had noticed. But the knowing look on Craig's face indicated he was aware of her reaction. No doubt, this kind of thing happened to him all the time.

"We set to go?" said Ricardo, totally unaware of what she'd been feeling. Willow nodded, grateful for the diversion.

As they walked outside, Craig sidled up next to her. "Bet I beat you. If I do, you've got to go out with me."

"That's never going to happen," she said, wishing she'd been more serious about her game lately. No way was this guy going to get the best of her.

"Why don't we let the lady go first?" Ken said, when they'd pulled their carts up to the first tee.

"If I have my choice, I'd rather be last," she said. "I haven't played in a while, and I need to loosen up with a few swings."

"All right," Ken said, bobbing his head. "How about you, Craig? Ready to play?"

Craig pulled out a five-wood from his golf bag, and took a couple of practice swings. Then, he swung, hit the ball dead on and stood with the others to see where it went. It rose in the air, curved, and landed in the rough right next to the fairway.

"Not bad," said Ricardo. He took a couple of practice swings and hit the ball straight down the middle, several yards beyond Craig's ball.

Ken followed. His ball landed close to Ricardo's.

Willow told herself to relax, that it was just a game even though Craig was grinning at her. She took a couple more practice swings and then hit the ball. It, too, flew high and straight, landing close to Ricardo's ball.

"Beginner's luck," Craig murmured as they headed back to their carts.

Ricardo heard him. "Willow's no beginner," he said. "She's …

"Never mind," said Willow, cutting him off. "It's just a game."

Ricardo caught on and gave her a discreet wink. "You're right. Just a game."

As they went from one hole to another, Willow hid her amusement at the way Craig worked to try to make every stroke perfect. She liked a little competition.

At the end of nine holes, Ken said, "I don't know about you guys, but this heat is draining. If you don't mind, can we end the game here?"

Craig gave his father a troubled look. "Are you all right, Dad?"

"Just a little overheated," Ken said. "Next time, we have to get an earlier tee time. I'm showing my age."

Craig handed his father a cold bottle of water that he took from the small cooler he'd placed on his cart. "Here, cool down a little." Their conversation soon turned to Alec.

"How's he doing?" Ricardo asked. "It's such a shame. He had such good plans for the inn going forward." He turned to Willow. "Plans that included you. He's very proud of all you've done. Your being here means a lot to him."

"Thanks. He's been awfully good to me. I appreciate it. I'd do anything for him," she responded with a sincerity she felt from her head to her toes.

"Do you think he can hang on to see the hotel sold?" Ken asked. "Every time I talk to him, he seems determined to make his plans come to fruition." Ken was Alec's accountant.

"His health is failing, no doubt about it," Willow said.

Craig studied her. "So, you're one of the Desert Flowers, like Lily?"

"Yes, that's what Alec calls us. Like Charley's Angels in that television show. It may seem silly to some, but, like I said, each of us would do anything for him and will fight for his cause."

"Are you ready to play again, Ken? Or do you want to stop?" Ricardo asked him.

Ken gave them a sheepish look. "I'm sorry, but I think I'd better stop. I'm not feeling well."

Willow watched concern fill Craig's face. "Let me drive you home," he said to his father. "I'll get my car later."

"Okay. That sounds good," said Ken.

The four of them were quiet as they headed back to the club. Willow saw how caring Craig was with his father and decided he wasn't all bad. Just one of those guys who liked women too much. Or vice versa.

"Don't worry about me," said Ken to Ricardo and Willow. "I think I'm just dehydrated. Craig will take me home. But I think we need to set up this same foursome for next week at an earlier time. I, for one, sense a little contest going on."

Craig turned to her. "Dad's right. This game isn't over. It's to be continued. I wasn't my best today, but I still think I can beat you."

She laughed. His determination to outdo her had made the game exciting. And, though she, too, hadn't done her best, she was still ahead of him by four strokes.

She was still in a good mood when she returned to Alec's house. But when she went indoors, she found her mother crying in the kitchen and Rose and Lily outside on the patio talking quietly.

"What's wrong?" she asked, her heart pounding.

"It's Alec. He's taken a downturn. It's been suggested Hospice be called in. This time, he agreed." Her mother threw her arms around her. "I'm guessing it's down to days, not weeks."

Willow hugged her tight, feeling sick to her stomach. She

knew it was bad. Alec had been doing so well. Getting weaker, yes, but not willing to have Hospice called in.

She went outside and sat down at the table with Rose and Lily. "Do you think Alec will make it through the next couple of weeks, when the sale will go through?"

"It's hard to say," said Rose. "But if he doesn't rally, I'm going to call Hank and ask him to come home."

"I told Brian I need to stay here until I know better how things are going. Thank heavens for Anna. She's very willing to help out," said Lily, biting her lip. "There's been so much death lately. Too much."

Willow took hold of Lily's hand and gave it an encouraging squeeze. Poor Lily was still suffering the loss of her sister and dealing with the fallout from the death of Brian's ex-fiancée. The reality of Alec dying had hit her hard, but Willow knew him well enough to understand it wasn't totally tragic, because he hoped to be with his beloved Conchita and their unborn child.

"Your mother told me you were substituting for Alec for his weekly golf game," said Rose. "How'd it go?"

Willow shrugged. "We had to end it early because Ken Kincaid wasn't feeling well."

"Is that Craig's father?" said Lily.

"Yes. He seems like a nice man. Ricardo Morales was there too."

"I love his wife, Loretta," said Lily. "She's the office manager at the law firm and is a wonderful person who keeps the office humming. Craig adores her because she's more or less taken over the role of mother after his own mom died several years ago."

Willow listened without comment. Craig Kincaid had a whole lot more to him than she'd originally thought. Though she liked that idea, she was definitely not going to be one of a long line of women he dated and dropped.

The nurse who'd been tending Alec approached.

Heart pounding, Willow jumped to her feet. "Alec?"

"Alec is doing okay for the moment. This disease can be tricky. It's still a matter of good days and bad. But the bad days are beginning to outnumber the good ones by a lot. He's asked to see the three of you."

Willow followed Rose and Lily into Alec's private quarters, her heart heavy.

Alec was lying in his lounge chair. He gave them a weak wave. "Ah, my Desert Flowers. I'm glad you're here. I wanted to thank you for the work you've done while I'm still coherent. It seems I'm on the homestretch with this disease."

Willow swallowed hard, telling herself to keep it together.

"Having you all here has worked out better than I thought. Watching you bloom working to help me reach my goal for the Desert Sage Inn has been a privilege. You, Rose and Lily, have found good men who love you. Willow, I put you up against Brent Armstrong so you would understand your own ability and see how strong you are. As I've always thought, you will do well in the hospitality business by being you, the daughter of two of the finest people I know. But I'm a bit old-fashioned and my plans for you include someone else. You'll understand in time."

Willow gave him a tender smile. She loved how Alec was always looking out for her.

Rose leaned down and kissed Alec's cheek. "You sweet matchmaker. You planned all of this for us?"

Alec laughed. "Well, I could only do so much. The rest was left up to you." He became serious. "I have other plans for the three of you after I'm gone."

Lily took hold of his hand. "I'm happy to do whatever you ask. I could never repay you for all you've done for me." She grinned. "Really? You thought Brian and I would end up together?"

His broad grin filled his shrunken face. "Like I said, I could only make sure you met and worked together."

Willow looked at Rose and Lily and began laughing. Thank heavens, he hadn't picked Brent as a love interest for her but as an example of someone who'd never had the right to call her names and make her feel like an outsider and who couldn't begin to measure up to her now. But what else had he planned for her? For them?

CHAPTER ELEVEN

ROSE

As she left Alec, Rose breathed a sigh of gratitude that she, Lily, and Willow had been given time to spend with this remarkable man, but she still wasn't ready to say goodbye.

Alec playing matchmaker? Only someone like him, with his knowledge of and caring for other people, could get away with it. She knew he'd done it out of love. And maybe a little guilt for cutting off his relationships with Lily and her. Willow was different. She was more like a daughter, which is why he'd given her the opportunity to learn how strong, how capable she was. His next idea for Willow could only be wonderful.

Lily caught up to her. "Can you believe that Alec purposely set us up? And with such amazing results?"

Willow joined them. "What do you think he has in store for me? And for the three of us?"

"Heaven only knows," said Lily, chuckling. "I can't wait to tell Brian that he was part of Alec's agenda for all of us." She sobered. "One thing is for sure. Alec could never have foreseen the positions Brian and I now have. And with a baby on the way? All too unexpected."

"I'm glad the nurse thinks Alec will be able to hold on for a while longer," said Rose. "But I'm going to call Hank to check on his schedule. He's looking into some financial and legal matters, thinking about our upcoming marriage."

"Guess I'd better get back home," said Lily. She picked up her purse and headed out.

Willow turned to Rose. "I'm going to get changed and go into the hotel to talk to John Rodriguez about how I can enhance my chances to get to stay at the Desert Sage Inn after it's sold. Knowing how close the ending is, I'd better do that now, not later."

"Not a bad idea. I'm going to work on my blog and then call Hank."

"How's 'You Deserve This' doing?" Willow asked her. She loved Rose's online blog talking about cool places to visit, where to eat, new clothing trends, and other things of interest to people too busy to investigate on their own.

It's going great," said Rose. "As long as I keep posting and interacting with my thousands of followers, it continues to grow."

"It was such a smart idea and it seems to be paying off," said Willow.

"Thanks," said Rose. She'd set up the business to provide an income when she was between consulting jobs helping small businesses establish social media platforms. It was a lot of hard work but fun too. She felt her posts about the Desert Sage Inn had helped to convince the Blaise Group that the prospect of turning two of their other hotels into parts of the Corona Collection would be profitable. People loved to find a special, upscale hotel at which they could pamper themselves—one of the ideas behind "You Deserve This."

Inside her room, Rose took a moment to look out the window at the desert landscape. The texture of the land, the cacti, and other desert plants served as an entrée to the foothills beyond. She loved the bright bougainvillea and other flowers that brightened the view. But it was the majestic mountains in the desert that always filled her soul. Their presence was a reminder to her to be strong. She wondered if Willow felt the same way.

She sat and went to work researching new places to eat in the area. When Hank returned, she'd ask him out to dinner for the sake of research. Thinking of him, she lifted her phone.

Her call went to voice mail, asking her to leave a message. Rather than do that, she decided she'd wait and call him later.

CHAPTER TWELVE

WILLOW

Sitting in John's office waiting for him to get off the phone, Willow's thoughts spun. With Alec's health fading, she needed to know if she had a real chance of being given a management position at the new Desert Sage Inn. More than ever, she was hoping to be able to tell Alec of her success before it was too late.

John got off his call and turned to her. "Willow! Good to see you. What can I do for you?"

"As you know, I'm planning to stay in the area after the hotel is sold. My wish would be to stay at the Desert Sage Inn working in a management position. Do you think that's possible?"

He shook his head. "I honestly can't say. I've been offered the position of general manager at the Desert Hotel Royal in Phoenix, and I'm going to take it. I have no idea who the Blaise Group is going to bring in here. My guess is that it's someone at one of their other hotels. Just as they've done for me, they like to keep their staff moving around so that each property has fresh ideas and management from time to time."

"It makes sense," Willow admitted. "But what about the position of assistant manager here? Any ideas?"

He studied her and sighed. "My guess is that after they assign someone as general manager, they'll offer either you, Brent, or Trace the position of executive assistant manager. I've made it clear I think you should get the position here at the inn, but it's a family business, which means it's probably going to be Brent or Trace. I'm sorry, but that's what I suspect."

"Thanks for being truthful," said Willow, trying to put on a brave face when she felt like pounding his desk in frustration.

"I'm happy to write recommendations for you for any job you seek," said John. "I admire your work ethic and your talent."

"Thanks. That's a beginning. I'll start looking for another job and may need your help." Willow got to her feet. "After working here, I realize I love operations much more than teaching."

"I'm sure you were an excellent teacher, and I know how good you are in management," John said, rising and shaking her hand.

Willow left his office and decided to go to the Premio Inn to see if there was any possibility of working there. Managing that nearby, small upscale inn would be a second-best dream come true.

As she drove up the long drive to the Premio Inn, she thought of subtle improvements she'd make to the entrance to enhance the sense of arrival. Pulling up to the white-stucco building with its red-tile roof, she was struck again by the stunning simplicity of the inn. A long, wide veranda lined the front of the building offering conversational groupings of rocking chairs, small tables, and comfortable wicker chairs. She knew from her last visit that since no cars were allowed to park in the front circle, a valet would quickly whisk her car away to a parking area off to the side. She also knew as attractive as this building was, luxurious, private guesthouses behind it were where celebrities and other wealthy guests preferred to stay. The use of these lovely guesthouses at high rates helped to maintain a steady flow of income.

Willow left her car with the valet, entered the inn, and went to the front desk, hoping to speak to George Hartmann, the owner and manager of the property.

The young man behind the desk shook his head. "Sorry. Mr. Hartmann is out of town and will be gone for a couple of weeks. But I will let him know you stopped by."

Willow handed him her business card. "Thank you."

Feeling defeated, Willow returned to her car and headed back to Alec's.

As she pulled her car into the garage, she noticed her cart, still loaded with her clubs. Thinking of the challenge match with Craig Kincaid, she decided a round of golf was just what she needed.

By late afternoon, only the toughest of competitors were willing to face the heat of the day to either practice or play a game.

Willow pulled her cart into the parking lot outside the pro shop and selected a few clubs to take with her to the practice range. She walked into the shop, paid for a bucket of balls, and exited through the other side of the shop and headed to the practice range. At the sight of Craig among the number of people swinging away, she almost turned around. But, determined to hold her own, she moved forward to a spot not too far from him.

When he noticed her, he grinned and walked over to her. "Guess you need a little practice, huh?"

"Yes, and you, too," she said, hiding her laughter. She'd seen his concentration when taking a swing and knew she had him worried.

"I asked Ricardo to give me some pointers but he refused. He said, this contest was between the two of us. What's going on? Did you already try to hire him?"

"No, I didn't. But if that's how he wants to handle it, that's okay with me." No way was she going to tell him how good she once had been, because she, too, needed to work on her game.

After Craig walked away, Willow selected one club and took a few practice swings with it. Then, all thoughts of others evaporated as she concentrated on her swing, trying to get a rhythm going, a natural feel to her movement. Growing up, she'd used golf as an escape from the teasing she'd faced in high school for being too smart, too pretty, too fat, too thin. The sport and Alec's gentle guidance had kept her from giving up on herself. Her parents had used examples of how they handled their own social mistreatment to instill in her an acceptable way to cope and a sense of self-worth.

She was so lost in her memories she startled when she realized Craig was standing near her. She whipped around. "Why are you watching me?"

He looked surprised and then bobbed his head. "I was just going to ask you if I could buy you a beer at the club."

"Oh, sorry. I have a lot on my mind."

"So? Want that beer?"

She sighed. No way could she practice with him standing right there. "Okay, that sounds good." If she hadn't been in the dry desert air, she'd be sweating like crazy.

She carried her clubs and the half-empty basket to the shop. Inside, she turned to Craig. "I have to put my clubs away and move my cart. Why don't I meet you in the bar?"

"Fair enough. I'll save us a table."

After tucking her clubs into her bag and moving her cart, she headed toward the far end of the building where the bar and café were situated. It felt good to be back in the familiar territory.

When she walked inside, it took a moment for her eyes to adjust to the dim lighting. Craig, she saw, was standing at the bar, talking to the attractive blonde behind it.

She walked over to them. “Hello, Mandy. How are you?” Willow said in a quiet, measured tone. Mandy had been part of the “in crowd” in high school and was someone Willow had never admired.

“Hi, Willow. Heard you were working here. I haven’t seen you around here for ages,” Mandy said. “You’ve been away, haven’t you?”

“I’ve been living on the east coast, but, obviously, I’m back home now.”

“For good?” Mandy asked, glancing at Craig.

“Yes. I hope to find a job here after finishing up a project for the inn.”

“Oh, I see.” She focused her attention to Craig. “Like I said, we have to get together sometime. Give me a call.”

He gave her an agreeable smile. “Okay. How about two drafts?” He turned to Willow. “Pale ale sound good?”

“Sure,” Willow said, ignoring the glares Mandy was shooting her way.

“Coming up,” said Mandy. “But, Craig, I’m off early tonight. Will you be at Jasper’s?”

“Probably. Why don’t I hook up with you there?”

Willow walked over to a table with Craig and faced him. “Sorry, I made a mistake. I’ll catch up with you at the game next week.”

“Wait! You’re going to leave?”

“Yes.”

He caught up with her. “What’s going on?”

“I made a promise to myself to stay away from players. Sorry, but my time is too valuable to me.”

While he stood gaping at her, she hurried out of the bar before she could make a bigger scene.

On the ride back to Alec’s house, her thoughts centered on

Craig. She understood why women were attracted to him. The man oozed sex appeal. He was magnetic. Her arm had almost caught on fire just shaking hands with him. Definitely someone she didn't want to get involved with. Especially at this time with the hotel about to be sold and Alec fading fast.

CHAPTER THIRTEEN

ROSE

When Rose finished work, she realized it was the perfect time to call Hank. She pictured him with Samantha about to put Leah to bed at her eight o'clock bedtime. The call rang and rang. She was about to hang up when Sam answered breathlessly, "Hello, Rose?"

"Hi, is Hank there?" she asked, wondering why Hank couldn't answer the phone himself.

Sam hesitated. "Actually, he's not. He's out on a date ... not really a date ... with a friend at a charity event for Nikki's hospital. I was supposed to go but didn't feel well enough."

"So, he asked this ... friend ... to go with him?" Rose kept her voice steady but she was shaken.

"Yes, Martha Wentworth and Dad dated before he met you. They're just friends now. He was in a last-minute rush to leave and forgot his phone," Sam said. "I didn't want you to worry, which is why I picked up. Is there anything I can help you with? Or should I just give him the message that you called?"

"Actually, don't bother telling him I called," Rose said. "I'll wait until he calls me."

"Oh, okay," said Sam. "He'll probably be late, so I'm guessing it'll be sometime tomorrow. How are things out there? We can't wait to get back to the desert. But I know how hot it is, and we'll wait until it cools down a bit."

"It'll be lovely to have you here," said Rose, wondering why Hank hadn't called her before he left for the evening with another woman.

CHAPTER FOURTEEN

LILY

Lily headed to the law office with mixed feelings. Though she was feeling well with her pregnancy, other matters made life difficult from time to time. This morning, Izzy had been whiny since getting up, and Ollie was unusually quiet. She thought it might have something to do with a Disney movie that had featured children with their mother. Lily had quietly talked to each of them about how much they were loved, but she knew she needed to do more than that during a time like this. Thank heavens, Anna was her cheerful self when she arrived to take care of the kids. She soon had Izzy and Ollie telling her about the tricks Jake was learning. The dog was a wonderful companion to both children.

Brian was in Austin dealing with his real estate agent selling his condo. She'd offered to help him pack up, but he thought it was more important for her to be at home with the kids. He was right, of course, but the burden of responsibility was heavy.

As she entered the office, those thoughts fled. She went to Loretta to see what had happened in her absence and to get an idea of what work she'd be handling today.

Loretta looked up at her. "There's Lily! I'm hoping you're ready to dig into a couple of projects I have lined up for you."

"Of course," Lily said, perking up.

Loretta waved her to a chair nearby and leaned over toward her. "First, tell me about Willow. Though I haven't seen her in a long time, I understand from Alec and Ricardo that she's both intelligent and beautiful." She lowered her voice. "Apparently, she's doing a number on Craig. When I asked him about her, he mumbled something about difficult women and walked away without answering."

Lily observed Loretta's gleeful smile and laughed. "I wouldn't go there if I were you. Willow doesn't put up with BS from anyone."

Loretta clasped her hands together. "Perfect. I love her!"

Lily grinned. *Come to think of it, Willow and Craig together? Dynamite!*

Throughout the day, Lily was amused by the thought. But no matter how she felt about the idea, she wouldn't mention it to Willow. If Willow wanted to talk to her about it, she'd be happy to do so.

CHAPTER FIFTEEN

WILLOW

With the golf game coming up, Willow decided she'd better sneak in some practice on the putting green. While it was still early, she got up, dressed, grabbed a cup of coffee, and climbed onto her cart. As she drove down to the hotel, her thoughts centered around the job situation. She still had a few days before she could expect to hear from George Hartmann at the Premio Inn. And though both she and John Rodriguez knew she was better qualified than either Brent or Trace, her chances of staying at the Desert Sage Inn were two: slim and none.

Sighing at the fact that her whole life seemed to be on hold, she told herself to take everything one day at a time. That philosophy worked well for others; it was time for her to use it too.

By the time she wheeled into the parking lot by the pro shop and club, she was in a better frame of mind. She got off the cart and loosened her shoulders. Some time spent putting would, she was sure, shake off her uneasy feelings.

She carried her putter and several golf balls to the space behind the club where a beautifully maintained putting green sat.

When she turned the corner of the building, she jerked to a stop. Craig was there.

He looked up at her and frowned. "What are you doing here?"

She gave him a steady stare. "The same thing you are—

practicing. That is, if you're willing to share the green."

His mouth twisted, but he bobbed his approval.

Telling herself to keep her cool, she walked over to the green, dropped the balls on the smooth surface, and waited for him to putt.

She watched as he planted his feet beside his ball, wiggled his butt a little to get settled, and tapped his ball. It rolled toward the hole, kissed it, and rolled on by.

Pressing her lips together to prevent a laugh from emerging, she waited while he tapped his ball into the hole and walked away.

Willow reminded herself that when playing in a tournament, it was important to block out everything but the ball, the hole, and the grass in between. She studied the lay of the land to help determine the contour of the green and grain of the grass and tapped the ball. It rolled a little too fast, then slowed and calmly disappeared in the hole.

Smiling, she went to retrieve it.

"Good shot," said Craig. "I looked you up online and know you won a state championship in high school. So, you're no beginner like you pretend."

"I never pretended to be a beginner. You're the one who called my shot beginner's luck if I remember."

"Yeah, well, I was being nice."

"Humph," she replied, bending over to retrieve her ball.

"I challenge you to a short match," said Craig, smiling. "The best of seven balls. Loser buys coffee."

Fired up from her success with the first one, Willow studied him and grinned. "Okay. You're on."

"Don't worry," said Craig, giving her a challenging look. "I'm not a washed-up champion player. I'm just an ordinary golfer. So, the chance of your winning is pretty even."

Willow couldn't help the way her lips curved. Craig was so

outrageous that he was actually funny. She could feel adrenaline pumping through her. She loved a challenge like this.

As she watched Craig get better with each ball and tie the score, Willow was suddenly afraid she might lose the challenge. She blocked everything else out of her mind and concentrated on getting the ball in the cup.

"I won!" she shouted. She was waving her fist in the air with triumph when she realized Craig was moving toward her with open arms. Before she could stop him, he swung her up in his arms and twirled her around.

"Even though I lost, that was a terrific shot. Good for you! Now, how about a cup of coffee?" He set her down and gave her a hopeful look.

"Sure, why not? I earned it," she said, recalling the feeling of accomplishment past golf games had given her. This was a fun competition she couldn't wait to tell Alec about. He'd always loved listening to her account of her games whenever he couldn't be there to see for himself.

The thought of Alec never seeing her play again pierced her like a sharp pick. Before she could stop herself, she was crying.

"What's wrong?" Craig asked, wrapping her in his arms.

All the fears, hopes, and disappointments of the past months prevented her from doing anything but releasing them in a torrent of tears.

Craig rubbed her back while she fought to control herself. But the feeling of strength that emanated from him giving her comfort was so overwhelming she pressed closer.

After catching her breath and finding herself in his arms, she pushed away. "Oh, no! I'm sorry. So many things have been going on ... I didn't realize ..."

He gave her a teasing grin. "Really? I thought you were just feeling sorry for my having lost."

She laughed, feeling foolish, yet somehow better. "Is that cup of coffee still on? I guess I need it." She was glad that no one else had seen what had happened at this early hour.

They went inside the club, sat at the bar, and ordered cups of coffee. The middle-aged man behind the counter glanced at her. "Everything all right, Ms. Sanchez?"

Willow smiled at him. "Yes, thank you."

Craig slung an arm across her shoulder. "I should be the one upset. Not her. She just won the bet, which is why I'm paying."

The bartender studied him, then faced her. "Ah, to be young again. This coffee is on me."

He placed a mug of the hot liquid in front of each of them.

Craig lifted his and clicked it against her raised mug. "Here's to more golf together."

"Okay. Deal." She swallowed and let out a sigh of contentment. Still remembering how she'd felt in his arms, she vowed to play her best. Craig needed to know she wasn't just another woman in his life, even if she was beginning to think he was a nice guy.

Willow returned to Alec's house, shaken by her morning time with Craig. Just when she was determined not to get involved with him, he did something sweet like holding her when she was having a complete meltdown. And instead of making fun of her, he'd helped her deal with her embarrassment.

Taking a chance on Alec being awake and alert, she headed into his private area of the house.

His lips curved when he saw her. "Playing this early?"

"Yes," she said, pulling up a chair next to the recliner he preferred over a hospital bed. "I wanted to get some more practice before your weekly game. Craig Kincaid and I have an ongoing challenge to settle between us."

"Ah, I see," he said, smiling. "You and he are quite evenly matched, I'd guess. And in more ways than one."

Willow sighed. "I don't know what to think about him. He makes me mad one moment, and then he can be very kind. What can you tell me about him? You've known him since he was a kid and are still friends with his dad."

"Ah, so that's how it is?" The smile that had been on Alec's face reappeared and widened. "Good."

"What do you mean?" said Willow.

"I've wondered about a connection between the two of you. Craig is a great young man who needs someone steady at his side. He was very attentive to his mother when she was dying of cancer. He still keeps a careful eye on his dad but has been blatantly foolish about other women since his mother passed a number of years ago. His father has talked to me about Craig's behavior, and we both agree he'll change when he finds the right young woman. Loretta has been keeping watch over him, reining him in from time to time. He has a lot of people who love him."

"I understand why," Willow said.

"Bennett Williams hired him more or less as a favor to Ken, but soon discovered how brilliant Craig is at his job. He can't say enough good things about him."

"Thank you, Alec. That gives me a better idea about him. I needed to hear that."

Alec reached over and gave her hand a squeeze. "If it matters to you, I like the idea of you two together. You're a strong, kind, loving woman. Exactly what he needs. And he's a steady, kind, loving man who likes to have fun."

Willow's jaw dropped. "Are you giving me your blessing?"

Alec sighed sadly. "If I don't do it now, I may not be able to. I trust you to choose any partner wisely. Though I may not be around to see it, the thought will make me happy."

"Trace wants me to date him," Willow blurted out. "But I don't think I'd ever fit in."

"Willow, you have every qualification to be part of any family, including his. Let your heart choose for you."

Sighing, Willow got to her feet, kissed Alec on the cheek, and forced a brave smile. "I love you, Alec, for always watching out for me."

"Love you too," he murmured, not bothering to wipe the tears off his cheek.

CHAPTER SIXTEEN

ROSE

Rose was surprised by an early morning text from Hank:

"Decided to return to Palm Desert early. We need to talk. I'll get in this evening and meet you at the house."

Heart pounding, she studied the words and tried to tell herself not to panic. The fact that he went out with a friend and hadn't called her back didn't mean there was anything to worry about. Still, she decided to take a swim. Slicing through the water always calmed her mind.

She put on her bathing suit, grabbed a towel, and headed outside. No one else was around. Grateful for the solitude, she tossed her towel aside and dove into the pool. As she began her laps, she told herself to relax and enjoy the exercise.

Sometime later, she slowed her strokes and turned on her back to gaze up into the sky. A few puffy white clouds hung above her like dollops of whipped cream. Though the day was already warm, she loved the thought of being outdoors doing something like this most days of the year.

As she floated in the water, her limbs relaxed and she opened her mind to thoughts of Hank. The fact that they'd moved so quickly to become engaged had seemed natural, so right. Even now, thinking of the time they'd spent together, she knew their relationship was special. Rather than worry about what was going on with Hank, she vowed to keep herself from falling into the trap of thinking what they shared wasn't real. It was a matter of trust. If it turned out she couldn't trust him with other women, she might as well discover it now.

She climbed out of the pool and shook the water out of her hair and the worry out of her head.

That evening, as a surprise, Rose stood outside the baggage claim area of the Palm Springs airport waiting for Hank. He'd been gone only a few days, but she'd missed him like crazy.

When a group of deplaned passengers headed her way, she stood on tiptoes to look for him. She saw him walking toward her, his eyes on the phone he held in his hand.

"Hank?" she called.

He looked up at her and grinned.

She moved toward him as his gait sped up. When they met, he swept her into his arms.

"Hey, there! I missed you."

"Enough that you couldn't call me back?" she said, smiling.

"More than that," he responded calmly. "Let's get my bag and then we need to talk."

"Okay. Is this about last night?"

His jaw tensed. "Yes."

Rather than ply him with questions like she wanted, Rose waited for Hank to retrieve his luggage, and then they walked to her car in the parking lot without saying anything.

Hank tossed his bag into the backseat, climbed into the passenger seat, and turned to her. "I don't want to move to Atlanta. I notified my real estate agent to officially put my house up for sale. We'd talked about it before, but I've made up my mind to move on."

"Oka-a-ay. What happened?" Rose said.

"Sam told me she mentioned to you that I was with Martha Wentworth. I want you to understand that this was a social thing, a gala, to benefit the hospital where Nikki works."

"Yes, that's what she said."

"Well, the evening turned into a disaster. First of all, I don't like events like that, and I didn't like being with Martha. Her telling people she was trying to convince me to stay in Atlanta just felt all wrong. She made it seem as if we were together. My life as I knew it there is over. I've chosen to be with you, and we're happy out here."

"Yes, we are." Rose knew there had to be something more to the situation. "What else?"

Hank sighed and looked away. "Martha told me that my wife, Leigh, had picked her out to be my next wife, that us being together was something Leigh wanted for both of us. I told her to forget it, that I was happily engaged, that I didn't appreciate her behavior, and that I didn't care if she was Leigh's choice for me. She wasn't mine." Hank swallowed hard but gave her a steady look. "She said some terrible things about you. Apparently, she looked you up online and knew from a friend about you and Alec and your ex. She mentioned you a time or two to others we were sitting with. I got fed up with it, asked a friend to see Martha home, and left."

"Oh, Hank, I'm sorry. I don't know what she heard about me, but I have nothing to be ashamed of. Yes, I stupidly married someone I knew was wrong for me, but that isn't a crime. And you know all about Alec and me. Contrary to anything ugly, the relationship between him and me is still lovely."

"I know that, Rose. You've done nothing to merit her maneuvering. When we go back to visit the kids, I want nothing to do with her and many of the people I used to associate with. In the meantime, I want you to know how much I love you."

He leaned over and cupped her face in his hands. "You're

the best thing that's happened to me in a long, long time. Being here with you is all I want."

Rose melted into his kiss, happy she'd been right about him all along.

CHAPTER SEVENTEEN

WILLOW

Willow headed down the hill in her cart wondering how Craig would behave toward her. If he'd told his dad and Ricardo how weak she'd been, sobbing on the putting green with him, she'd be wounded.

When she parked her cart and went into the café to find them, she noticed the look of concern Craig gave her and was pleased when he simply said hi.

Ken and Ricardo got to their feet.

"Morning, Willow. Are you ready?" said Ricardo.

"Yes." She turned to Ken. "How are you feeling?"

"Great. I've had plenty of water and brought some extra bottles with me."

She waited for Craig to say some teasing remark, but he remained quiet.

"Today, Ricardo and I are going to share a cart," said Ken. "Why don't you and Craig share one? The club has asked us to use as few golf carts on the course as possible."

Rather than say something to him about his obvious attempt to put her and Craig together, she simply said, "Okay. Craig can load his clubs on my cart." She had no intention of letting Craig drive her around the course, making her feel as if he, not she, was in charge.

Once Craig got his clubs settled on her cart, he climbed aboard. "Okay. Let's go. If we're lucky we can beat them to the first hole."

She glanced at him. "Are you always this competitive?"

He grinned. “Not unless I have twenty bucks on the game.”

Knowing he could well afford the money, she laughed. “No bets with me?

“How about ten dollars? I don’t want you to lose more than that. There’ll be plenty of games ahead. Loretta, our office manager at the law firm, told me that my partner, Bennett Williams, won’t be able to play in this group for the next few weeks, and I’m to take over for him.”

“Oh, that’s nice for you,” Willow said.

“Yeah, we try to mix work and pleasure as much as we can. The whole purpose of living in a place like this.”

“That’s a great way to think about things. The hotel business can be very time-consuming with guests arriving and leaving and demanding things throughout the day.”

“But you love it,” he said—a statement not a question.

“Yes. It’s something you either love or hate,” she replied.

“Law can be boring, but I like working with different people, helping to solve their problems.”

As Willow pulled the cart to a stop by the tees on the first hole, they gazed at one another and smiled.

Ricardo walked up to them. “Are you two all set to play now? Ken and I have been waiting for you.”

Willow blinked in surprise, totally unaware of how slowly they’d been traveling. Laughing, she hopped off the cart. “I’m ready to beat Craig at his game.”

“Lucky for her, we bet only ten dollars,” said Craig, drawing a club out of his bag.

Later, as the four of them sat in the club café, Willow couldn’t stop the goodwill bubbling inside her. She hadn’t had this much fun since she could remember. She and Craig were evenly matched as were Ricardo and Ken. There had been a few tense moments when she was sure she was going to lose to Craig, but pride made her blot out her surroundings and get down to work. And when at the end of the game, the four of them shook hands, she was pleasantly surprised to see Craig's eyes widen at the sizzle of energy between the two of them.

"I understand we'll be playing together for a while," said Ken, looking pleased. "Why don't I buy the drinks this time? The rest of you can take turns in the future."

"That's fair," said Willow, sipping on the lemonade she'd ordered. Beer might come later in the day, but for now, she needed to be on her toes to compete with Brent and Trace at the office.

As if her thoughts had conjured him up, Brent strolled into the restaurant. "There you are!" he cried, pointing to Willow. "I've been looking for you."

The other three stared as Brent marched over to her.

"What can I do for you?" Willow asked, trying her best not to snap at him.

"They're going to announce the new executive assistant manager for the inn. We've been asked to come to John's office." He curled his lip. "If you can manage to get away."

"It's a favor for Alec," she said, then mentally scolded herself for trying to make an excuse. It was none of Brent's business what she did outside work.

Brent continued to stand there.

"Please tell John I'll be there shortly," said Willow.

"Who are you?" Craig asked Brent.

Brent smirked. "Probably the new exec assistant, Brent Armstrong."

Craig glanced at her. "Is this for real?"

She shrugged, pretending she didn't care about the job. "We'll see."

"You heard the lady," said Craig. "She'll be there. Now, give us some privacy."

"And you are?" Brent said.

"Craig Kincaid." Willow wondered if he'd introduce the other two men, but he didn't, which indicated to her how annoyed Craig was with Brent's attitude.

Brent stood a moment longer then, with a barely concealed glare at Craig, turned and moved away.

Craig turned to her. "You've actually had to work with this guy?"

"Unfortunately. His cousin, Trace, is a nice guy, though. The three of us have been reviewing operating policies and procedures for the last several weeks."

"Hm-m-m." Craig gave her a thoughtful look.

"I've heard hotel employees, especially the guys in the pro shop talk about what a jackass this guy is," said Ricardo. "I certainly hope he isn't the one chosen to stay on here."

"If Alec has any say, he won't be," said Ken. "He and I chatted the other day. His cousin, Trace, seems to be a different story. Alec likes him."

Willow stood. "I guess I'd better call John and then get freshened up. Do you want to come with me and grab your clubs?" she said to Craig.

He shook his head. "I'll get them later. I'd better call into the office. Ben might have more flexibility, but I have to squeeze this into my schedule."

Willow left them and quickly called John.

"Take your time, Willow. I thought I'd order lunch into the office, and we can talk then about how we all go forward."

"Oh, okay." Willow was dying to ask him to give her a hint but knew how unprofessional that would be. The verdict wouldn't change because of a private conversation.

###

Dressed appropriately in a lightweight skirt and matching linen jacket, Willow entered John's office. During the time she had to shower and dress, she went over a number of scenarios in her mind. Most of them not promising. Though she was disappointed by the thought of not remaining at the inn, she reminded herself of a saying her mother had always told her:

"Things work out best for those who make the best of how things work out."

I can do this, Willow told herself as she took a seat in front of John's desk, between Brent and Trace.

John faced them, his smile less than normal. "Mitch Armstrong called this morning to tell me a decision has been made as to which of you has been selected to carry on here at the inn. One of you has been named as executive assistant manager with rights to sit on the board. The other two will be given opportunities elsewhere."

Willow could feel the tension rolling off the men on either side of her. She took a deep breath and let it out slowly.

John spoke. "Trace, you will stay here at the inn. Congratulations!"

Willow felt John's words buzzing in her ears like annoying pests. She was every bit as competent as Trace. Before she had more than a moment to think this, Brent erupted like a loud, noisy volcano, screaming as he jumped up from his chair. "This is wrong! I did every bit of the work that Trace did. Even better!"

"As a matter of fact, I'm pleased with the work *all* of you did," said John calmly. "I don't make the decisions. The Blaise Group board has spoken. It would behoove you to sit down and listen."

Brent sent Trace a look of hatred that sent a shiver through her. She glanced at John. He'd seen it too.

"Are you going to be willing to stay for lunch and learn of other opportunities or not, Brent?" John asked.

Brent plopped down in his chair and sat with his arms crossed in front of him.

A knock at the door broke the tension in the room, shattering the quiet.

Trace got to his feet and went to open it.

A waiter stood outside with a tray of sandwiches, snacks, and cold sodas on a rolling cart.

"Come in," called John. "You can set that tray down on the small conference table in the corner."

After the waiter left, John motioned them to the chairs at the conference table. "Sit down and let's enjoy our lunch while we discuss what's going to happen next."

Willow lowered herself into a chair willing herself to stay calm even as disappointment stabbed at her.

When they were all seated, John said, "Help yourselves. And while you do, I want to say a big congratulations to Trace. I think you'll be a fine addition to the new staff here. I understand Lou Molina is transferring here while I replace him at the Desert Hotel Royal." He turned to Brent. "You will accompany me there."

"As what?" snapped Brent.

"As executive assistant manager," John replied, and Willow knew how disappointed John was for the decisions he had to announce for the company. "But without the attitude."

"And me?" Willow said.

"Mitchell is going to come to Palm Desert for the weekend. He has a special project in mind to discuss with you."

Willow let out the breath she'd been holding and gave him a pleading look.

John shook his head. "I don't know anything more than that."

Brent gave her a look of satisfaction that she wanted to slap off his face. But she forced herself to remain calm. She remembered her earlier private conversation with Mitchell and told herself not to worry. He liked her and her work. But couldn't someone have given her at least a hint?

Throughout lunch, John talked about Brent's move to Phoenix and Trace's move to Palm Desert. "Right now," John said, "I'd expect each of you to stay in your new location and position for at least a year. When Mitchell comes this weekend, he'll meet with you privately to give you more details. An announcement will be made in certain publications about Trace and Brent," John explained. "The board asked me to give you three advance notice about it." He turned to Willow. "I don't know what they have planned for you, but I'm sure it's good news."

Willow remained quiet, but a part of her felt sick at the idea of losing out to Trace. Thank God it wasn't Brent.

After John dismissed them, Willow gathered her things and prepared to leave.

Trace came up to her. "I'm sorry to disappoint you by getting the job. You're every bit as qualified as I am."

"I know, but you worked hard for the position, and I can't take issue with that," Willow said. "Congratulations."

"I'm sure something good is headed your way," Trace said. "My father has been impressed by your work, and he isn't an easy person to impress."

"Thanks. Guess I'll find out this weekend."

"Will you go out with me to celebrate? As awkward as that may seem, there's no one else that would understand what I'm feeling."

She laughed. There was no point in being bitter. "Sure. Why not? I'd be celebrating too."

"Great. I'll pick you up at six. This time, we'll go out. How does Mexican sound?"

"If you mean Tico's, you're on!"

His smile sent a twinkle to his eyes. “Thanks, Willow. I really mean it.”

“See you later.” She gave a little wave and left before she allowed her disappointment to show.

That evening, promptly at six, Willow heard the doorbell and walked to the front door. After swimming off her frustration that afternoon, she’d showered and pampered herself with perfume, lotion, and extra attention to her skin. She knew she looked good as she went to greet Trace.

She opened the door and gaped at Craig. “Hi! What are you doing here? I’m expecting someone else.”

Craig’s glance swept over her with appreciation. “I’m here to pick up my golf clubs.”

“Oh, yes. Sorry, I forgot I was carrying them around on my cart. Let’s get them now.” She led him to Alec’s garage and opened one of the overhead doors. Built for four cars, the garage had plenty of space along the sides for extra storage. Her cart was there.

They walked over to it.

As Willow went to lift his golf bag out, Craig reached around her and took hold of the strap of the leather bag.

She glanced up at him and caught the look on his face as he murmured, “M-m-m. You smell good.”

“Thanks,” she said, laughing when he made a point of sniffing.

“So, who’re you expecting? Not that creep from the café this morning, is it?”

She shook her head. “His cousin, Trace.” She heard a car in the driveway and said, “Here he comes now.”

Trace waved at them and pulled up behind Craig’s vehicle. He got out and faced them as Willow and Craig walked toward them.

"Hi, Trace. This is a golfing friend," said Willow. "Trace Armstrong, meet Craig Kincaid."

With interest, Willow watched the two men size up one another as they shook hands. Both men were handsome. Whereas Trace was tall and thin, Craig's broad shoulders and muscular body made him seem larger than he actually was.

"Trace is going to become executive assistant manager for the inn," Willow said. "So, he'll be moving here permanently for a year at least."

Craig shot her a look. "I thought that was the job you wanted."

"It was. But this weekend I'll learn what job the Blaise Group is offering me instead."

"But you wouldn't move, right?"

"Yes. I've decided to stay here no matter what."

"Good," said Craig and Trace together, bringing a smile to her face.

CHAPTER EIGHTEEN

WILLOW

Trace and Willow waved goodbye to Craig, and then Willow said, "Wait here while I get my purse. I won't be long."

"Don't worry. I'll stay here no matter how long it takes."

"Such gallantry," she teased and hurried inside the house.

"Who's that?" her mother said, pulling back from a front window and holding out her purse to her.

"That's Trace Armstrong," Willow said. "He and I are going out to dinner."

"Very handsome," her mother said. "Alec told me about him and his cousin."

"What did he say about them?" asked Willow, surprised Alec would discuss them with her.

"He said you have some big decisions ahead of you. That's all."

Willow stared at her mother. Getting no reaction, she shook her head. "You'd think I was a teenager," she grumbled.

"No, sweetie, it's not like that. It's only that we all love you so much." She gave Willow a quick hug. "Now, go and have a good time."

Willow opened the door and stepped outside.

Trace walked up to her, cupped her elbow and led her to his car.

Willow could feel her mother's eyes on her as Trace held the door for her as she slipped into the passenger seat. Her mother would like that he did that.

"Ready to go? Tico's should be in full swing. It's a great evening to be outdoors."

"I love their food," she said, deciding to relax and have fun. The day had been disappointing, but that wasn't a reason to ruin the evening with someone she was anxious to get to know better outside of work.

As Trace had suspected, Tico's was alive with people packed in the bar and spilling outside. Trace gave his name to the person at the door of the restaurant, and a waitress whisked them away to a table for two outside under the shade of a tree whose branches hung over the edge of the patio.

"Great seat," Willow commented as Trace helped her into a chair.

He grinned. "I told them this was a special evening."

"It is?"

He became serious. "I hope so. Now that the issue of placement at the inn is settled, I want the chance to get to know you better. After all, we'll be living in the same town."

They placed drink orders—a Texas Margarita for her, draft ale for him.

"Want an order of guacamole to start?" Trace asked.

"Sounds good," she said.

After the waitress left, Trace said, "Thanks for helping me celebrate. I know you deserved the position at the inn, so whatever my father has in mind for you, I'm sure it's good."

Willow sighed. "I hope so. I feel very obligated to Alec, and I want him to be proud of me and my work."

"How could he not be?" Trace said.

She studied the sincerity on his face. "How can you and Brent be so different?"

He chuckled. "People ask me that all the time. I'd say it has a lot to do with my parents. You've met my dad. This weekend,

I'm sure you'll meet my mom, my step-mom actually. But she's raised me and my sister since I was very small."

"A sister?"

"Yeah. She's the head of the design department for the hotels and a real dynamo. She doesn't use her last name, though, which is why you might not have recognized her as part of the team."

"Very different from Brent."

"Yeah, Brent is the youngest of two brothers. His older brother was killed in an auto accident when Brent was only twelve. That's why Uncle Duncan puts so much pressure on Brent. The truth is Brent will never live up to the memory of his brother."

"Families are complicated," said Willow.

Trace nodded his agreement. "Especially if they work together in a corporation like ours. Not fun. I've always felt I had to work harder than those around me or else people in the industry would think I was just handed an opportunity."

"Yeah, I get it," said Willow. "And you still love the industry?"

He smiled at her. "Yes. The same as you obviously do."

Their drinks came.

"Here's to the hotel industry!" Trace said.

They clicked glasses and sipped silently.

In the quiet, they heard a familiar voice say, "I hope the table you give me is the best in the house. I'm here to celebrate my big promotion."

Willow froze.

Brent and a young woman she didn't know were following a hostess to the far end of the patio.

Trace watched them with her. "Can I just say that I can't wait for Brent to be shuttled out of town? I'm hoping people forget his name so I can just work here in peace."

"It must be difficult for you," Willow said with sympathy.

"You have no idea," Trace said.

"We agreed to see where any relationship might take us, though I have to be honest and tell you I'm not looking for anything like that at the moment. My job situation is still up in the air, which means I need to get my life in order, and I want to be there for Alec during his final days.

"Fair enough," said Trace. He reached across the table and took hold of her hand.

She looked into his handsome, sincere face and sighed. He was everything she'd always thought she'd wanted in a man—kind, smart, and fun. Maybe, after everything settled down, she'd be able to focus on her life going forward. Until then, she had several things to work out.

The next morning, she went to Alec's wing of the house to check on him. Though Hospice had been called in, one of the nurses told them he had time left. Each day with him was precious to Willow. As a young girl she'd enjoyed and appreciated the attention he'd given her. Now, as an adult, she understood the parenting role he'd played in her life, giving her opportunities that she might never have had. But the idea of her parents and him discussing her future, including the Armstrong young men, made her uneasy.

Alec was awake and sitting up in bed reading when she was ushered inside his quarters.

"Willow." He held out his hand.

She took it, wrapping her fingers around it, realizing how emaciated his whole body had become. "Good morning," she said cheerfully, hiding the shock she felt at seeing him this way. He'd always been such a large presence in her life.

"Your mother told me you went on a date with Trace Armstrong,"Alec said.

"Yes, she told me you and she talked about Trace and Brent."

"She was concerned about them. I assured her that as far as I knew Trace was a fine young man but Brent was not," said Alec.

"I see. Trace and I had a good time last night. He's definitely interested in me. Though I agreed to consider dating him in the future, I told him I wasn't ready for a relationship right now."

"That sounds like a good plan," said Alec. "No need to rush into anything. Mitch called me yesterday to give me the news about the position at the inn. I believe he was right to give it to Trace."

"You do?" Willow felt a stab of hurt.

"Yes. He has something better in mind for you. He and I agreed on it."

"You did?"

Alec's lips curved into a satisfied smile. "We did."

"Are you going to tell me what it's about?" Willow asked.

Alec shook his head. "It's not up to me to do it. I want you to know how proud I am of you."

Tears stung Willow's eyes. His words meant so much to her. "I have you to thank for all the opportunities you gave me."

"You're the only daughter I had in this lifetime," he said, and she knew he was thinking of his unborn child.

"Are you sorry you never remarried?" she asked. "You might have had more children."

Alec studied her. "Marriage is right for some people and not for others. I hope you don't think you have to rush into marriage in order to have a full life. Think of Rose. She's been alone most of her adult life."

"Until now, when she's thrilled to be engaged to Hank."

"Exactly," said Alec. "You're an intelligent, incredible woman, Willow. Take your time before deciding on what the future outside of work may or may not hold. You're still young."

Willow felt the tension and worry of the last few weeks melt away. "You're right. Just because Rose and Lily's lives have changed, I shouldn't allow myself to feel like I need to rush into a relationship right now."

"That's my girl," said Alec. "When the time is right and the person is right, you'll know it."

"*Mami* and *Papi* won't ever condone my playing around though."

"Of course not. You're not that kind of woman. Remember, you don't want to be foolish. You're going to wait until the right man comes along. Pedro and I have already agreed that whoever you might choose in the future has to be a very special person."

"You make it seem as if I'm not smart enough to do this on my own," Willow protested.

Alec patted her arm. "We're talking about it now because I won't be around to see it. Your parents have always been very generous that way, allowing me to be part of your life." He didn't bother to swipe at the tears that fell onto his cheek. "It's been such a privilege."

Willow hugged him carefully. "For me too," she whispered. "I love you."

After Alec settled back against the pillows in his bed, "I love you, too."

Willow left the room quickly, unable to hide her own tears.

CHAPTER NINETEEN

LILY

Lily awoke early, rolled over and stared at Brian, in awe of the fact that they were married. So much had happened in her life that some mornings she woke up still thinking she was back in New York working at her old law firm.

Brian sensed her looking at him and grabbed her, causing her to stifle a scream.

"I've got you!" he whispered before planting his lips on hers.

She wrapped her arms around his neck and nestled closer. At the sign of his readiness, she sighed with anticipation. The chemistry that had brought them together had grown with their marriage. She was thinking of stripping off her nightgown for a little fun when she heard the padding of feet behind her.

She turned to face the intruder and smiled when Izzy rubbed her eyes and climbed into bed with them.

"Is it time to get up?" Izzy asked.

Lily shot a look of disappointment at Brian and said, "I guess it is."

"Are you working today?" Izzy asked, cuddling with her.

"Yes, a short day only," Lily said. "But Anna will be here."

"I love Anna," said Izzy.

"Me, too," said Lily climbing out of bed. Anna was a nice addition to the daily routine. Lily already thought of her as a new friend. They usually shared coffee in the morning before

Lily left for the day. During conversation, Lily learned that Anna's two daughters lived elsewhere, and she felt lonely without them.

As Izzy and Lily walked to the kitchen, Jake emerged from Ollie's room and followed them to the sliding door and barked to go outside.

Ollie, dressed in pajamas, soon followed, and went into the backyard with the dog.

While Lily got out cereal and fruit, Izzy sat quietly at the kitchen table. "Is Mommy in the sky?"

Lily searched for the right words. "Is that what someone told you?"

Izzy nodded. "Anna said she's in heaven." She pointed to the sky.

"Well, that's how some people feel about dying. I like to think your Mom is watching over you and loving you right here with us."

"I can't see her," said Izzy.

"No, but if you close your eyes you can remember what she looks like, can't you?"

Izzy closed her eyes. "Yes, she's here."

Lily wished things could be as easily handled with Ollie. He'd confided he had a fear of being placed in the ground. She'd talked about a body being just a shell for the spirit of the person inside, but that was another worrisome thought for him. The psychologist she'd been in touch with promised to help.

Ollie came into the kitchen. "I saw a lizard out in the backyard!"

"Oh, good!" Lily said, smiling and ruffling his hair. She, herself, hated the thought, but knew how much Ollie enjoyed them. He was very proud of having his own lizard, Leo, in the house.

As the kids were eating, Lily sipped on coffee and checked the calendar on her phone. She had a short day at work but would spend some time at Alec's. There, she hoped not only to see him, but to meet with Rose and Willow.

Brian came into the kitchen, his hair still wet from the shower. "I have an early morning meeting. Mitch is flying in today, and John and I have to discuss change of management. Trace will be the new executive assistant manager at the inn."

Lily's jaw dropped. "Not Willow? How could that be?"

Brian shook his head. "I don't know, but I'm sure there's something more to it."

He kissed her on the lips, lingering a bit, and then said, "I'll see you tonight in time for dinner unless Mitch wants to meet with me."

"Okay, I understand. Have a nice day. I love you."

"Love you too." He walked over to the table, gave Izzy a kiss on the cheek and cupped Ollie's cheek in his hand. "Love you two little guys."

"I'm not little," Izzy announced.

"I'm bigger than you," said Ollie with a note of scorn.

Laughing, Brian waved to the three of them and left.

Later, Lily bid the children and Anna goodbye excited to have some adult time in her world. After the baby came, she planned to stay home for several months at least. From there, she'd re-evaluate, but after seeing how quickly Izzy had changed in those early months and years, she didn't want to miss out on anything.

Now, she entered the office, eager to begin. She was enjoying the part-time position because she never knew which project she'd be working on.

Loretta greeted her warmly. "How are you? And how are those adorable children of yours?"

Technically the kids weren't hers yet, but the adoption process was moving forward, and in Lily's heart, they already were her children. "They're doing great, considering what they've both been through. Each day is better and better."

Loretta waved her closer. "Tell me more about your friend, Willow. Since we first talked about her, Ricardo told me he loves playing golf with her and says she's a perfect match for Craig."

Lily laughed. "I can well imagine that she is. Aside from being beautiful, she's smart and not about to let any man get the best of her."

They stopped talking when Craig approached. "What's going on?"

"Getting caught up for the day," Lily answered innocently.

"Hey, Lily," said Craig. "What's up with Willow? She introduced me as a golfing friend to this guy, Trace, who she's dating."

"Uh, that's what you are, right? A golfing friend?" Lily bit the inside of her cheek to keep from laughing.

"Well, yeah, but ..."

"Then, what's the problem?" Lily asked, unable to resist.

Craig started to say something, then turned around and walked away.

Loretta winked and mouthed the words, "He's got it bad."

Lily clamped her lips together to keep the bubble of laughter inside.

CHAPTER TWENTY

ROSE

Since Hank had returned from Atlanta with the idea of living in Southern California for most of the year, he and Rose had alternated between buying a home in the mountains or one on the coast. They figured they could always stay in a hotel in Atlanta if Sam and Rob or Nikki were too busy to have them stay at either house. Things were changing too rapidly to make a clear choice. Sam and Rob were already thinking of buying a place in Palm Desert, and Nikki wasn't sure she wanted to stay in Atlanta either.

Rose had worked all her life, and the idea of facing choices like this was exciting. As long as she and Hank were together, she was flexible about living in most places that attracted him. Behind all the excitement of thinking of the future with him was the somber knowledge that when she finally moved in with him, Alec would be gone.

On this bright, early morning, Rose's thoughts remained on Alec as she swam in the pool. She'd stayed with Hank at his rental house until late but had returned to Alec's house to sleep. It might seem silly to others, but she thought of it as a way to honor Alec's trust in her to come to Palm Desert to help him. The personal side of it was that her being nearby during his waning days was in thanks for all he'd done for her both years ago and now. He'd even had a hand in her meeting Hank.

Stroke after stroke, her body glided through the water effortlessly. No matter where she and Hank lived, she wanted a pool. She'd forgotten how her soul craved swimming as a way to sort things out in her mind.

At the sound of a splash beside her, she glanced over to where Willow was coming to the surface, her long, dark hair flowing behind her like silken wings.

"Good morning," Rose said with affection. She had grown to love the younger woman. "When you're through swimming, let's talk."

"Okay." Willow began swimming away on her back.

Rose got out of the pool and wrapped a towel around her. Last night, swimming with Hank, she hadn't bothered with a bathing suit or wrapping a towel around her. She'd been shy about her body when they first started dating, but under Hank's admiration, she'd grown comfortable with it and with him.

She walked into the kitchen for coffee. Juanita was there, fixing something for breakfast for the night nurse who was now off duty. Willow's mother was the perfect hostess to all the nurses who came to provide care for Alec.

"Good morning, Rose. Care for anything to eat? I can fix eggs for you," she said.

Rose gave her a quick hug. "No, thanks. A cup of coffee is all I need right now, but I appreciate the offer." She poured herself a cup of coffee and took a seat at the kitchen table.

"How's Alec doing?" she asked the nurse.

"He's still very alert, but I imagine as his disease progresses, he'll need more medication. That might take away some of his awareness. It's sad because he's such a charming man."

Her stomach squeezed with worry and sorrow gripped her. Trying to cope, Rose got to her feet. "Guess I'll go outside and watch Willow swim."

Juanita came up to her. "You talk to her, Rose. She needs

some encouragement."

Surprised, Rose turned her attention to Juanita. "Because she didn't get the position at the inn?"

"That, and more," said Juanita. "She looks up to you, you know."

"I love her," said Rose. "Let me see what's going on."

CHAPTER TWENTY-ONE

WILLOW

Willow glanced up as Rose returned to the patio. Thinking it might be a good time to talk to her, she climbed out of the pool, snatched her towel, and strode over to the table where Rose was seated. "Have a minute?"

"Sure," said Rose. "Grab a cup of coffee and we can talk."

Willow went inside to the kitchen, poured herself a cup of coffee, and walked back outside filled with anticipation. It was rare to get a moment alone with Rose, and she intended to take advantage of it.

As soon as she sat down, Rose reached over and patted her hand. "I'm sorry. I just heard that Trace got the new position at the inn. I know you wanted it. How are you feeling about it?"

Willow shrugged. "I was disappointed, of course, because I know damn well that I'm every bit as qualified as Trace. But both John and Alec, even Trace, have mentioned something else for me that might be better. We'll see. Mitchell is flying in this evening, and I'm scheduled to meet with him tomorrow. Until then, there's nothing I can do."

"At least Brent didn't get the job," said Rose. "What's going to happen with him?"

Willow shook her head. "Poor John. Brent is going with him over to the Desert Hotel Royal in Phoenix. Lou, the resident manager there, is coming over to the Desert Sage Inn. Lou is very nice and very sharp. It'll be good."

"Does Alec know about all the changes?" Rose asked.

"Yes. I talked to him. He and Mitchell have agreed on my new position. I can't imagine what it is. But if things don't work out, I'll try to find a job here in the valley. I'm definitely staying. In fact, I might see about renting Brian's condo. His lease is up soon, and that's something I could do until I know more about the future. We'll see."

"Lily loved his condo. At one time, she was thinking of trying to buy it."

"Yes, I know," said Willow. "I'm not sure what I'm going to do." She swallowed hard. "I went out with Trace last night to celebrate his promotion."

"You did?" Rose said, looking surprised.

"We'd agreed earlier to see if a relationship between the two of us was something we both wanted on a long-term basis." She took a sip of her coffee and let out a sigh that spoke of her indecision. "I want to get settled in a job before thinking of it."

Rose studied her. "Are you feeling under pressure to do something because of the way things have turned out for Lily and me?"

Willow shrugged, unsure how to answer. "Maybe. I'm in my early thirties and have always wanted to find the right man. I've been worried about getting involved with Trace, but with Brent gone, it might be easier."

"Do you want my honest opinion?" Rose asked.

"As always," Willow said. She grinned. "I'm sure you're going to give it to me anyway."

Rose chuckled. "I'm not good at holding my tongue."

"So, what do you think about Trace and me?" Willow drew a deep breath and waited for Rose to respond.

"If you have to ask, you must have a lot of questions in your mind." Rose's green-eyed gaze bore into her. "Does this have to do with Brent and the way he tormented you in college?"

"In part. But there's more. Brent's not someone I see including in holiday get-togethers," Willow answered. "That and the way my ex-boyfriend's parents thought I wasn't good enough for their son."

"But you're good enough for anyone. Right?"

Willow straightened in her chair. "Absolutely. The question is, are they good enough for me?"

Rose clapped her hands with delight. "Great answer. Something you'll have to find out for yourself. But, Willow, you don't need to be in a relationship or married to be happy. I spent many years alone living happily by myself."

"Didn't you ever get lonely?" Willow asked.

"Yes," Rose confessed. "There were times when I was, but I knew I didn't want to be in a relationship until it felt totally right. What has happened between Hank and me is a gift from the gods of love. I never expected it."

"Okay, you've helped me to decide," said Willow, grinning. "I'm going to date Trace and see what that feels like over time. But I'm not forcing anything. He's just a nice guy, and I like him."

"Whoa! Are his kisses just nice? Like Dan's?"

"No," said Willow, laughing. "They're hot!"

"Good," said Rose. "I think you have some interesting times ahead. I'm here if you want to talk."

"Thanks," Willow said, grateful for this chat with someone she'd grown to love and respect.

At loose ends, Willow decided to get out on the golf course before the day heated up. She got dressed and headed out. Since playing with the three men, she'd decided to work on her game, maybe play in some local competitions.

She drove into the parking lot at the pro shop. Maybe, if

she was lucky, she could get paired with someone else, or be able to join a foursome.

Inside, she chatted with the staff and asked if there was an opening.

"As a matter of fact, a woman called and is waiting for an opening. As long as you're willing to play with her, we can book the two of you together. We don't allow singles to play when we have a waiting list."

"No problem. I'm willing to play with anyone, unless they're a beginner." .

"This woman will be perfect," said the young girl behind the counter. "Let me give her a call, and if you can wait a few minutes, I'll book the two of you for the next available tee time."

"Okay." "I'll look around the shop to see what new things you have."

"We've got a sale going on. Check out the back room," called the girl, punching in a number on the shop's phone.

Willow was happily browsing when she heard her name being called. The staffer behind the counter waved her over to where a pretty Asian woman was standing. "Willow, meet Suzi, your golf partner today."

Willow held out her hand. "Pleased to meet you ..." she waited for the woman to announce her full name.

The woman returned Willow's smile. "Just call me Suzi...it's easier that way."

"Thanks. I'm Willow Sanchez."

The woman's eyes widened. "Oh, nice to meet you."

Willow headed outside with the woman, admiring her energy as they both trotted to their carts. It was hard to guess her age, but a couple of gray hairs shone among the black ones.

They rolled up to the first tee and got out.

"You go first," said Suzi. "I've been traveling and need to loosen up a bit."

Willow took a few practice swings and then hit the ball straight down the fairway.

"Great shot," said Suzi. "I'm impressed. I hope I don't slow you down."

Willow waved away her concern. "Take your time. I need this morning away from work."

"What do you do?" Suzi asked.

Willow explained that she'd been doing a special project for the hotel. "I'm just about through with it and will be looking for something else. But I've decided to stay here in Palm Desert."

"It's a lovely place except, perhaps, in the heat of the summer. But then, I suppose residents go to the mountains to cool off."

"Yes, they're conveniently close."

Suzi teed off. Her ball didn't go as far as Willow's, but it went straight.

Pleased she wasn't playing with a novice, Willow relaxed, happy to be outside doing something she loved.

The morning passed pleasantly. She and Suzi talked about general things, but after her question about why she was here was rebuffed, Willow understood that Suzi wanted her privacy. Content to keep it that way, Willow simply enjoyed being with her. Though she wasn't as good a golfer as Willow, Suzi held her own.

When they finished, they were both hot and sweaty. "Can I buy you an iced tea, beer, or soda?" Willow asked.

Suzi shook her head. "Thanks, but I think I'll just leave. I can't wait to have a shower."

Willow chuckled. "Sounds good to me too. Thank you for a pleasant morning. Have a nice afternoon."

Suzi gave her a little wave, climbed on her cart, and drove away.

Willow did the same.

On the drive to Alec's house, Willow decided to check in with Lily to see about Brian's condo. Besides, with Lily working and spending time at her home, Willow had missed her.

CHAPTER TWENTY-TWO

LILY

Willow's text asking if she could stop by brightened Lily's afternoon. She and Anna had established a routine with the kids for quiet time in the afternoon. For Izzy, it meant naps, though that term was never used. Ollie used the time to read, which meant Lily would have the freedom to visit with a dear friend.

Willow arrived within minutes of her text.

Lily studied the woman standing at her door smiling at her and her heart opened with affection. "Hey, girl! C'mon in!"

She signaled Jake to sit, opened the door, and ushered Willow inside so she could give her a big hug. "I'm very glad you're here. It's quiet time for the kids so we can talk. What can I get you to drink? Iced tea? Lemonade?"

"Iced tea sounds great," Willow said. "I played golf this morning, and I'm still hot."

Lily led Willow to the kitchen. "By the way, I think a certain someone was miffed that you introduced him as a golfing friend."

Willow frowned. "Who? Craig?"

"The one and only," said Lily, still amused by the expression of disbelief on Craig's face when he'd told her. Willow was such a good jolt to his ego.

Willow shook her head. "Craig is a nice guy, but I don't want to get involved with him. He's the kind of man who's not going to settle down until he's old and set in his ways. Who wants that?"

"I agree he isn't ready to settle down. Loretta complains about it all the time," Lily said, as she poured two glasses of iced tea.

Lily cleared the kitchen table of a craft project she'd been working on with Ollie and offered a chair to Willow.

Willow sat and faced her across the table. "I wanted to talk to you and Brian about maybe subleasing his condo. He still has time left on his lease, doesn't he?"

"Yes. But now that he's settled here in this house, I'm sure he'd like to talk to you about it. I believe an extension is available if you're interested."

"I might be. Until I know what my job is, I can't be certain. But as Alec is getting worse, I need to start thinking of plans."

Lily patted Willow's hand. "I was very disappointed that you didn't get the new position at the inn. Thank heavens Brent didn't get it, but still, as much as I like Trace, the position should have gone to you."

Willow made a face. "I worked hard for it. But then, so did Trace. He and I have decided to set that aside and consider dating in the future. Brent is someone I dislike, but that doesn't mean I shouldn't give Trace a chance."

Lily studied her. "I like your thinking. It's only fair. I remember being judged by my mother's behavior, and I didn't like it."

Willow's dark-eyed gaze settled on her. "How are you doing with everything? You must miss Monica. And though you seem to be doing a great job with the kids, it has to be hard."

Lily's mouth trembled, and she looked away to get her emotion under control. "I still think of Monica every single day, of course, especially with Izzy here to remind me of her. The idea that another person caused her death infuriates me. And then I get angry thinking about how Monica willingly met him sure she could be in control for once." Lily shook her head sadly. "It's all a lot to deal with."

"A lot of changes for you," said Willow patting Lily's arm with sympathy.

Though her stomach was still knotted with grief, Lily forced the threat of tears away. "I don't know what I'd do without you and Rose and Juanita. While my sister has been taken away, I've been given the three of you."

They turned as Izzy padded into the room rubbing her eyes and carrying the stuffed bunny Juanita had given her. Izzy smiled at Willow, then walked over and climbed into Lily's lap.

Lily hugged her tight. "Have a nice rest time?"

Izzy asked sleepily, "Can I have some juice?"

"Sure. Why don't you run and get your brother while I get juice and crackers ready for you."

"Okay," said Izzy. She jumped down from Lily's lap and ran from the room shouting, "Ollie! Ollie!"

"She's so adorable!" Willow exclaimed.

"Thanks," agreed Lily. "Both kids are doing well considering. They have a special bond, probably because of all they've been through. And Brian's been a big help."

"That's nice, but, Lily, you're the one they count on most. What's it going to be like when the baby comes?"

Lily sighed. "I can't imagine. At least we have time to get used to the idea."

Ollie and Izzy returned to the kitchen.

While Lily was pouring juice and setting out two small plastic bowls of fish crackers for the kids, Willow received a text.

After reading it, Willow looked up at Lily, wide-eyed. "Mitchell is in town and wants me to join him for dinner at his house. I'd better leave, I have to get ready."

"Shouldn't he have given you more notice?" Lily asked.

Willow gave her a thoughtful look. “He and Alec talked about the job he wants to give me. Maybe he wants to be sure to give me a chance to talk it over with Alec before ...” her breath caught ... “before it’s too late.”

The thought hit Lily hard. Her eyes filled.

CHAPTER TWENTY-THREE

WILLOW

Willow left Lily's house with mixed emotions. Seeing Lily with the kids, the way she'd hugged Izzy and how she'd ruffled Ollie's dark hair in caressing strokes, Willow understood how much she wanted children of her own. Not right away, of course, but with a man who could provide her with a loving home and a fulfilling relationship. Someone who understood the hospitality world she lived in. Someone who made her tingle.

She hurried back to Alec's house intent on looking her professional best. Mitchell might make it appear it was a friendly dinner, but she knew better.

Alec was sleeping when she arrived at the house. Willow wandered into the kitchen and was glad for the opportunity to talk to her mother, who listened to her plans for the evening. "I'm sure it's good news, *Cariña,*"

"I certainly hope so," Willow said. "I don't want another disappointment." She gave her mother a hug. "Wish me luck. I have to go and get ready."

Willow hurried to her room. Though she had a couple of hours before she was to be picked up, she wanted to look her best.

She climbed into the shower focusing now on the business at hand. What job could Mitchell have in mind for her?

Later, after a shower and fussing with her hair, Willow sat before the dressing table in the bathroom applying makeup. She hardly wore any, preferring instead to leave it at eye shadow and mascara and a soft shade of glossy lipstick. Bold red colors on her lips didn't suit her.

She slipped a pair of simple silver hoops in her ears, and going to her closet, she selected a black skirt and a sleeveless silk blouse in a light shade of green that Rose had helped her pick out. The silver and turquoise necklace tastefully dressed up the ensemble. Black, strappy sandals lengthened her already long legs.

She gave herself an appraising look and turned away.

Later, that opinion was confirmed when Trace picked her up and let out a long, low whistle. "You look beautiful!"

"Thank you," she said, hiding her nerves as she shut the front door behind her and walked with him to his car.

He helped her into her seat and ran around the car before sliding in behind the driver's wheel.

"I have strict instructions not to talk business with you," said Trace. "But I'm as curious as you are about the job you're going to be offered."

"Guess we'll soon find out," said Willow, again wondering why everything was very last minute. But then she knew how busy Mitchell was with business deals that had nothing to do with her.

Trace drove up to the front of the house Willow had earlier admired. Like Alec's house, this one-story, tan-stucco home on a well-manicured lawn spread out in interesting angles and curves like a beautiful butterfly resting on a leaf. Alec had once told her that because someone had money, it didn't mean they had good taste. In this case, both money and good taste were in evidence.

Willow drew in a breath and let it out slowly, telling herself to relax as Trace helped her out of the car. Though Mitchell was intimidating as her boss, she'd already seen that he was a nice man. And Trace had already told her how much he loved his stepmother.

She and Trace walked up to the front door together. Before Trace could knock, the door was flung open.

Willow glanced at Mitchell and stared at the woman at his side. "Suzi?"

Suzi gave her an impish grin. "When I told Mitch about the lovely young woman I met this morning, he insisted I find a way to let you know who I am. I'm Suzuki Armstrong, Mitchell's wife and Trace's stepmother. But my friends call me Suzi." She waved them inside. "Welcome, Willow."

Still stunned by the news, Willow stepped into the front hall.

Mitchell held out his hand. "I'm glad you could come. As I told Suzi, I didn't think it was fair to keep you in the dark. That's what happened to Hank and Rose if I recall."

Willow shook his hand and chuckled. "Yes." Well aware of how that relationship developed, she couldn't help glancing at Trace, but he was busy petting the black and tan dachshund who'd barked for attention.

"How sweet!" she said, turning to the dog. She bent over to pat it and accepted the warm kiss the dog gave her hand.

"Heidi is very affectionate," said Suzi, her dark eyes shining. "But please don't feel obligated to pay attention to her." She picked up the dog and laughed when Heidi kissed her cheek.

Willow laughed at the pure, loving energy of the little dog. "I love dogs, but I'm not used to them. I didn't have one growing up. My parents both worked, and they didn't think it was fair to leave a dog alone all the time."

"Willow's parents work for Alec Thurston. They've done so for years," Mitchell explained.

Suzi looked at her. "How nice. He's such a lovely man."

"Yes, he's been very good to me and my parents," said

Willow. Neither Mitchell nor Suzi showed any sign of the haughtiness that had sometimes greeted her in the past when her parents' work was mentioned.

Feeling comfortable, Willow followed Suzi through the house and out to the patio in the back. Whirring fans suspended from the overhanging pergola kept the air moving, providing enough of a breeze to make it pleasant. She loved warm evenings like this.

Suzi motioned her to one of the chairs. "Please make yourself comfortable. I'll be right back. I have some appetizers for us."

"And I'll take drink orders," said Mitchell. "Trace tells me you like Texas Margaritas or red wine, a pinot noir if available."

Surprised, Willow said, "Thank you. Either is fine."

"I have a special Oregon pinot noir that I hope you'll try. We're thinking of offering it at the Corona hotels."

"I'd be happy to taste it for you," Willow said, pleased by the idea. Though she wasn't as well trained as some, she'd been told she had a refined palate and knew good wine.

Trace lowered himself into a couch near her chair and turned to her. "I'm glad you could come here and meet my mother. I had no idea you'd already met."

Suzi walked over to them carrying a tray that held several small plates filled with a variety of appetizers. She set the tray down on the coffee table in front of Trace and turned to Willow.

"I hope you'll forgive me for not introducing myself properly. When I'm visiting one of our hotels, I prefer not to let people know who I am. It gives me a chance to evaluate service and surroundings privately for my husband. I'd heard your name, of course, but didn't think I should say anything relating to business."

Willow heard the sincerity in her voice and observed the kindness in her face. "I'm glad to know you. Especially since I work with Trace and Brent."

Suzi exchanged glances with Trace and took a seat on far end of the couch. "I understand Brent has been very difficult to work with and has shown unacceptable behavior toward you in the past." Her lips thinned. "I'm well aware of how hurtful that can be."

"Uncle Duncan and my mother don't get along," Trace said.

"And his son is someone who I feel should not represent the company," Suzi said. "But I can only advise my husband on things."

Mitchell, who'd been taking care of drinks at the outside bar turned to her, carrying two glasses of red wine. "My dear, I treasure your thoughts."

A look of affection passed between them, and they both laughed.

Trace glanced at her and winked. "They're always like this."

Willow was reminded of her own parents' behavior. Maybe she'd judged Trace's situation too quickly.

Mitchell went to the bar and returned to hand Trace a bottle of beer and sat in a chair with what looked like a gin and tonic for himself. He raised his glass. "Here's to health and happiness."

"Yes," said Suzi. "For us all."

Mitchell studied Willow. "This evening is time for a social gathering. Tomorrow morning, we will talk business."

Though Willow was anxious to learn more about his job for her, tonight, being here at his house, wasn't the time or place for it. Rather than think about it, she concentrated on getting to know Trace and his parents better.

Conversation centered on the highlights of living in Palm Desert, different vacations the family had taken together, interest in Willow's teaching job, and a general getting-to-know-you talk.

Willow was amused by the fact that though Suzi was a small woman, she was definitely in charge of the tall, strapping, handsome men around her. It turned out that she was the one who'd suggested to Trace that he attend the hospitality program at the University of Nevada, Las Vegas rather than Cornell.

"It's unfair, but being so close in age, Trace has had to overcome the obstacle of being Brent's cousin through the years," said Suzi.

"I have a lot of cousins but don't have that problem." Willow hesitated and then turned to Trace. "I don't envy you that challenge."

"Willow, tell me more about your relationship with Alec," said Mitchell. "He thinks of you as a daughter."

Willow puffed out a sad breath. "His wife and my mother were cousins, which is how we came to know one another. After his wife died, Alec needed help to keep going. My parents kept an eye on him, and he turned to them for help, both physical and emotional. I sometimes feel as if I grew up with three parents, not two."

"Alec is an interesting man, a talented one. I respect him tremendously," Mitchell said.

"Yes, he has a lot of admirers."

"Including the three of you Desert Flowers, as Alec refers to you."

Willow felt her lips curve. "Rose, Lily, and I have been able to do the job Alec asked us to do. You don't know how happy that makes me."

"And me," Mitchell admitted. "The Corona Collection of Fine Hotels is a superb addition to our portfolio of hotels. There's been some dissension about it, but I'm convinced it's going to be very good for the Blaise Group."

"Wait!" said Suzi. "I want to know more about the Desert Flowers. I love the idea that you three women were hired by Alec to work for him."

"Yes, it's quite an honor. We've all played a role in Alec's life, and we were happy to be given the chance to do something for him. Rose Macklin has her own well-respected blog called You Deserve This, as well as her own marketing consultant business. Lily Walden once worked as Alec's assistant and recently left work at a law firm to help with details of the transaction, and I'm working under Brian Walden, along with Brent and Trace, to assist with the transition."

"Very good," said Suzi, grinning at her. "Trace told me he cooked dinner for you one evening."

"We ended up cooking it together," said Trace, "trying out all the cookware and other things you bought for the kitchen."

"It's a beautiful kitchen," said Willow. "I like to cook, too, but haven't had a chance to do much of it here while I stay at Alec's house."

"Anytime you're in a cooking mood, you're welcome to use the kitchen here," said Suzi, smiling at her. "We won't be spending much time here this summer, but I hope we return in the fall."

"Thanks," said Willow, well aware what a generous offer it was for a woman to share her kitchen with another.

Conversation continued smoothly through cocktail time and into dinner.

By the time, Trace drove her home, Willow was as taken with his parents as she was with him.

After agreeing to meet with Mitchell the next morning, Willow said goodnight and thanked them both for a wonderful evening.

Still aglow from the pleasant time, she climbed into Trace's car feeling more comfortable about the idea of dating him.

Instead of taking her up the long driveway to Alec's house, Trace kept following the back road of the property. "Do you mind if we sit and talk out here where we have privacy?" Trace asked her.

"I don't mind at all. With nursing staff coming and going, and my parents sticking close to Alec, I assure you we wouldn't have any privacy in front of Alec's house."

"Will you continue living at his house after he's gone?"

"No. I'm thinking of subleasing Brian's condo and maybe extending the lease until I get a better idea of what's going to happen to me."

"I wish I could help, but Dad won't talk about your job, not even to me," Trace said. "I know it's something good, though." He pulled to a stop on the edge of a lighted area and turned to her. "Willow, my parents like you a lot. I'm glad because I care about you."

She faced him, seeing the strength of his jaw, his fine features, the sincerity in his eyes, and felt a connection to him. When he pulled her close and brushed his lips against hers, she closed her eyes and told herself to relax and enjoy his kiss.

When they pulled apart, they stared at one another with pleased expressions.

"Nice," said Willow. She'd felt comfortable in his embrace.

"I'm falling hard, Willow," said Trace, cupping her cheek in his hand and letting his gaze settle on her.

"Me, too, but as I told you earlier, I want to go slowly," she said. "My life is full of several unanswered questions right now. Later, when things are settled, I'll be able to think about the future. Us. Until then, let's simply enjoy being together getting to know each other before we move too fast."

His frown morphed into a smile. "Okay, then. But I want

another kiss. Come here."

Once more his arms surrounded her and his lips met hers. Sighing with happiness, she allowed herself to think of a future with him.

CHAPTER TWENTY-FOUR

WILLOW

Willow awoke feeling as if she'd been trying to run in deep sand and going nowhere. Thoughts of her upcoming meeting with Mitchell played tag in her mind, keeping her from sleep. After he'd invited her to come to the house early tomorrow morning to meet with him, he'd lowered his voice and informed her their meeting was to remain confidential.

During the night, she'd tried to think of scenarios that would require secrecy. But nothing made sense.

Too nervous to eat, Willow got up, showered, and dressed for the meeting in conservative business clothes, wanting to look as professional as possible.

In the kitchen, she kissed her mother good morning, said goodbye without giving any details, and left the house.

As always, driving through the town, she admired the quiet of the early morning before residents and visitors filled the shopping areas. As the heat rose, more vacationers did errands in the morning and then rested or napped in the hot afternoon.

Driving up the long drive to Mitchell's home, Willow thought of the people who lived in this beautiful house. Suzi was a pleasant surprise. She'd liked her when they played golf together, but seeing her as Mitchell's wife and Trace's stepmother, she liked her more. Observing Trace with his parents, both respectful and at ease, she thought how lucky he was to have them.

She parked her car in the front circle, got out, and drew a deep breath. If she didn't like the offer he was about to make her, she'd be honest and tell him so. She'd worked in Boston because she thought it was the right thing to do. But being here at home, doing work she loved, she knew she wouldn't take just any job. It had to feel right.

As she was making her way up the flagstone walkway to the house, the front door opened and Mitchell waved to her.

Willow hurried to him. "Good morning."

"It's going to be a hot one. Come on inside. We'll talk in my office." As they crossed the threshold, he turned to her. "Can I get you water? Coffee?"

"Water would be nice," Willow said, her throat dry from nerves.

He led her to his office and said, "I'll be right back with water."

She took a seat in one of the two leather chairs flanking the gas fireplace and admired her surroundings. On either side of the fireplace, along the entire wall, dark-stained bookcases held books, photos, and what looked like a collection of story tellers from Native American tribes. The other walls, painted a warm tan, held a number of beautiful paintings of contemporary art. Across from her, three long windows offered a distant view of the mountains that was even more beautiful than the paintings. Along the solid wall to her left, sat a sleek wooden desk made of walnut, she guessed, with a modern, brown-leather office chair behind it.

Mitchell returned, handed her a cold bottle of water, and kept one for himself. "There. I figured this was easier than dealing with glasses and ice."

"Thank you," said Willow smiling. Only a hotelier would apologize for bottled water. She opened hers, took a sip, and set it down on a coaster on the side table next to her.

As she waited for Mitchell to do the same, she clutched her hands and told herself to relax. When he finally turned to her, she braced herself.

"What I'm about to tell you is strictly confidential," he began. "The Blaise Group is in the process of buying another hotel. Not everyone knows about this, not even my brother at the moment. But when he returns from vacation, he'll be informed."

Willow wondered what part she'd play.

Mitchell gave her a steady look. "I believe you know the property. The Premio Inn."

Willow let out a puff of breath. "It's a lovely small inn."

"I agree. I've been meeting privately with George Hartmann. He's ready to retire and is now willing to sell. He's brought up your name several times as someone we need to talk to about the process. Alec has also approached me about it. Both men agree with me that you should be made manager of the inn after the sale goes through. In the meantime, I want you to head the transition team during the time you train to be the new manager."

Manager? Not executive assistant manager? Manager? Wow! Willow forced herself to remain in her chair, though she wanted to leap in the air with joy.

Mitchell steepled his fingers in front of him. "The inn will be the smallest component of the Corona Collection, but its value is very obvious. We need someone to run it who knows the community, is able to interface appropriately with well-known guests, and most of all, knows the hospitality business thoroughly. We're moving quickly to make this happen before we lose Alec. It's a wish of his to see this take place. With procedures worked out for making the Desert Sage Inn part of the new collection, adding the Premio Inn to it is much simpler."

Willow's throat thickened with emotion. She swallowed hard. "I'd very much like the opportunity to manage that property. I've done some research on the inn, its history, and how well it has performed. I'd even approached George about running it after he retired."

Mitchell bobbed his head. "He's done his own research on you and has discussed this opportunity with Alec, who not only is an admirer of your talent but loves you as well."

Willow blinked rapidly to hide the sting of tears. She was thankful to Alec for his continued support, but deeply devastated by the idea of losing him.

Mitchell gave her a minute and then said, "I, too, have liked what I've seen of your performance and your work ethic, and I am confident you are well qualified for this promotion." He gave her a warm smile. "I'm sure when some of the board members meet you, they'll agree."

"Duncan won't like it," said Willow, feeling freer to mention it after last night's discussion.

"No, he won't. That's one reason we're moving Brent to Phoenix, so you won't have any interference from him. Again, a matter of confidentiality."

"So, I'm not to mention it to anyone?" said Willow.

"Only those you can trust, like the other two Desert Flowers," said Mitchell. "If it becomes known, and a battle within the company takes place, the sale might not go through, and you won't have a position with the Blaise Group."

"I understand," said Willow. The worst part would be maintaining silence while Brent taunted her about not having a job. But for a prize position like this, she'd forgo the urge to tell him.

"I'll send you an outline of what your duties will be along with a pay package, and an employment contract. Once that's signed, we'll make an announcement about your promotion to manager of the inn. I expect the sale to close next week." He shook his head. "I apologize if this seems awkward, but I think it's best handled this way. Families can be complicated."

Willow nodded. She wanted, no, needed everything in writing.

"Okay, then," said Mitchell. "I'll send a contract along with the other information, and we can meet soon. Perhaps as early as the beginning of next week if you're amenable. That gives you only a couple of days."

"That shouldn't be a problem," said Willow, suddenly overcome with the enormity of what had just been offered to her. The first person she wanted to talk to was Alec.

She and Mitchell stood and shook hands. "I'm pleased to welcome you aboard, Willow. We'll meet here Monday. I'll have Brian Walden and Simon Nickerson, my attorney, join us, should you or I have any questions."

"Thank you," said Willow. "I'm very excited about the opportunity and have a few ideas about some of the changes you might want to make to the property. Nothing extraordinary. Just a lot of little ways to improve what is already a wonderful inn."

Mitchell chuckled. "I love your enthusiasm. See you later."

Willow left Mitchell's house feeling as if she could fly. Managing the Premio Inn was a dream come true. She'd hoped to get the job on her own but having it as part of working within the Blaise Group was better. They were known for having good benefit packages and very competitive pay scales. Maybe instead of renting a place, she should begin looking at buying a house for tax purposes. A lot to think about.

Back at Alec's house, Willow went to check on him.

A nurse opened the door to his private section of the house.

"How is he?" she asked.

The nurse shook her head.

"Can I talk to him?" Willow asked, her heart thumping with alarm.

"Sure. He might respond to you." The nurse waved her through the living space and into Alec's bedroom where he lay in a hospital bed positioned by the window so he could look out at the landscape he loved.

Willow held back a sob as she studied the shell of the man who'd loved and laughed and enjoyed life very openly.

Alec looked up at her and a smile, more like a grimace, stretched across his sunken face.

"You talked to Mitch?"

"Yes," she said, as she crossed the room and gently held his hands. "He told me that you and George Hartmann talked to him about my running the Premio Inn. Thank you." She ignored the tears that blurred her vision.

"I know you'll do me proud," said Alec. "You're going to be the best manager they ever had." He closed his eyes.

Willow stared in horror at the struggle it took for Alec to breathe.

He accepted the oxygen mask the nurse placed over his nose and color returned to his cheeks.

"Let's give him a chance to rest," said the nurse quietly.

Willow bent over the rail and kissed his cheek.

His gaze followed her as she stood by his side for a moment before turning and walking away.

In the kitchen, she found Rose and Lily talking at the table. They looked up at her.

She tried to smile in return but couldn't. Tears streamed down her face.

"You just came from Alec's room?" Lily said, giving her a

sympathetic look.

"It takes such an effort for him to even breathe. I don't see how it can go on much longer." She grabbed a tissue and wiped at her eyes before joining them at the table.

"Lily and I were just discussing it. We want to remain close," said Rose. "The nurse suggested we do so." She took hold of Willow and Lily's hands. "Remember, we're Alec's Flowers, here for him."

"Yes," said Lily tearfully.

Willow swallowed hard and nodded. They could do this together. She got up and poured herself a cup of coffee.

"Did you hear about your new job?" Rose asked.

"Yes. I've just come from a meeting with Mitchell. I have permission to tell the two of you, but it's confidential information. If it gets leaked out, it might not happen," said Willow.

Lily's eyes widened. "I won't tell anyone. Not even Brian."

"You can tell Brian because he'll be at the meeting when we talk about plans. But, Rose, please don't tell Hank or anyone else."

"Not a problem," said Rose. "Tell us what's going on."

Willow took a sip of soothing coffee and filled them in, scarcely believing her own words.

"That's terrific, boss lady!" said Rose. "You're perfect for the job!"

"Yes," agreed Lily. "You'd already looked at the property as something to manage."

"I thought I'd be an assistant, not become the manager right away," said Willow. "That's the part I find very surprising."

Rose reached over and patted Willow's hand. "You're every bit as capable of doing that as anyone I know."

"It's a job I can't wait to start," said Willow. "A dream come true, really."

"What about Brent and Trace? Do they know?"

Willow shook her head. "No. They're not going to know anything about it until I've signed a contract. The contract will state that I'll lead the transition team as I begin the training to manage the property. I'm sure George will be a help to me."

Lily grinned at her. "I'm so happy for you. Is there anything I can do to help you?"

Willow gave her a thoughtful look. "I've decided to look at houses. Instead of renting, buying makes sense for the tax benefits alone. You can help me. You did a fantastic job with the house for you and Brian."

"At the time I wasn't sure the house would be mine. But I made sure I liked it," said Lily laughing. "I'll give you the name of my real estate agent. She's very good and not at all pushy."

"Such a sweet yet sad story how you ended up with a growing family," said Rose to Lily. "You look great. No one would guess you're pregnant."

Lily caressed her stomach. "I've been lucky. I feel good. A little queasy from time to time but nothing worse. Thank heavens, because with Izzy and Ollie around, I don't know how I could manage everything if I were sick."

"So many changes for us all," said Rose, smiling at them. "By the way, Willow, how did your date with Trace go?"

Willow couldn't stop a smile from spreading across her face. "It was great. Trace is a good guy, and I love his parents. The woman I played golf with the other day is actually his stepmother, Suzi or Suzuki Armstrong. She's delightful, and Mitchell is totally relaxed and happy with her.

"That's wonderful. I'm happy for you," gushed Lily. "Another romance."

Rose caught the corner of her lip and sighed.

"What?" said Willow, trying not to be annoyed. Rose

tended to see the downside of things.

"I just don't want you to get hurt," said Rose. "Mitchell might be different from his brother, but they're from the same ambitious family. I'm just telling you to be aware of them. That's all."

"Oh, but ..." Lily said.

Willow cut her off. "Rose is right. Working for the Blaise Group makes things a little different, more complicated. But I like Trace, and as I agreed, we'll see where it takes us. Especially now that I know we'll both be living in Palm Desert."

CHAPTER TWENTY-FIVE

ROSE

An uneasy feeling crept through Rose as she heard Willow talk about dating Trace. She hesitated and then warned Willow against the idea of family members being so different. At one time she'd worked in a similar situation. She'd thought she knew and understood them all and had later been blindsided by the one person she'd thought she could trust to support her work. The man who'd requested her to put together an entire promotion package had then gone ahead and presented her ideas as his own. When she tried to speak up about the injustice, she was immediately shut down by him and the others. She left the job taking as many materials and as much of her pride as possible. But it had been a hard, painful lesson.

She listened to Lily's happiness about her new situation, genuinely pleased for her and turned to Willow once more, hoping she'd be protected from the personnel squabbles that were certain to arise from time to time. The fact that Willow would have a signed contract for the job as manager of the Premio Inn before Duncan could step in and ruin it was reassuring. But she knew Duncan well enough to understand that his ego would always make him interfere with decisions that didn't please him.

On top of everything else, Rose was delighted to learn that Willow, like Lily, was going to stay in Palm Desert. She and Hank had been house hunting but hadn't found anything they both liked. Now that they'd decided to live there with a getaway location elsewhere and had learned that Samantha and Rob might consider buying a place of their own here, they wanted something nice but not too big.

She studied the two women who'd become as close to her as sisters and raised her coffee mug. "I love you guys!"

Willow and Lily raised their mugs.

"Here's to the Desert Flowers!" said Willow.

"Always!" added Lily.

Rose blew them each a kiss, feeling as though she could face anything with their support. Even saying goodbye to Alec.

CHAPTER TWENTY-SIX

WILLOW

Like Rose and Lily, Willow stayed close to Alec's house. The papers from Mitchell were hand delivered to her, and though she looked at the contract and other materials, her thoughts remained on Alec. It helped to know he was receiving excellent nursing care. Though he was lucid from time to time, it was clear to everyone that his body was shutting down.

Lily and Rose returned to their old rooms, and the three of them took turns checking on Alec. Juanita and Pedro also were present, obviously saddened by what was happening.

One of the nurses approached the five of them in the kitchen. "It's time," she said quietly, sending a shot of panic through Willow. She didn't want to say goodbye; she wanted a miracle to happen and have Alec tell her it was all a mistake, that he was feeling better.

Her mother took her hand and gave it a squeeze. "Come with us."

All five of them went to Alec's quarters and into his bedroom. He lay in bed, his eyes closed. She glanced at the sorrow on the faces of the others and gazed at Alec, tears blurring her vision, wetting her face.

One by one, they bent and kissed his withered cheek.

Willow felt, rather than saw, Lily take one of her hands, Rose the other. Then they, with her parents, encircled Alec's bed like guardian angels. Each, she knew, had special reasons to love and honor him.

They hadn't been there long when Willow, along with the others, saw Alec still. And very clearly, she understood that the soul of Alec Thurston no longer resided in his ravaged body. She let out a small cry and began to sob.

They gathered in a group.

"Now, let's pray that Alec is reunited with Conchita again. It was his dream," said Juanita. "I have to believe they're together again."

They each bowed their heads for a moment of silence, and then they filed out of the quiet room together.

Still shaken, wracked with grief, Willow followed the others to the kitchen.

"Now we celebrate," said Willow's father, though his eyes shone with tears. "I promised Alec I'd open a bottle of champagne so the five of us could celebrate his life." His voice caught. "More will come later to be shared with friends, but he wanted this time to be for what he thought of as his personal family." He glanced at each of them. "For the five of us."

Juanita went to the butler's pantry and brought out five tulip glasses. "A little sip for you, Lily, enough to give him a toast. Yes?"

"Yes, of course," Lily said, bursting into fresh tears.

Pedro opened a bottle of champagne—Dom Perignon as Alec had requested, Pedro explained—and poured some into each glass. With trembling hands, he gave Willow a slip of paper. "Please read this for me. I cannot do this."

Willow had seldom seen her father this emotional. She took the paper from him, opened it, and said, "Alec has written a toast for us."

Rose shook her head. "Very typical of him to want everything just so."

"Go ahead, Willow, read it," prompted Lily, sniffling.

"Okay." She took a deep breath and began to read:

> "Dear ones, the five of you are my special family and I was glad to have you in my life. Take a moment to celebrate all that we've shared. I want you to always feel the closeness between you that has developed over the past months. I've made certain requests of you.
>
> "My first is that you enjoy a glass of delicious champagne to celebrate our love and friendship. Though I'm sorry to leave you, I've waited a long time to once again be with Conchita and our baby girl. Be happy for me, not sad. Laugh and be silly, remembering our times together. We've had some good ones, haven't we?
>
> "I've made a second request. As Rose and I discussed, she will oversee all arrangements for the celebration of life service and following reception. Juanita and Pedro have already agreed to help her.
>
> "I'm requesting you, Lily, to assist the lawyers in carrying out my instructions as stated in my will.
>
> "And, Willow, I'm requesting that you, Rose, and Lily, work together to oversee the foundation I've formed in Conchita's name to help young mothers of Spanish origin who need a financial boost.
>
> "More will become clear. But for now, I depend on you, my beloved ones, to do for me what I cannot do for myself. I love each and every one of you."

Willow blindly handed the note back to her father. Fresh tears rolled down her cheeks.

"All right," said Juanita, "let's take a moment and remember what we loved about Alec, who became such a part of our lives." She lifted her glass. "Here's to Alec! *Vaya con Dios*!"

"Yes!" said Rose. "Let's honor his wishes and enjoy our memories of him. We have a lot of work ahead of us. I, for one, will be forever grateful for having known and loved him." Her voice shook. She sank onto a kitchen chair looking anything but joyful.

Willow took a seat beside her, thinking of all the mornings she'd spent there with her fellow Desert Flowers plotting and planning ways to help Alec.

Lily, Juanita, and Pedro joined them at the table.

"So many memories," said Juanita. "Conchita and I were close cousins growing up. When I learned she was pregnant, I planned a trip to see her. But before I could get there, I heard she'd died. Pedro and I came as quickly as we could following the horrible news. Alec was a mess. He wouldn't eat, couldn't sleep, and started drinking. We helped him get through the worst of his pain, but I knew even then he would forever be haunted by what had happened to his beloved wife, my beautiful, sweet cousin."

"Yes," said Pedro. "There were days I didn't think Alec would survive."

Juanita gave each of the women a tremulous smile. "Each time I thought he might slip back into his deep depression over what had happened, one of you played a happier part in his life."

"He was a good man," Pedro said. "An honest one."

Willow bobbed her head in agreement along with Rose and Lily.

"Now, we celebrate him," said Pedro, rising to refill their glasses.

The quiet in the kitchen was soon broken by the arrival of a representative from the funeral home, more staff from Hospice, and people to remove the equipment from Alec's room.

Pedro and Juanita left the kitchen to help. Willow stayed behind with Rose and Lily.

Lily let out a long sigh that spoke of her sorrow. "It's never easy to say goodbye, but I'm especially devastated by the recent deaths of two of the people I love."

Willow patted her back. "It's been a hard time."

"I'm touched by Alec's thinking of the five of us as his true family and glad we had this special, private moment together," said Rose. "Both the memorial service and the reception at the hotel are going to be packed with people."

"You and he discussed it?" Lily said.

"Yes," said Rose. "It was bittersweet. He wants people to celebrate his life, though his many, many friends will be sad at his passing."

"He was a very special person," said Willow. "My life would have been very different if he hadn't taken an interest in my education, made me realize the hotel business is what I wanted to do, and gave me the confidence I needed to make it happen."

"Among other things, Alec showed me how to navigate a kinder life I never knew growing up. He encouraged me to reach out and grab hold of new things, new opportunities," said Lily.

"For me, he was the one person who made me believe I was loveable after growing up with parents who made me feel otherwise." Rose leaned forward. "I want to honor him the best way I know how, but I'm going to need your help with the plans he laid out for us."

"Not a problem," said Willow. "When is everything to take place?"

"His body is to be cremated. Later, we will scatter his ashes. For now, at Alec's request, his service will be held at the Church on the Corner as soon as possible. I spoke with them a few days ago when I knew Alec didn't have much time left. We talked about days of availability and I booked the church and the minister for Monday afternoon."

"That gives us only a couple of days to get ready," said Willow.

"Yes, but everything is planned," said Rose. "I reserved the ballroom at the hotel for that evening, thinking we could change it, if necessary."

"Alec knew?" Lily said.

"Oh, yes," said Rose. "He's the one who insisted on it." Her eyes filled. "As always, the host with the most."

"A true hotel person," said Willow, her voice shaky. This whole situation was forcing her to think about her parents. Still young in their fifties, the day would come when they, too, would be gone. The lesson for her was simple. Life was too short to be unhappy.

"Okay," said Rose. "Let's take a few more minutes, then the three of us have to start making calls. Alec and I have put together a long list of friends and business acquaintances." She lifted her glass of champagne. "Here's to Alec!"

"And the Desert Flowers," said Lily.

The three of them clicked glasses together. They'd started out not knowing one another and were now friends and part of Alec's special family.

Willow sat in her room with her list of people to call, wondering what to say. Rose had said to keep it simple, but

Willow knew each time she relayed the news it would feel like a stab to her insides. Filled with determination, she set to work.

A couple of hours later, Willow felt totally drained. She'd completed her calls. Though most people on her list weren't shocked by the news, they had to tell her over and over again what a great man Alec was, how he'd helped them, or just that they were sorry to lose an outstanding person like Alec in a world full of people who weren't always kind or caring.

She changed into shorts and a sleeveless blouse, put on hiking boots and went to the kitchen to grab a bottle of cold water.

Her mother looked at her. "The casita?"

Willow nodded. She needed the climb to the little cabin Alec had built to get away from the pressures of business and life, in general. Through the years she and others had used it for a quiet retreat. She needed it today, more than ever.

CHAPTER TWENTY-SEVEN

WILLOW

Outside, the heat was rising, which would make the climb up the steep side of the foothill behind the hotel property that much more rewarding. Willow set off to grieve and remember.

As she climbed the path into the foothills, she recalled the first time she'd gone to the cabin with Alec and her father. It had been an educational experience, learning about some of the desert plants, birds in the area, and desert creatures, including rattlesnakes. She gazed at a desert iguana and thought of Lily's son, Ollie, who loved little lizards like this.

A red-tailed hawk circled in the sky above her, gliding in circles with what looked like pure laziness, but was, instead, preparation for a strike against a poor, hapless creature below.

Visitors often missed the beauty of the area, she thought. But then, many came for golf, swimming, dining, and shopping, and that was good too.

She kept her head down studying the ground. Small stones and rocks underfoot sometimes made it slippery.

When at last she reached the turnoff for Alec's casita, she looked up and stared in surprise at the man seated on a bench outside it.

"What are you doing here?" she asked,

Craig Kincaid gave her a solemn look. "My dad told me about Alec. I wanted to be here. Come sit. There's plenty of room for you."

Willow walked over to the wooden bench he'd placed

outside the cabin and took a seat, still breathing hard from the climb. She took a sip of water and stared out at the hotel grounds below, collecting her thoughts.

After she'd cooled off a bit, she turned to him. "Why here?" she asked, genuinely curious. Craig was the last person she'd expected to see.

He let out a long sigh and continued staring down into the valley below. "Alec brought me here shortly after my mother died." When he turned to her, she saw his eyes were shiny with unshed tears.

She waited for him to continue.

"My mother was a beautiful person. I don't mean just on the outside, but on the inside too. When she got cancer and knew she didn't have much time to live, I felt so damn helpless because there was nothing that I could do to change it." He swallowed hard. "I did a lot of stupid things, got into trouble. Alec helped me see that I was hurting my family and friends by acting that way."

"That sounds exactly like him," Willow said softly, understanding how that could've happened.

Craig gave her a shaky smile. "Loretta tells me I have more growing up to do. I think I owe it to both my mother and Alec and others to begin to do that. I visited with him privately a week ago, and we talked about a lot of things." He pressed his lips together, and Willow knew he was trying to keep his emotions in check. "I admired him more than I can say."

"Me, too," said Willow softly. She placed a comforting hand on his thigh and let out a trembling sigh.

He slid an arm around her shoulder. "He laughed when I told him you called me a golfing friend. Know what he said? He told me it was a good place to start."

She giggled at the way he'd said golfing friend, as if it was an insult.

He grinned. “I like to hear you laugh.”

“Alec has asked us not to be sad but to celebrate his life. It’s not going to be easy to keep that in mind. I called a whole lot of people to let them know about the service and reception. No one was happy to hear the news.”

“Well, if it’s any help, you can talk honestly to me about it anytime. Some people expect you to pretend everything’s all right during times like this. I know better. It eats you up inside.”

Willow realized she didn’t know Craig at all. She looked up to study his face. His gaze met hers. Her heart raced as he studied her before he leaned down to kiss her. Instead of moving away like she thought she should, she closed her eyes. The soft but sure touch of his lips set off a surge of feelings inside her. The kiss felt comforting, like a balm to her injured heart and just as quickly shifted into something so riveting, so primal, that she could only respond.

He drew her closer. “Ah, Willow,” he whispered.

Her eyes flew open. When she realized what was happening, she pulled away. It wasn’t the time or place for something like this.

She jumped to her feet. “I’m sorry. That should never have happened.”

Quickly, before he could stop her, she ran down the trail away from him. The idea of taking a private moment to think of Alec and turning it into some kind of tryst was abhorrent to her. Alec deserved better behavior than that, she told herself, willing away the feelings that Craig had aroused in her.

She looked behind her, wondering if Craig would follow. But he wasn’t in sight. Probably as disturbed as she, Willow decided, making her way down the hillside in regular pounding steps.

When she got back to Alec’s house, she hurried to her

room, unwilling to talk to anyone until her emotions were under control.

The next two days flew by as Willow assisted Rose, Lily, and her parents with arrangements for the service and reception for Alec. Each felt committed to making them the best they could be.

On Monday, Willow prepared to file into the church and take her place at the front with her parents as Rose and Lily stood by with Hank and Brian. Drawing a tired breath, she saw Mitchell, Suzi, and Trace sitting in a pew with Duncan and Brent. Her mouth grew dry. Though she'd cancelled the meeting with Mitchell, she hadn't read through the employment contract and other materials he'd given her, much less signed anything, with all that was going on.

Her father offered his elbow and she took it, giving her mother room to walk on his other side. Careful to keep her gaze down so she wouldn't have to see the looks of sympathy on everyone's face and begin to cry, she moved forward.

The interior of the church was as simple, as unassuming as its name. Wine-colored carpeting covered the aisle between the rows of plain wooden pews. At the front of the church, a white, embroidered runner crossed the top of a wooden altar on which a simple brass cross sat between two white, flickering candles. A large, round, stained-glass window with an abstract design was centered in the back wall above the table and cast colorful beams of light across the congregation.

A minister wearing a dark robe waited to greet them. To the left and above him a choir dressed in black robes sat ready to sing when the appropriate time came.

Alec hadn't been a deeply religious man, but Willow knew he'd appreciate the setting—meaningful but not ostentatious. Two wicker baskets on either side of the steps leading up to the altar were filled with greenery and assorted white zinnias, anemones, primroses, daisies, and an assortment of desert flowers. Again, simple but meaningful.

The service went quickly as memories of Alec flashed in and out of her mind, like a film strip of events she'd shared with him growing up. She listened as several friends and business people spoke about Alec. Rose had agreed to speak for the five of them, and now she rose and went to the front of the church.

As if she was in a vacuum, Willow saw Rose's mouth move, heard the hum of sound, but failed to focus on her words. Nobody could say anything to take away the sting she felt inside. As Craig had commented when she saw him at the casita, the knowledge that she would never see or talk to Alec again was eating her insides. She glanced across the aisle to where Craig was sitting with his father, Bennett Williams, and Loretta and Ricardo Morales. She realized then how meaningful being a golfing friend had been to Alec. Craig caught her eye, but she quickly looked away.

Forcing herself to focus, Willow observed the way Rose's lips quivered and knew she, too, was struggling with the idea of losing Alec.

"Alec Thurston was a man of honor," Rose said. "If he told you something, you could count on it to be true. Nothing proved this more than his devotion to the memory of his wife and unborn daughter. That devotion will continue with the formation of his memorial to them, The Conchita Charitable Foundation, whose purpose is to offer financial assistance to women of Spanish descent in business. Alec Thurston, we will miss you, but will carry you in our hearts as we continue your work in both word and deed."

Rose's face was contorted with grief as she made her way back to the pew to Hank.

The choir rose. To the sounds of lush music and earnest voices, Willow whispered, “Goodbye, Alec. I love you.”

She didn’t realize tears were streaming down her face until her father handed her a tissue. She wiped at her eyes and drew a deep breath. She knew the days ahead would be full of challenges, but she’d face them with a need to prove that Alec’s confidence in her would not be in vain.

She followed the others out of the church and headed over to the hotel to make sure the arrangements Rose had made according to Alec’s wishes were carried out as professionally as possible.

CHAPTER TWENTY-EIGHT

ROSE

Exiting the church, Rose held tight to Hank's hand. His silent encouragement as she'd spoken in the church had kept her from breaking down and crying. She loved that about him—how his presence steadied her, made her believe that she could do most anything.

She saw Willow leave and relaxed, knowing she'd make sure everything was being taken care of at the inn. Alec had been very specific about making the reception a happy one, a classy experience for those he cared about. In the meantime, her role was to see that everyone was invited to the gathering.

Lily was mixing with the crowd, standing next to Brian, as they both spoke to people they knew or were meeting for the first time.

Mitchell and a pretty Asian woman approached her with Trace. Introductions were exchanged. Rose observed their faces, seeing their genuine care, and thought of Willow. They seemed like nice people. Her good humor wavered when Duncan and Brent joined them. But even they seemed saddened by Alec's lost battle with the cancer he'd fought so hard.

"Please join us at the inn," said Rose. She turned as Juanita came over to her.

Placing an arm around her shoulder, Rose introduced Juanita to them, noting the surprise on Duncan's face. *What a jerk.*

"Alec always talked about you and your husband in glowing

terms," said Mitchell, shaking Juanita's hand. "Especially your cooking."

Juanita laughed. "You know what they say, 'A way to a man's heart is through his stomach.'"

Mitchell chuckled. "What will you do now that Alec is gone?"

"It's a little premature to talk about it, but Alec, Pedro, and I have a plan."

"I'll see you at the reception," said Duncan to Rose. "I have to go speak to Bennett Williams."

Rose turned as Simon Nickerson, the attorney for the Blaise Group approached.

After giving his condolences to her, Simon addressed Mitchell and Suzi. Trace had wandered off.

Rose left them to their conversation and went over to Lily and Brian. "Nice service," Lily said, giving her a hug. "Thank you for speaking on our behalf, sharing our thoughts and love for Alec. It went well."

"Thank heavens, Hank was facing me, cheering me on. I've never done that kind of thing before and didn't realize how difficult it would be."

"Willow is handling things at the hotel, but we better join her," said Lily.

"Yes, the crowd is leaving here and heading there," Rose said, searching for Hank. He was talking to Duncan and didn't look very happy.

CHAPTER TWENTY-NINE

WILLOW

Willow stood at the door of the ballroom greeting people, keeping an eye on the wait staff who were arranging food on the buffet tables at each end of the room. The bar was set up in two different places along the back wall. Waitresses and waiters stood by to take orders and pass food around. As sad as the occasion was, Alec had wanted to make sure that good food and free drinks would be enjoyed by all, offering an irresistible choice of everything from oysters on the half shell and caviar to more native offerings like stuffed peppers and southwestern egg rolls filled with chicken, black beans, tomatoes, and spicy seasoning. On the buffet tables, a steamship roast of beef sat at one end of the room, while a whole ham and roast turkey sat at the other end. The buffet tables also offered assorted vegetables, casseroles, rolls, sauces, and condiments—enough to keep anyone from leaving hungry.

When she saw Craig and Ken Kincaid approaching together, her heart filled with gratitude that Alec had had such a good friendship with them both. When Ken kissed her on the cheek and murmured his condolences, it seemed natural for Craig to do the same.

Unaware that Trace and Brent were not far behind, she was startled when Brent leaned down as if to kiss her. Quickly, she stepped back.

His look of surprise morphed into anger. "What? I'm not good enough?"

"Whoa," said Trace, placing a hand on Brent's shoulder. "Don't make a scene. Just keep moving." He gave Willow an apologetic look and guided Brent forward.

Understanding, Willow let out a sigh. Someday, she was sure, both Brent and his father, Duncan, would get a comeuppance. It couldn't come soon enough.

As more people streamed into the ballroom, Willow soon forgot the incident and concentrated instead on making sure everyone had the refreshments they wanted. When Lily and Rose joined her, she relaxed and made an effort to circulate among the groups, checking on the servers who silently made their way through the crowd, serving appetizers and taking drink orders.

She was standing by one of the buffet tables when Trace walked over to her. "How are you doing?"

"I'm okay," she said. "Anxious to see that everyone is taken care of, as Alec had wanted."

"It's a great reception," Trace said. "Sorry about Brent earlier. He makes it very difficult at times."

"Yes," Willow answered. She could read in Trace's face and hear in his voice how much he wanted to kiss her.

They stood smiling at one another.

Craig joined them breaking the tender moment.

"Oh, here's your golfing friend," said Trace. "Hi, Craig."

Willow bit her cheek to keep from laughing at the way Craig rolled his eyes. She knew how much he hated that term.

While the two men talked, Willow slipped away to check on Lily who was looking disturbed by the conversation she was listening to between Bennett Williams and Duncan Armstrong.

"Hey, what's up?" she asked Lily.

Lily moved her aside. "They're talking about the grand reopening of the hotel, which is about to happen. Duncan is now demanding they change the date so Brent can be part of the ceremonies."

Willow sighed. "Somehow we have to put a stop to him always messing around with things that have already been decided. It's a power play. I get that. But it makes work for everyone else."

Lily elbowed her. "Why are you here talking to me when two handsome men were vying for your attention?"

Willow laughed. "They're just guys I know. Trace and I went out a couple of times, but until my new job is made public, I'm going to play it cool, even with him. I don't want anything to disturb my plans."

"I understand. Until Brent is out of the picture, it may be safest to play it that way." Lily smiled as Brian headed toward them.

Willow watched as they kissed. Seeing the adoration in Brian's face and the cute way Lily's cheeks turned pink, she hoped she'd share that very same feeling with someone special in her life.

"I know you want to stay until the very end," Brian told Lily, "but I'm leaving to go home and give Anna a break. It's technically her day off."

"Good idea. I'll join you when I can."

As Brian walked away, Lily turned to her. "He's such a good dad. We were both worried about being parents, but he's done a great job of taking on that role. He's going to be a big help with our baby too."

Willow made a mental note to think about that aspect in moving forward with Trace or anyone else.

Rose joined them. "Things are going well. We have plenty of food, conversation is brisk, the bars are busy, and people are reminded of what Alec did to make the inn what it is today."

"I hope the Blaise Group contingent is well aware of that as they move to take the property over. The Desert Sage Inn might have a relaxed atmosphere, but behind it is excellent service and a well-run operation," said Lily.

"What are you Desert Flowers talking about?" asked Hank, with a teasing grin. "Are you making trouble?"

"Not yet," Willow said, and the four of them laughed.

After the last of the guests had left the inn, Willow, Rose, and Lily went to Hank's suite, kicked off their shoes, and relaxed on the couches or in chairs in the living area.

"Ah, that feels good," said Lily, stretching out her legs from an overstuffed chair and wiggling her toes.

Willow threw herself across the cushions of the couch she'd chosen and sighed happily. "Nice to lie down."

Rose moved her shoulders all around and leaned back against the cushion on her chair. "I'm suddenly so tired I don't know if I can make it back to Alec's house."

"When are you going to move in permanently with Hank?" Willow asked.

A smile creased Rose's face. "Tomorrow. I'm glad I was able to stay at the house during Alec's last days and while we were making today happen, but now I want to be with Hank."

"You really love him," Willow stated. It wasn't a question.

Rose nodded. "Very much." She winked at Willow. "It'll happen for you. If I'm not mistaken, two handsome men are already interested."

"Yes," agreed Lily. "But as you told me earlier, Willow, I think you're right to not worry about that for the moment. You want to get your life in order with your new job first."

Willow sat up and faced her two best friends. "I still don't trust the Blaise Group's proposal until everything is signed, sealed, and delivered, as they say."

"You don't trust Mitchell?" Rose said, giving her a look of surprise.

"I don't trust his brother Duncan," Willow replied.

"He was already trying to move the date of the reopening of the inn so Brent could be part of the ceremonies," said Lily.

"I don't know what Hank was discussing with Duncan earlier, but he didn't look happy," said Rose. "Somehow, we Desert Flowers have to do something to take him down."

Willow exchanged glances with Rose and Lily, delighted by the idea.

The next afternoon, Willow walked into the Williams and Kincaid law office hoping she wouldn't run into Craig. She had a few questions about the contract and other information Mitchell had given her, and Bennett had agreed to look them over.

The young man behind the reception desk took her name and buzzed Bennett, announcing her arrival.

Loretta Morales entered the reception area. "Good afternoon, Willow. I'll take you back to Bennett's office; he's on the phone." Her gaze settled on her.

"Thanks," Willow said.

"Too bad Craig is out of the office. I'm sure he'd like to see you," said Loretta, as she hurried Willow along the hallway.

Willow remained quiet and then they were facing the door to Bennett's office.

"Thank you, *Doña* Loretta," Willow said and, at Bennett's signal, entered the office. She knew from the golf foursome how much Loretta loved Craig, even felt responsible to his deceased mother to keep an eye on him, but Willow had no intention on getting pulled into that situation.

Bennett said goodbye to whomever he was talking to and indicated a chair at the small conference table in his office.

"Let's take a look at what you have," he said, rising from behind his desk and joining her at the table.

While he looked over the contract, Willow took out her sheet of notes and questions. She wanted to make sure she had an escape clause should things not go according to the contract, mainly because she didn't trust all the people at the Blaise Group. Until Duncan and Brent were under control, she felt she needed that protection.

After Bennett had looked over the simple contract, he turned to Willow. "It's surprisingly short and fairly straightforward. We might want to strengthen the non-compete issue in your favor, but all the confidentiality and non-disclosure clauses seem fair. What did you want to discuss?"

She confided her feelings about Duncan and his ability to interfere with the smallest of things. "I want to know I have the authority to run the Premio Inn as I see fit, that if any questions come up there's a formal, structured way to address them without someone calling me on the phone or making an impromptu visit. I can see both Duncan and Brent trying to do that to undermine me."

"That might be worrisome," said Bennett. "Let me work on this for a while. We can set up a meeting tomorrow or the day after. Better to protect yourself than to let it be up to chance and common decency. In the meantime, you'd better warn Mitchell that your meeting with him will have to be pushed off another day or two. I'm sure he'll understand. With all that you and the other Desert Flowers have been asked to do, you haven't had time to focus on this."

"Thanks," said Willow, letting out a sigh of relief. "I've learned that it's best to make a stand when you're first hired rather than try to insert something new into an agreement later on."

"I agree. I'll have Loretta call you tomorrow morning to set up a time to meet," said Bennett, getting to his feet.

Willow stood. "Thank you for taking the time to see me. I appreciate it."

He gave her a sad smile. "Anything to help you. I still can't believe it's finally come to an end for Alec. The longer he lived, the more I hoped he would continue to keep the disease at bay."

"I know what you mean," said Willow fighting tears. "Alec has always seemed like a super hero to me."

Bennett walked her to his door, and she left, realizing her life going forward would never be the same without Alec in her life.

CHAPTER THIRTY

ROSE

Rose awakened, rolled over, and reached out to touch Hank. The dear, wonderful man had been very supportive and understanding while she'd camped out at Alec's house during his waning days. Soon, they'd begin to plan their wedding. In light of his recent trip to Atlanta and the incident with Martha Wentworth, Hank had decided he wanted a destination wedding for the few people he wanted to invite. A fresh start, he'd claimed. Rose was more than happy to go along with it as long as his daughters, her fellow Desert Flowers, and Juanita and Pedro attended.

Now, Hank turned to her, caressed her cheeks and pressed his lips to hers. She closed her eyes, loving the taste, the feel of them. At fifty-two she'd wondered if she'd ever know this feeling of handing over her soul and finding it filled with love for a man who made her feel complete.

"M-m-m," Hank murmured. "Who knew I'd find a mermaid in my bed."

She chuckled happily. They'd played a game in the pool last night, with Hank taking the part of Sea Captain while she was the mermaid he discovered on a sailing trip to a far-off tropical island. Thinking of it now, a flush of heat raced to her cheeks. Good heavens, she was crazy about this man!

Later, after a shower and sipping a cup of coffee, Rose got ready to go to the meeting at Bennett Williams' office for the reading of Alec's will. She imagined the only reason for her to be there was to hear about the establishment of The Conchita

Charitable Foundation. She, like Lily and Willow, would see that the small foundation was handled properly. The thought made her happy. She felt as if she already knew the pretty, sweet woman who'd captured Alec's heart completely. Pictures of her were on display in Alec's part of the house. Always had been.

CHAPTER THIRTY-ONE

LILY

Lily hadn't realized how exhausted she'd feel after the service and reception for Alec were over. Still, she gamely got out of bed and prepared to meet with Bennett regarding Alec's will. She was to make sure Alec's wishes in the will were followed. She couldn't imagine any problems with it; the charity he'd set up would, she supposed, be the main beneficiary. Still, she knew personal items would have to be taken care of.

Bennett had requested that she, Rose, Willow, Juanita, and Pedro meet this morning to hear the reading of the will. Anna, bless her heart, had promised to watch the kids though she, too, must be tired after spending so much time with them lately. They adored her, which made leaving them much easier.

After getting breakfast started for Izzy and Ollie, letting Jake outside, and fixing the coffee maker for Brian, she headed into the bathroom.

Brian was there, drying off from his shower, when she entered the room. He was bracing his body against the sink to compensate for the stump of the partial leg he'd lost to war in Afghanistan. She took a moment to admire his strong, virile body, his cute butt. Though their marriage was still new, she sometimes found herself surprised to see him like this. She dreamed of being happily married but had never realized exactly how much she'd been missing.

Brian studied her in the mirror and turned to her with a

smile. “You look happy this morning.”

She laughed. “Happy to see you.”

Brian leaned against the counter and pulled her to him.

She eagerly went into his arms, loving the secure feeling they gave her.

“I’m happy to see you too,” he murmured as one hand caressed her belly. “How are the two of you doing?”

She laughed. “We’re doing fine. A little queasy now and then, in the bathroom a lot, and ready for bed at night.”

“Sounds about right for an expectant mother.” He beamed at her and hugged her tight.

Still smiling, she pulled away, handed him the towel he’d dropped, and moved toward the shower.

“Too late for fooling around?” he said, wiggling his eyebrows at her.

“Sorry. I’m running late,” said Lily, not bothering to hide the regret in her voice. It was rare to have private time with him in the morning. These last few moments were ones to treasure.

Still glowing with happiness, Lily entered the law office of Williams and Kincaid, wondering what the day would bring. She was directed to a small conference room and discovered that the rest of the group was already there.

Bennett and Pedro stood when she entered, and with a wave of her hand, Rose indicated the empty chair near Bennett was for her.

“All right,” said Bennett, closing the door to the room and returning to his seat at the head of the table. “Are we ready to hear Alec’s bequests?”

Lily exchanged glances with the others in the room and, like them, nodded.

Bennett began reading the standard beginning of any will

and then slowed. "To Juanita and Pedro Sanchez, I leave a sum of five hundred thousand dollars, and the house in which they've been residing in the Miramar Estates neighborhood free of any mortgage that might still be remaining." He paused as the sounds of weeping from Juanita filled the room.

Reaching out to her, Bennett said quietly, "He told me many times how you and Pedro saved his life."

Juanita wiped her eyes with a tissue.

"Okay, then, let's proceed," said Bennett after clearing his throat. "As previously agreed, my house on the hotel property is to be sold to the Blaise Group for the sum of $3.2 million dollars. All proceeds from that sale are to be divided equally among my Desert Flowers—Rose, Lily and Willow—to thank them for their support and love during these last months as well as for earlier years. All items in the house are to be shared between my family of five. What they don't want can be sold or given away, at their discretion."

Lily couldn't help the gasp that left her lips. "Oh, my God! I never ..."

Rose shook her head. "That lovely, lovely man."

"I can't believe ..." Willow began.

"All three of you gave Alec more peace and happiness in these last months than any of you could ever appreciate," interjected Bennett. "Alec's only request was to do something with this money that makes you happy."

Lily sat back in her chair, stunned by the news. She could tell from the expressions on Rose and Willow's faces that they, too, never suspected such a thing.

While Bennett read a number of other sums of money given to loyal people on the hotel staff, Lily's mind spun as an idea came to her. She could hardly wait to talk to Rose and Willow about it. When Bennett discussed details of The Conchita Charitable Foundation, Lily straightened in her chair, certain she was right.

CHAPTER THIRTY-TWO

WILLOW

After Bennett concluded the meeting and left them in the conference room, Willow remained in her seat as stunned as the others in the room. Never would she have imagined such a gift as the one Alec had left her and the other two Desert Flowers.

She turned to them now. "What are we going to do with the money?"

"I have an idea," said Lily.

"Before you begin," said Juanita. "Let me tell you what I discussed with Alec."

They all turned to Juanita. "As part of the Conchita Foundation mission, we talked about the idea of providing meals to those who might need them. Pedro and I have already decided we'd like to find a building somewhere in the area where we could offer free meals to people in need. We'd start out slowly, offering meals a couple of times a week."

"That's perfect!" said Lily. "I'm proposing we Desert Flowers put half our money to work for the foundation. I never met Conchita, of course, but I'd like to do something good in her name because of what Alec meant to me and how he remained loyal to her memory."

"Maybe we could do something with that money that would be a wise business move. Something like purchasing the building that would provide food like Juanita and Pedro want, but would also serve as an office for the foundation," said Rose.

"That's a good idea," said Willow. "If, for some reason, the food idea doesn't pan out in the long term, we'd always have the investment in the property."

"We have lots of planning to do," said Lily. "I'm happy to work on it at home. I've been wondering what I'd do when I can no longer be at the law office because of the baby and more and more activities for the other two."

"It's going to take all of us to make something like this happen," said Rose. "We can meet on a regular basis."

"We already have the skills," said Willow. "Rose, you are the perfect person to handle all publicity, creative ideas and community involvement. Lily, you're very good at putting together ideas and coming up with a step by step plan." She turned to her parents. "You know enough people in the community and through church to understand what is needed. And I'm happy to work on budgets and other financial matters. "

The five of them smiled at one another. They were still a team. No longer was Alec there to guide them, but he would remain the reason for doing this work.

Only later that afternoon, did Willow realize what an opportunity Alec's gift was. It meant that if the hotel business didn't work out, she'd always have a reason to stay in Palm Desert. With this in mind, she returned to Bennett's law office to talk about the contract with the Blaise Group.

"What do you think?" Willow asked Bennett. She was sitting once more with him in his office at the small conference desk. Her employment contract was on the table between them.

"I've suggested a few rather minor changes, but other than that, the contract is pretty standard, quite fair," Bennett said. "If for any reason, you leave the company and go to work for someone else, the confidentiality agreement should be no problem. However, I've changed the non-comp clauses to read that you have the right to provide for yourself anywhere else, including in the Coachella Valley. It's too onerous of them to think they can control your life that way."

"What about adding a clause about how disagreements are handled?" Willow said. "If Duncan or Brent tries to undermine what I'm doing, I need a recourse for action."

Bennett gave her a solemn look. "Yes. That's wise. So, I've added something to the effect that should there be any disagreement on their part as to how you're managing the property, threatening the contract, the board's sole remedy is to appoint Mitchell Armstrong and two others from the board to discuss it with you."

Willow thought about it. "Okay. I like it."

They talked about some of the finer points, and then Bennett said, "I think it's safe for you to go ahead and sign the contract. Be aware, though, that no one here, not even Duncan, knows about this unless you've told them."

"Duncan isn't going to be happy," said Willow, already hearing in her mind how he would rant about not being included.

Bennett gave her a steady look. "By the way, I don't know if you're aware, but Duncan wanted to move the date of the grand reopening of the Desert Sage Inn as part of the new Corona Collection. I understand that isn't going to happen, but any talk of the Premio Inn has to be delayed until after that celebration."

The thought of such maneuvering to accommodate personal issues made Willow question her choice, but she quickly brushed that thought away. Some businesses had their own unique problems. She could work around this one.

###

When she returned to Alec's house, she found her parents, Rose, and Lily sitting at the kitchen table. Lily was at her laptop typing away while Rose was dictating something.

"What's going on?" Willow asked, taking a seat beside them.

"Per the will, we are able to choose anything we want from the house before it's sold to the Blaise Group," said Rose. "We're all going to have to go through things and remove anything we choose for ourselves."

"We're making an inventory list of everything. What we don't want will be auctioned off or given away. Any money from the sale of items will go to the Foundation," said Lily.

"Is there a rush on doing this?" asked Willow. "I've decided it would be smart for me to buy a house instead of renting a condo and I'd like to find one before I make a decision on what things I can use from this house."

"No problem," said Rose. "I'm in the same boat. Hank and I are looking at a couple of houses tomorrow. We're pretty much decided on the kind of neighborhood. We just need to see what's available."

"I didn't think I'd want anything," said Lily. "But I'm changing my mind. I don't like the idea of someone else not appreciating the lovely things here." She tapped her computer. "When we're done going through all of the rooms, listing everything there, I'll leave the list in the kitchen and we can each sign up for anything we might like."

"Then we'll make arrangements to sell or give away the rest,"said Rose.

"Yes," said her mother. "Every penny of the sale will be used for the Foundation and the beginning of the new food kitchen."

"We've got to come up with the right name for it," said Willow. "What do you think, Rose?"

Rose grinned. "How about something simple, like Juanita's Kitchen?"

Pedro, who was normally quiet, clapped his hands. "Excellent. Juanita means God is Gracious and Gift from God."

"Yes, our being able to work on this project is a gift from above," said Juanita. "I'd like to think of it as a gift from both Conchita and Alec."

The room grew silent as each of them in the room fought to control their emotions.

When Trace called Willow that evening for a date, she turned down his invitation and explained she needed time alone while she was dealing with the aftermath of Alec's funeral.

"Let me know if there's anything I can do for you, any way to help," he said.

She heard the sincerity in his voice and sighed. He was a good guy, but she had too much on her mind to worry about dating. She needed time to get her life in order without him being a part of it.

Willow went to the bedroom she'd used for the past few months wondering if the other women felt as she did about how their lives were changing once again because they'd all loved a man called Alec Thurston.

The next morning, Willow slipped on her bathing suit, grabbed a towel, and went out to the pool. She was alone in the house now, but she didn't mind. She felt Alec's presence, could almost see him watching her as she dove into the pool. Like Rose, she found swimming to be a great stress reliever. This morning she needed it. She'd tossed and turned all night, trying to figure out what she wanted for the future. Independence for a while at least, a nice place to live, and a job she loved. All within her reach.

In the pool, she felt tension leave her as her muscles began to work. With Alec's money she could afford a house with a pool. Nothing too fancy, but highly livable with space to grow. Funny, when she thought of a house, she didn't imagine any guy living there.

She kicked harder, wondering what was wrong with her. Was no man ever going to be good enough? Both Trace and Craig were interested in her, but she was too tired, too drained to think of it. She was lost in thought, moving briskly through the water, when she heard someone call her name. She jerked to a stop, treaded water, and looked up to see Rose smiling at her.

"Hey, there! What are you doing here?" Willow asked, pleased to see her. She climbed out of the pool and wrapped a towel around herself.

"Just thought I'd see how you're doing all alone in this big house," Rose said, smiling. "I was missing our morning coffee together."

"How sweet. You said you and Hank are going house hunting this morning. Any ideas for me?"

"As a matter of fact, I do have one. There's a new development in the foothills Hank and I are looking at, and I thought you might like to go with us. From what we've read and what the real estate agent told us, it's a good time to buy there. Prices will only go up."

"Would you mind if we were neighbors?" Willow said, giving her a steady look. "We'll be working together on Foundation stuff."

"Mind?" Rose laughed and shook her head. "I'd be thrilled if I knew we could get together some mornings for coffee."

Willow breathed a sigh of happiness. She loved the idea too.

After looking at a few houses and then the newer homes for sale in a development called Rolling Hills, Willow decided she didn't want to live anywhere else. The views, the cooler air, and the idea of the developer keeping things as natural as possible appealed to her.

Hank and Rose decided to continue to look around, though Willow knew that Rose, too, had her heart set on Rolling Hills. Willow said goodbye to them and stayed with the real estate agent on site to see what kind of deal she could work out. She hoped to buy one of the less expensive homes, though the one she had in mind was large.

After taking time to return to the house, take some measurements, and list anything she might want to change, she was confident about her choice. Though with Alec's money and her savings she could pay for it in full, she decided to go with a mortgage to allow herself to continue a strong savings program. She'd spent enough time with Alec to know it was important.

When Rose and Hank returned to pick her up, Rose said, "Well? Are you going to do it?"

Willow grinned. "I am. I'm waiting to hear from the bank, and then I'll go ahead with it. I have first right of refusal on the house I want."

"Nice," said Rose, throwing an arm around her shoulder. "Hank and I are still talking about a house here, too."

Hank joined them. "Do you mind waiting a few minutes? I'm going to pick up some more information from the agent, and then we'll be ready to go."

Once Hank left them, Rose sighed. "I knew from the minute we walked into the show home at the end of the street that this is where I wanted to live. But I have to let Hank make the choice too. Hopefully, he'll decide sometime soon because the lease on the house he's renting is going to run out in a couple of weeks."

Hank and Rose dropped her off at Alec's house.

As she opened the front door and stepped inside, Willow's first instinct was to head to Alec's private quarters. Reality struck a blow, reminding her that he was gone. Breathing deeply to steady herself, she walked into the kitchen and found her mother sorting through cupboards.

"It's going to take a while to prepare this house for sale," said her mother. "We'll have to work together to clear everything including little things like kitchen items."

"Yes, I know," said Willow. "That's why Rose and I are trying to go ahead with plans to buy a house. We each have some items we'd like from here, and it's time for us to move out anyway."

Her mother wiped her hands on her apron. "How did it go?"

Willow sat at the kitchen table. "I've found the home I want to buy. It's in a new development in the foothills. I have first right of refusal. Ordinarily, I'd talk to you, Dad, and Alec about it, but I'm pretty happy with the deal I've got. All the money I'd saved to buy a condo in Boston is still in my savings account. Now I have enough funds for a healthy down payment."

Her mother handed her a glass of lemonade and sat down beside her. "Ken Kincaid is the financial advisor your father and I use. It might be a good idea to talk to him to see how best to handle the purchase of the house you like. It'll be a while before Alec's will is probated and before this house is sold."

Willow was not at all surprised by her parents using a

financial advisor. Still, it pleased her. Her father, in particular, was very conservative with his money, had always been.

"Thanks. I'll call and see if I can get an appointment right away." She liked Ken. And if her parents and Alec trusted him, that was good enough for her.

"So many changes," her mother said, a sad note to her voice. Then her face brightened. "But a lot of good things too." Her lips curved. "Juanita's Kitchen has a nice ring to it, don't you think?"

Willow laughed. "I do. It's good to know your talents are recognized, and this is a perfect way to do it. Leave it to you and Alec to come up with the idea of something like this." Tears stung Willow's eyes, surprising her. "It seems very empty not to have him here."

"I know. His life, though well-lived, was just a part of what might have been, if Conchita and the baby had lived. She was such a magical person—beautiful and bright. Like a gift of a shell from the sea, he used to tell me."

"Do you believe he's with her now?" Willow asked.

Her mother nodded. "I do."

Willow stared out the window. "You and *Papi* are like that. Together for always."

Her mother chuckled. "Possibly. But there are days when I wonder." She reached over and squeezed Willow's hand. "Marriage is a lot of work. That's why it's best not to force any relationship."

Willow's eyes widened. "Oh my God! Do you think that's what I've been doing?"

"No." Her mother shook her head. "But this is a vulnerable time for you."

"I know. That's why I've told Trace I'm not going to see him for a while. I need a break from thinking about all that."

"Good," said her mother. "After you make your call, want

to help me empty cupboards? We'll put everything out on the table so we can all choose whatever we want."

"Don't you think all of the cooking things should go to you to use for the food kitchen?"

Her mother stood and smiled. "That would be nice, but I can't make that choice without approval from the others."

"Okay. I'll be right back. I want to make that call to Ken."

CHAPTER THIRTY-THREE

WILLOW

The next morning, Willow sat in the small conference room Ken Kincaid's assistant had left her in waiting for him to get off the phone and join her. She stared at the black and white photos of early scenes of Palm Desert, awed by the way a beautiful area had grown from barren desert. The hum of the air conditioning in the office reminded her of the work it had taken to get the city to its present stage.

"Ah, Willow. Sorry to take so long." Ken walked into the conference room and held out his hand. "Glad to see you. How can I help?"

Willow smiled and shook his hand. "I need some advice. I'm about to purchase a home, and with money coming from Alec's estate, I need help planning for the future. My mother suggested I call you."

"Ah, yes. Your parents have been clients for years. Such good people."

Pleased, Willow proceeded. "First of all, I want your advice on the purchase, and then I need help in coming up with a plan for a mortgage. I've saved diligently through the years, thinking I'd stay in Boston, and I have funds for a down payment. But, perhaps, we can talk about it."

"Sure," said Ken. "Let's get you set up as a client and we'll go from there. We'll take a look at everything, and you can decide how best to proceed. How does that sound?"

"Great," said Willow. "I want to plan for the future."

"I suppose that will include a spouse and children."

Willow shook her head. "Not for a long time. I want my independence. I'll be starting a new job, a job I really want."

Ken's eyebrows rose but he calmly handed over some paperwork. "Either way, it's important for you to be self-sufficient."

Willow liked his advice already.

The days passed in a flurry as Willow prepared to settle in a new house while helping to take apart Alec's. Fortunately, her mother had worked with Alec and Ken to go through files, drawers, and personal papers after Alec knew he was dying, so none of that work had to be done.

Still, it was never easy to break apart a house that had been lived in for over twenty years. It was interesting to see what the others wanted from the house. As for herself, Willow requested the kitchen table and chairs which she considered the heart of the home and her friendship with the other Flowers. She also asked for the furniture from the suite that had been designated for her at Alec's house, thinking it would make a beautiful guest room in her own house. Rose and Lily, too, decided to keep the furnishings in their suites as a means to remember their time there.

One by one things were either chosen or the group made a decision to sell it or give it away.

Though Hank and Rose's house wouldn't be ready for a while, Willow offered to have them temporarily store anything they wanted in her garage. It would be convenient because Rose had finally gotten her house in the same neighborhood of Rolling Hills.

"I think we ought to have an estate sale and give hotel employees first chance at it," said Lily one day.

They all agreed that an estate sale should take place as soon as possible and set to work pricing and preparing things for sale.

On a bright, hot morning, Willow stood with Rose and Lily in various rooms of the house where furniture, artwork, lamps, and soft goods were displayed, waiting to make sales. Her mother was stationed in the kitchen, though everyone else had agreed most items from there needed to be set aside for later use in Juanita's Kitchen, as the project was now officially called.

As she watched various furnishings being carried out of the house and loaded into cars and trucks, Willow thought of how meaningless possessions were following death. Yet, she was happy to have the few things she'd chosen from Alec's house. They'd be placed in her house along with other gifts attached to memories of others. That was what made them very special to her.

With the success of the estate sale, very few things remained to be given away. Alec's clothing and shoes had already been donated, and his automobile long since given away to a charitable auction for cancer research.

After a truck from a donation center departed with the last of the items from the house, Rose, Lily, and Willow looked at one another, drenched in sweat, and automatically headed out to the patio. Juanita joined them with a plastic pitcher of lemonade and four paper cups.

"The cleaning crew comes tomorrow, along with the appraiser," she said. "Then, my sweet ones, we're done here."

"Hardly seems possible that in a few months our lives have changed," said Willow. She gazed at Rose and Lily.

Rose grinned. "I'm happy I came to Palm Desert for many reasons. Part of it is meeting all of you. And Hank, of course."

"You're blushing," teased Lily, and Willow joined in the laughter.

"What about you!" declared Rose. "Brian, Ollie, Izzy, and now a baby."

Lily laughed and patted her rounded stomach. "Such blessings. Especially at night when one of them needs attention."

Willow grinned, seeing the love and pride on Lily's face.

"And Willow," said her mother, her eyes twinkling with humor. "You are about to fulfill your dream of managing a hotel and you now own a house of your own, within easy reach of your mother."

"Fortunately, not that close," said Willow, playing along. But she, too, was grateful to be back in Palm Desert.

"No word yet from Mitchell?" Rose asked.

Willow shook her head. She'd anxiously awaited the announcement of the purchase of the Premio Inn and her appointment to run it. With more delicacy than she'd thought possible, Mitchell was holding off until she was ready to focus on it. She suspected it had to do more with keeping Duncan from spoiling plans than anything else. But she was still grateful.

"I have a feeling that he's waiting until after the grand reopening and the right moment when neither Duncan nor Brent is around to spoil it all."

With the grand reopening party coming up, she felt at a loss. The Desert Sage Inn was now a Blaise Group hotel with Trace assigned to the position she'd once wanted. She'd been given the job at the Premio Inn, but until it was announced she'd feel insecure about it. She trusted Mitchell and would refrain from telling anyone else about it as he'd asked. It was an unorthodox way to run a business, but knowing Duncan and Brent as well as she did, she understood. She had to get through the party officially ending her connection to the Desert Sage Inn.

CHAPTER THIRTY-FOUR

WILLOW

A couple of evenings later, Willow dressed in a sleeveless, black-linen sheath and slipped on a pair of high-heeled sandals and stepped back to inspect herself in the mirror. The silver and turquoise Native American necklace stood out against the background of black and matched a broad band of silver and turquoise at her wrist. Dangling silver earrings sparkled at her ears barely visible beneath her long, straight, dark hair.

She sighed thinking of the reception ahead. This was the night she'd both looked forward to and dreaded. Though she vowed to keep her emotions under control, she knew it would be difficult. How do you say goodbye to dreams you've held onto all your life?

Knowing she had no choice but to act the gracious guest, she went out to the garage and climbed into the new, white SUV she'd purchased. She'd heard the governor had been invited to the grand reopening and had politely declined, but the mayor and four of the five City Council members planned to attend. Several Hollywood stars were on the list as well as numerous prominent people in the hospitality industry. In most ways, it should be a pleasant evening.

She pulled up to the front of the hotel. A valet hurried over to her, held the door, and assisted her out of the car. She handed him the car fob and headed inside, drawing calming breaths.

In the lobby, an easel displayed a large sign declaring the

Desert Sage Inn was now a part of the new Corona Collection of Fine Hotels. A number of staff members, dressed in the new tan uniforms she'd researched for use in all the Corona properties, greeted the arriving guests.

"Hello, Willow," said someone she recognized from the management team. "Welcome to the Desert Sage Inn. We invite you to join the others in the ballroom for a wonderful evening."

"Thank you," she said pleasantly, noting how well spoken, how sincere the staff member sounded.

At the entrance to the ballroom, Trace stood greeting guests. When he saw her, his eyes lit with pleasure. "Hi, Willow. You look stunning as always." Before she could stop him, he leaned down and kissed her on the cheek. "A special welcome to you. Enjoy the party."

"Thanks, I will." Though a part of her wanted to turn back at the thought of the Blaise Group taking over the inn, she'd stay and be a gracious guest in memory of Alec.

She entered the ballroom and looked around to see who else was there. Spying Sarah Jensen standing and talking to another woman, she maneuvered her way through the throng to say hello.

Sarah looked up, saw her, and smiled. "Ah, Willow! You look beautiful! It's nice to see you! It's been a while."

"Too long," said Willow, giving her a quick hug. "How does it feel having Eric home?"

"Too wonderful to describe. When a loved one is away serving in the army, the stress of knowing he could be hurt is constant. Now, with that weight off my shoulders, it feels good not to worry."

"I'm happy for you. Two different deployments to assignments overseas would be hard for any spouse to handle. I'm happy for you both."

"Me, too," said Sarah. "He was going to come tonight, but he's staying home with Henry. Poor kid has a cold and wasn't feeling good."

"I'm sorry. I was anxious to meet him. But we'll make it another time." Sarah's little boy was about to turn three and was, no doubt, loving having his Daddy home.

"Call me for coffee," said Sarah. "Though Eric is around, I still need to get out of the house now and then."

Rose walked over to them. "Nice party, huh?" She handed Willow a glass of red wine. "I saw you come in and knew you'd need this."

Willow laughed and accepted the wine. "It's just that this will always be Alec's hotel in my mind."

Sarah introduced the woman standing with her to Rose and Willow as Nan Becker. "Rose and Willow are two of the Desert Flowers, as Alec used to call them," she went on to explain.

"Oh! I've heard about you," said Nan grinning. "I love the idea of the three of you women teaming up. In fact, my daughter who attends the high school told me about the motivational talk you gave to the girls there. She came home all inspired to become the best student she could to get into a nursing program."

Willow and Rose glanced at one another and grinned.

"The pep talk was Lily's idea," said Willow. "Here she is now!"

Lily hugged the three women and smiled at Nan as she was introduced. "Lovely party," she murmured. "I noticed a few starlets circling the room, and I was introduced to the mayor." She turned to Rose and Lily. "I'm meeting with her next week about finding a space for Juanita's Kitchen."

Willow laughed. Lily was the most organized person she knew.

"Great. We'll meet after you speak to her," said Rose.

Willow left the women to take a look at the food preparation. The offerings were not much different from the reception held for Alec. Still, it was nice to see such a complete spread of delicious food.

She'd just put a cold shrimp in her mouth when she felt movement behind her and turned to find Duncan waiting to talk to her. Swallowing as best she could while wanting to choke, she waited for him to speak.

"I'm sorry you won't be with the hotel here, but Trace is very capable," Duncan said, with an unexpected note of sincerity. "And Brent will do well in Phoenix. I'm not sure what you plan to do next, but whatever it is, I wish you well."

Willow swallowed and dabbed at her mouth with a tissue. "Thank you, Duncan. This is a lovely party."

"Yes. Quite appropriate, I think. You and the Desert Flowers did a good job for Alec. I'm sorry he's not here to be part of the celebration."

"Me, too," said Willow quietly, appreciating Duncan's unexpected kindness.

Trace approached. "I'm off door duty. How about sitting and sharing some food with me?"

Willow held up a hand to ward off the idea. "I'm just going to pick at food as I make my way through the crowd. But thank you."

Trace's cheeks colored and his lips thinned. "Okay. I'll give you a call. I'd better go check on some of our other guests."

As he abruptly turned on his heel and walked away, Willow watched him as he stopped to talk to a couple of young women who'd tried to get his attention. She wasn't at all sure how she felt about him.

She stayed at the reception for an hour greeting friends and meeting others. And then, even though the evening was still young, she slipped out of the room.

When Willow returned to her house, she wandered through its rooms touching a chair, a couch, the kitchen table, wondering what the future would bring. As she'd told Ken, she liked her independence. Still, she knew she didn't want to be alone forever. Alec had shown her in many ways how lonely that was. She gazed at her pool and decided to take a swim. The sun was going down, but it was still warm. She changed into a bikini and stepped outdoors.

She was just about to dive into the pool when she heard the doorbell. Frowning, she paused.

When it rang again, she reluctantly headed for the front door.

"Hello? Who's there?" she called behind the locked door.

"It's me, Craig. Sorry it's late, but I'm dropping off some papers my father wanted you to have."

She opened the door a crack. "Okay." She threaded her hand out through the doorway and then stepped back when Craig pushed the door wider.

"What's up?" His gaze traveled over her body, and an appreciative look settled on his face.

Fighting her response, observing him in his business suit and thinking of a kilt, she forced herself to focus. "Uh, the papers?"

"Oh, yes. I almost forgot." He held out a large brown envelope and waited for her to take it. "My father told me about your meeting with him."

Her eyes widened with surprise. "What?"

"No personal financial information. He'd never do that. He mentioned that he admired what an independent woman you are and how you want to remain that way. He likes the fact that you're focusing on the new job you've been given and says you're very smart. Anyway, I'm glad you're staying in Palm Desert."

"Thanks. Me, too."

Craig shuffled his feet, cleared his throat, then said, "Will you go out with me tomorrow? I'd like to take you to dinner. No strings attached."

She hesitated.

"Just as friends," said Craig.

Willow recalled how much fun she'd had with Craig playing golf together. "This wouldn't be a date?"

Craig shrugged. "Not really. You want your independence; I don't want to be involved with anyone. We can have fun without worrying about taking it to the next step."

"But you can have a real date with any girl in the valley. Why me?"

He shook his head. "It's gotten to the point where if I ask a woman out, she thinks I'm on my knees proposing. I'm not kidding. I just want to go out without any pressure."

Deciding she had nothing to lose, Willow said, "Okay. Friends, fun, and NO SEX."

"Okay by me." Craig grinned. "If things change, I'll let you know."

"All right. Deal." She held out her hand and Craig shook it.

"Great. I'll pick you up tomorrow at six." Craig gave her a little salute and walked away.

Willow closed the door and leaned against it wondering if she'd been foolish. Could going out as friends work with Craig Kincaid? He'd sounded serious about not wanting to get involved. She'd seen how other women draped themselves over him and supposed it would get tiresome and why he'd want to go out with someone who was safe.

Pushing aside thoughts of what she hoped wouldn't be a bad decision, she opened the envelope and leafed through the papers. First thing tomorrow morning, she'd study them. Now, as she'd planned, she was going for a swim.

CHAPTER THIRTY-FIVE

WILLOW

Willow lay in bed staring at the lemony ribbons of early morning light that reached out to her from between the louvers on the window blinds. She sometimes still found it hard to believe she owned her own house. After years of scraping and saving, she'd always thought she'd buy a condo in Boston. She was glad that hadn't worked out. This, being home with family and new friends, was a much better choice for her.

She stared at the blank walls in the bedroom. She'd been waiting to get through the job of clearing out Alec's house before deciding on artwork for her house. Now that the work at Alec's was completed and she owned a few of his paintings, she was ready to begin to mount them and purchase others to accompany them. The oil painting she'd selected from Alec's house—a beautiful desert scene—would hang over the fireplace in the living room. A couple of smaller paintings would fit in nicely in the guest room or in her office.

She was keeping to neutral tones throughout the house leaving her the fun of brightening the interiors of the rooms with varying colors in soft goods and other décor. Her decorating was far from completed, but she intended to take her time to make sure everything was exactly the way she wanted. It pleased her she didn't need approval from anyone else.

After pouring herself a cup of coffee, Willow grabbed the papers Craig had delivered and sat at the kitchen bar to look them over. A sense of pride filled her at the investment portfolio she and Ken had developed. When Alec's money came in from the sale of the house, she'd use most of it for investing. The rest would purchase things she needed for the house. She wouldn't have any debt to speak of except the mortgage. She thought of Alec's generosity and hoped he somehow knew how grateful she was.

Her phone rang. *Mitchell Armstrong*.

She eagerly clicked on the call, hoping the announcement of her appointment would be made soon, and she could start her new job. "Good morning!" she said cheerfully.

"Hello, Willow. I'm afraid I have some bad news. We're being forced to delay the purchase of the Premio Inn, which means your start date has been pushed back."

Willow's heartbeat pounded in her ears. "May I ask why?"

"Duncan and another board member think we should totally redecorate the inn, make it look more like a Blaise property."

"But I thought it was going to be a real part of the Corona Collection. If so, it's perfect just the way it is. Maybe it could use a little refreshment of furniture in the lobby, but when I inspected the hotel some weeks ago, the inn was in beautiful shape."

"I agree with you. The issue, apparently, is with the native look of the inn."

"But that's its charm," countered Willow, feeling sick at the idea of destroying the panache of the inn.

"Again, I agree with you. But I have to allow the board members to take a vote on it. After agreeing to buy the property, they want to make sure it's going to be very much a part of our group of hotels. My lawyer has advised me to give them some time to visit both the Premio Inn and the Desert Sage Inn and make a judgement."

Willow felt like crying. Duncan Armstrong, like a thorn in her a ... foot, kept interfering with her success. Anger filled her at the thought. "My employment is not in jeopardy, is it?" she asked, her words as hard as desert rocks.

"Absolutely not," Mitchell quickly assured her. "I've defended our employment agreement and the board is behind you all the way."

"Is it because Duncan couldn't destroy that, that he's striking out at the plans for the hotel?" Willow knew she might sound out-of-line, but if she was going to work for the Blaise Group, she wasn't going to hide her thoughts or be bullied. That was the whole purpose of the special clause she and Bennett had added to the employment contract. Interference by Duncan was an issue she wanted to be able to shut down.

"I understand your frustration, but sometimes it's worth taking a little time on issues like this," said Mitchell. "I'm confident that once a few of the board members see the property in person, they'll better understand its charm."

"Will George Hartmann be there during their visit?" Willow asked.

"Oh, yes. He and Duncan have had words, and George is determined to do right by the property. Like Alec did for the Desert Sage Inn."

Willow immediately felt better. "Let me know if there's anything I can do to help."

"Thank you. I appreciate that," said Mitchell. "We'll talk soon. My hope is that any delay will be resolved quickly, and we can move ahead with plans to reopen the hotel as a part of the Corona Collection with you at the helm."

"Thank you," said Willow. She clicked off the call furious that once again Duncan had interfered with plans that included her.

Her phone rang again. *Rose.*

Willow answered the call and immediately began spouting off about the conversation with Mitchell.

Rose listened quietly then said, "Good morning, Willow!"

Willow laughed. "Sorry, but I had to get it off my chest. They're all going to drive me crazy!"

"Including Trace?" Rose's question hung in the air as threatening as a hovering hornet, making Willow feel as if she was about to get stung.

She let out a long sigh. "I don't know. I like Trace. His parents too. But the situation with him is becoming a lot more complicated now that I'll be working for the Blaise Group. And as I told both him and Craig, I'm not looking for anything more than friendship."

"Craig? I thought you weren't interested in him," said Rose.

"Only as a friend. We've had fun playing against one another in our golf games. He's not interested in me; he told me so. And I told him I'd be interested in friendship only. No sex."

"Whoa! Sex? What's going on? Are you going out with him?"

"We're having dinner together tonight. Just as friends. I'm not going to stay at home just because I'm not serious about him." Willow knew she sounded defensive but couldn't help it. She didn't want to explain to anyone else that she was willing to take a chance on Craig's friendship because he made her feel alive.

"Ah, I see," said Rose, with a hint of laughter. "I love you, Willow. Just checking on you and how you're doing in your new house. Ours won't be ready for a couple more weeks. Hank and I are flying to Atlanta to sort through things in his house to prepare it for sale. We've definitely decided to do it."

"Another home 'demolition' project? Better you than me," said Willow. "I'm still trying to get settled here."

"It's a big job, but it'll be worth it. We Desert Flowers are all going to be happy with our new homes in Palm Desert together. I just know it."

"I do love my house," Willow confessed. "That's another reason I'm not interested in a serious relationship with anyone. I finally have the freedom I want in a place I'm happy to call home."

"That's very important," Rose said. "I'm happy for you. I'll give you a call when I get back. In the meantime, may I ask you to do me a favor? Will you check on the progress of our house? They're down to doing all the finishing things like trim work and painting, but I like to know someone is keeping an eye on things."

"Sure. I'm happy to do that for you," said Willow. "It's convenient now that we're going to be neighbors."

"Thanks. It means a lot to me. I've got to go. See you when I get back."

After Rose ended the call, Willow stared out the window of her breakfast nook and sighed. Feeling lonely, she called Sarah Jensen. She'd been so busy with Alec's house and her own, she hadn't seen Sarah in some time, until last night. And now that Sarah had asked her to call and was taking time off from her part-time job at the Desert Sage Inn where she'd worked as assistant manager, she might be available.

Sarah's voicemail came on. Willow left a message for her, clicked off the call, and realized everyone else was busy with their own lives. She was about to head to the shower when her phone rang again. *Ricardo Morales.*

Surprised, but pleased to get a call from him, she picked it up. "Hello!"

"Hi, Willow. I just got a call from Ken Kincaid. He wanted to make sure we'd all continue to keep our games on Tuesday mornings. It's what Alec wanted."

"How sweet! Yes. I definitely will be there, continuing to take his place."

"Good," said Ricardo. "See you then."

Pleased by the thought, she clicked off the call.

She headed into her bathroom to take a shower, eager to feel the soothing effect of warm water washing over her. In just a matter of hours her emotions had run the gamut from excitement, disappointment, anger, and gratitude, to anticipation.

That evening, as Willow waited for Craig to arrive to pick her up, she reminded herself that friendship with him would be nice. Her close friends were busy and as much as she wanted her independence, she didn't want to be stuck at home all the time. She deserved a night out with someone who knew what her boundaries were. It was that simple.

Promptly at six o'clock, Craig arrived at her door. "Ready?" he asked, giving her a look of approval. "You look ... good."

"Thanks! You look pretty good yourself." She stepped outside and locked the door behind her, ready for an evening of fun. The last couple of weeks had been full of sorrow and tension.

"Where are we going?" Willow asked.

"How does Italian food sound?" he asked.

She grinned. "Are you talking about Mama B's?"

"The one and only," said Craig. "It's hard to get a reservation on a Saturday night, but I know the hostess there."

"Of course, you do," said Willow pleasantly. It was a good thing they'd agreed to be friends because she'd never want to be in a relationship where other women were such a big part of it. When she found the right man, she wanted to be certain of what the two of them shared.

Craig frowned. "What do you mean? Sheila and I went to

high school together. She's married to one of my best friends."

Willow placed a hand on his arm. "Craig, you don't owe me any explanations. We're just friends."

"Right," he said, looking surprised and then nodding his agreement.

He helped her into his car, a dark, oversized SUV.

Willow sat in the passenger seat while Craig walked around the car and then slid behind the wheel.

As Craig drove the short distance to Palm Springs, they remained quiet. It pleased Willow that they were able to enjoy the ride without feeling the need to keep up pleasant conversation.

At one point, Craig turned to her and smiled.

"What?" she said.

He grinned. "No nervous chatter. I like it."

She leaned back in her seat. "No need for it. It's just us."

He studied her a moment. "Guess you're right."

When they pulled up in front of a small, white-stucco building, a valet immediately approached the car, opened the door for Willow, and circled the car to talk to Craig.

Delicious aromas—a blend of garlic, olive oil, and other seasonings—wafted out from the kitchen and greeted Willow. Her mouth watered. She was already anticipating the delicious food that she knew awaited her. Mama B's was known for its veal dishes, grilled fish, fresh pasta, and famous red sauce. Dinner here was an expensive treat and one she intended to enjoy.

"Smells great already," said Craig, holding the carved wooden front door open for her to enter.

Inside, Willow stood a moment admiring the interior. Tables were covered with pale-pink linen cloths. Crystal goblets and wine glasses sparkled from the flickering candlelight that washed over each table, shining on the silverware and folded napkins at each place. Chairs and booth seats were covered in red velvet and offset the dark paneled walls. The carpet that covered the floor embraced red, pink, and green colors in a subtle, Oriental-style pattern and was both pleasing and different.

An attractive blonde smiled at them and moved forward to embrace Craig. “How lovely to see you!” She turned to Willow, eyeing her carefully as Craig introduced Sheila Gottridge to her. “You may remember Willow Sanchez. She’s back home in Palm Desert,” Craig explained. “She was a few grades younger than us.”

“I’m sorry, I don’t remember you. But perhaps you knew my baby sister from high school—Debbie Martin?”

“Oh, yes. Please say hi to her for me.”

“She lives in Ohio now, but comes back to visit in the winter. But I’ll tell her I saw you. Are you here for a visit?”

Willow shook her head. “No, I’ve left Boston where I taught college courses and have moved here permanently. I’ve been living and working at the Desert Sage Inn.”

“She’s bought a house near there,” said Craig.

“Oh, well then, you’re a native returned home. It’s always a good thing to hear,” Sheila said, gazing from her to Craig and back again, obviously curious about seeing them together.

“Tell Dan hello for me,” said Craig. “He owes me a golf game.”

Sheila laughed. “You might have to bribe him. He knows he can’t beat you.”

“Tell him I’ll let him win. It’s been too long since we’ve played.”

Sheila laughed again and turned to signal a waiter. “Please seat Craig Kincaid and his date. They’re at table thirty-two.”

Willow shook her head at Craig, wanting to make it clear this was no date.

Craig looked surprised, then grinned. "She's my good friend."

Chuckling to herself, Willow followed the waiter to a desirable table in the corner of the main dining room. Craig and she were never going to let the other win, whether it was a game of golf, or an exchange of words. That's what made being with him fun.

Willow was seated in a chair that allowed her not only to gaze outside but to keep her attention on the interior of the restaurant. She let her gaze roam and froze.

Duncan, Mitchell, and Trace were seated at a table not far from them.

CHAPTER THIRTY-SIX

ROSE

Rose sat with Hank in the airplane leaving Palm Springs, wondering what the next few days would bring. Packing up his home of over thirty years wouldn't be easy. Especially for his daughters, who were still getting used to the idea of their father marrying again and moving out of state. Still, she'd come to like Samantha and her sister, Nikki, and vowed to be patient as they all navigated through this difficult time.

She glanced at Hank snoring softly beside her and thought of all the changes in her life. The best of all was meeting him and falling in love with him. Though Alec would always have a special place in her heart, Hank was the man she'd been looking for all her life.

Her thoughts flew to Lily and Willow. They were the sisters she'd never had, the sisters she'd always wanted.

She chuckled softly at her earlier conversation with Willow. Though she might think she could be just friends with Craig, Willow was about to go on an emotional journey with him. The chemistry between the two of them simmered beneath the surface whenever Rose saw them together.

Rose stared out the window of the plane, gazing down at the mountains below, her thoughts remaining on the last few months. They seemed like an entire lifetime. Or maybe it was because she'd felt alive, as if awakening from a past that now seemed empty.

CHAPTER THIRTY-SEVEN

WILLOW

In the restaurant, Trace looked up and settled his gaze on her, his expression shocked. Willow gave him a little wave and then watched uncomfortably as he strode across the room and approached their table.

Craig set down his menu and stared up at Trace.

"Hi, Trace. You remember Craig Kincaid, don't you?" Willow said, hiding her dismay at the way the two men were glaring at one another.

"Ah, yes," said Trace, with an edge to his voice. "The golfing friend. What are you guys doing here?"

"We're just friends having dinner together," Willow said.

"A nice quiet way to enjoy each other's company," said Craig.

Trace's gaze pierced her. "But you said ..."

"Craig and I are just friends," said Willow. "Like I told you, I'm looking for nothing beyond that."

"Okay. I see. You're just spending time with your 'golfing friend'." Trace studied Craig and then he walked away, his back stiff.

Craig's face flushed but he remained quiet.

"Sorry for the interruption," Willow said. She picked up the menu the waiter had left at her place. "What are you thinking of having?"

"First off, I'm going to order wine," said Craig glancing across the room at Trace. "What would you prefer, red or white?"

She acted as if she wasn't aware of Craig's frustration. Trace calling him the golfing friend had struck a nerve. "I'd love a nice red, perhaps a pinot noir."

"Okay. They have some good ones." He signaled the waiter.

She waited while he conversed with the waiter and after he'd ordered wine, Craig sat back in his chair and studied her. "What's going on with you and Trace?"

"Nothing," Willow said. "Like you and me, we're just friends. We've gone on a couple of dates, but that's it. I don't want to talk about it. I'm here with you tonight for a delicious meal, like we agreed."

"You're right. Let's enjoy it."

Their wine came, and after going through the ceremony of smelling the cork and tasting the wine, Craig declared it a good one. The waiter poured some in her glass and more in Craig's.

After he left, Willow said to Craig, "Thanks for bringing me here. Mama B's is a very special place, and this is a treat."

"Even with the trio across the room?" Craig said.

"Yes. I don't want anything to ruin this evening. I intend to enjoy every bite of my food."

"You're not one of those boring women who have to mentally count calories before ordering anything?"

Willow shook her head. "I grew up with good food both in my house and at the hotel. I learned early on that delicious meals are gifts to be enjoyed."

He laughed. "God! I like you more."

She grinned. "If we're going to be friends, you'll find out I mean what I say."

They ordered their food and talked about growing up in the area. Craig was enough older that their paths had seldom crossed.

"My father said you used to play golf with Alec. Ricardo

worked with you, too. Right?"

"Yes. Alec paid him to give me lessons. I needed an outdoor activity like that. I was a total nerd in school."

He studied her. "I wasn't the best student. I could've done better, but I was having too much fun."

"You played football, didn't you?"

"Yeah. And I used to drive to the coast with friends to go surfing a lot." He took a sip of wine and focused on her again. "It wasn't until Ben Williams hired me as an intern as a favor to my father that I got serious about law. I'm sure Ben thought I'd change my mind, but after he realized I was serious, he helped me get into law school."

"And?"

"And I've been happy with my job. I like helping people."

"Me, too. In a different way, of course," said Willow. "But if I can make someone's stay at a hotel pleasing, it makes me feel good."

"That comes naturally to you. Look at your parents. They have been wonderful to Alec and helpful to anyone else they know."

Pleased, Willow leaned forward. "Have you heard about Juanita's Kitchen?"

He shook his head. "Is it a restaurant?"

"Sort of," Willow said proudly. "My parents and Alec have come up with a way to help area people in need by setting up a free-meal kitchen. My mother will help run it. Rose, Lily and I thought it should be named Juanita's Kitchen. Isn't that perfect?"

Craig lips curved. "It sounds great."

"It's hard to believe one man could make such a difference in so many lives," said Willow. "Alec was such a special person."

Craig gave her a thoughtful look. "He's a good example to

follow. After my talk with my father the other day, I feel like I'm ready to make some changes. I'm still trying to decide exactly what changes they'll be." He chuckled. "My father is hoping I'll settle down. We'll see. Like you, I like my independence."

"I get it. I really do." She sat back as the waiter placed a hot plate of food in front of her. She inhaled the aroma from the veal piccata she'd chosen and let out a happy sigh. "My dinner smells delicious."

"Dig in," said Craig, picking up his knife and fork. "My ribeye steak looks too good to wait another second."

They ate quictly, enjoying their meals with obvious pleasure. Again, Willow liked the idea that she didn't feel compelled to talk.

In the middle of their meal, Mitchell, Duncan, and Trace walked over to them.

"Sorry to interrupt," said Mitchell. "We just wanted to wish you a pleasant evening, Willow. We'll be talking soon."

"Good to see you," said Duncan, gazing from her to Craig before turning away.

"I'll catch up with you later," Trace said, his features softening. For a moment, Willow thought he might kiss her and was relieved when he turned and walked away.

Willow waited until they'd gone before saying, "What is it about Duncan that I don't trust?"

"Duncan is a snake. Be careful with him."

Willow was tempted to tell him about the latest snafu created by Duncan, but because the purchase of the Premio Inn was confidential information, she couldn't say a word. Instead, she merely nodded.

As they went back to eating, Willow liked the idea of Craig warning her.

Later, when it came time for dessert, Willow hesitated. "I'm stuffed, but I know how delicious any dessert is here. Want to split the Crème Brulée?"

"Sounds perfect," Craig said, setting aside the dessert menu.

The waiter took their order for dessert and offered a dessert wine to each of them, compliments of the restaurant.

"Thanks. Why not?" said Craig looking to her.

She shrugged. "I'll have a glass too."

The waiter and another staff member cleared their table, leaving the space between them empty. Through the lens of the wine she'd drunk, Willow stared at the man opposite her, realizing how truly handsome he was. She liked him even better after learning he was the kind of person who enjoyed helping others.

He caught her studying him, and an appealing rush of color filled his cheeks.

The waiter arrived with their dessert and wine.

"I brought two spoons," the waiter announced, giving them smiles.

As soon as they were alone, Willow dipped her spoon into the dessert and lifted it to her lips. She couldn't hold back a little groan of pleasure at the delicious creamy taste in her mouth.

Craig's gaze settled on her.

She set down her spoon. "Sorry. Go ahead. It's your turn."

Grinning, Craig lifted his spoon, scooped out a good-size portion of the mixture, and brought it to his lips.

Watching him eat, the way he closed his eyes with pleasure, she was shaken by the desire that hummed through her body. She picked up the wine glass that had been placed on the table for her. Sipping on the sweet wine, Willow hoped Craig wasn't aware of the way her body had reacted to him. She couldn't, she wouldn't mess with her plans going forward. She knew from the way Duncan had looked at her earlier that moving forward with her job wouldn't be as easy as she'd hoped. Even Mitchell's words to her had lacked the warmth they'd held for her at his house. No doubt he knew of Trace's disappointment at seeing her with Craig.

Craig finished the dessert, leaned back, and patted his stomach. "Delicious. All of it. How's the wine?"

"Very nice," she said. "A fitting end to such a wonderful meal."

"Good," said Craig. "It's been a great evening. More to come."

Willow shook her head. "Not for me. After a delicious meal like this I'm ready to go home, maybe take a walk, and call it a night."

"Okay," said Craig. "No problem. It's good for me to get home at a decent hour for once."

Willow heard the disappointment in his voice but wasn't about to change her mind. If their friendship was going to work, she had to be strong. The disturbing fact was she liked the idea of being more than friends with him.

As Craig pulled into her driveway, Willow tensed. *Should I quickly get out of the car to avoid any confusion about a goodnight kiss?* She opened her door.

"I'll get that," said Craig. "Loretta would kill me if she knew I didn't act like a gentleman toward you."

Willow waited for him to come around the car and help her, well aware that Loretta and Ricardo and their children were close to Craig and his father.

Stepping onto the paved surface, Willow gazed at her house, scarcely believing it was hers.

Craig took her arm and led her up the front walk to the door. "Thanks for a great evening, Willow. Let's do it again."

"Yes, that would be nice." She got out her key, slid it into the lock, and opened the door.

Craig stood looking at her, yearning in his eyes.

"Good night," Willow said. "I had a very nice time."

"Yeah, me too. It was fun." Craig continued to gaze at her.

"See you on the course," she said, trying to think of something to say while telling herself that friends don't usually kiss goodnight.

Craig shuffled his feet, then gave her a little salute. "Okay, then. Good night."

As he headed down the walk toward his car, Willow sighed, closed the front door, and locked it.

CHAPTER THIRTY-EIGHT

WILLOW

The next morning, Willow decided to go visit Lily. She'd spent the night tossing and turning, thinking about Craig and wondering if she was making a mistake thinking they could and should be just friends.

While she was still having coffee, her cell chimed. *Trace.*

"Good morning!" she said cheerfully.

"Willow, we need to talk." His voice was hard, his words crisp.

"About what?" she said, fidgeting in her chair.

"About us," said Trace. "I thought we had something special going on. You know how much I like you."

"I like you, too, Trace. That's why I'm being honest about wanting to be just friends at this time. After losing Alec I'm in a vulnerable place. On top of that, I'm facing a lot of uncertainties and want to be settled in my new job before I consider a serious relationship with anyone."

"Have you thought about what an advantage you'd have dating me," said Trace. "Considering a job and all."

Willow felt her nostrils flare. "Just what are you saying, Trace. That I'm not qualified to take care of things on my own?"

"No, no, but you know how my uncle Duncan is. If he knows you're in the group, he'll be a big support to you."

"I see ..." She didn't mention that Duncan rarely supported Trace. She could only imagine the type of response that would come her way if she said it. She felt a headache form at the base of her skull.

"I just want to protect you, Willow. Take care of you. Be with you."

Willow closed her eyes. His words, all of them, were wrong. She wasn't looking for a man to take care of her. She knew damn well she was as capable as he or Brent, and the job offer she'd already accepted was one she intended to keep with or without support from Duncan or anyone else. She trusted Mitchell to stand by the agreement he'd made with Alec.

"Are you there?" Trace asked.

"I'm here," Willow said, rallying. "But, Trace, to continue being honest with you, I don't think we should see one another socially again. We'll be working for the Blaise Group and can enjoy each other's company in that way, but that's exactly it. Another reason to stay apart."

"You can't be serious," said Trace. "You know how much I care for you."

"Yes, I know. I care about you. But this isn't the right time for me. I've told you that. It's truly a me-not-you situation. Goodbye, Trace. We'll talk another time, but I won't change my mind." Willow clicked off the call and with shaking fingers set the phone down on the counter. She hated confrontation of any kind. But she knew she'd done the right thing, even if it might be a problem going forward with her job at the Premio Inn.

As if she'd conjured him out of her thoughts, Mitchell called. "Hello, Willow. Duncan and I would like to meet with you later this morning. How does eleven sound? We'll meet in the small conference room at the Desert Sage Inn."

"I can do that," said Willow. "Do I need to bring any materials?"

"I would suggest having your employment contract with you."

"All right. See you then," said Willow, forcing herself to remain calm.

As soon as she got off the call, she phoned Bennett Williams.

He listened to her and then said, "I think you'd better have representation at this meeting. I can't imagine Mitchell would mind, and I think it's important."

"Mitchell might not mind, but his brother will," said Willow.

"I wouldn't worry about it. I think we're all fed up with Duncan's actions," said Bennett. "Including Mitchell."

"Thank you, Bennett. Will I see you at the hotel?"

"I'm afraid not. I have another meeting, but I'll send Craig. He should be able to handle it for you."

"Oh, but ..."

"No worries. He's very good at his job. Talk to you later. A client is waiting for me." Bennett clicked off the call, leaving Willow unsure how to handle the situation with Craig.

"Simply move forward," she said aloud. She'd been thrilled with the offer to run the Premio Inn. Nothing was going to interfere with that. And if she was going to do a good job, she had to face Duncan with confidence.

Willow went through her contract again, making notes. If she was to help oversee the conversion of the Premio Inn to a Corona Collection hotel, she'd have a list of suggestions ready. Might as well find out what Duncan had on his mind besides redecorating the property.

By the time Willow completed her work, she realized how late it was and hurried into the shower to get ready.

Fifteen minutes later, she was on her way to the Desert Sage Inn. Driving up to the front of the hotel she'd loved since she was a child, a pang of sorrow pierced her. The thought of Alec not being there and seeing a different logo on the nameplate of the hotel hurt. She left her car with the valet and went inside. Downstairs, outside the small conference room, she came to a halt. Craig was leaning against the wall smiling at her. "Hi. Bennett filled me in on the situation and I've taken a look at your employment contract. Ready to go?"

"Yes." She tried to chase away the image of him riding a white horse coming to her rescue. He was doing his job, nothing more, she reminded herself. Still, when they walked into the room together, she was grateful for his protection. Duncan and Mitchell were discussing something and Duncan was pounding the table.

When he saw them, Mitchell rose to his feet. "Good morning, Willow. Craig, I'm surprised to see you here."

"Bennett Williams had a meeting he couldn't change and sent me in his stead. As you may remember, he worked with Willow on the employment contract. It seemed only right that one of us attend this meeting."

Mitchell bobbed his head. "Understood." They shook hands.

Craig walked over to Duncan and shook his hand before settling in a chair next to her, facing the two men across the table.

Duncan turned his attention to her. "Glad we could meet, Willow, because I have several questions that I need to ask you before feeling comfortable about your appointment as manager of the Premio Inn. Understandably, I was upset that the decision was made without my input."

"Your questioning her doesn't change anything," Mitchell said to Duncan. "It was something we talked about, and when I approached the board, they were very excited about it. One of our board members, Harold Albright, is a regular at the Premio and said if George Hartmann wanted Willow Sanchez to take over for him, that recommendation was good enough for him and should be fine with everyone."

"Still, I should've been consulted before any vote was taken," Duncan protested.

"Duncan, you and I have talked about this before. The resolution has been made and approved. There's no going back and trying to change things. You have just one vote."

Willow noticed the muscles in Mitchell's jaw flexing and knew how angry he was.

"May I ask why you invited my client to this meeting?" Craig asked.

Mitchell glanced from him to her. "Part of the agreement of employment was having Willow be on the transition team. The purchase of the Premio Inn is about to take place. The transition, however, needs to be handled pretty much like that of the Desert Sage Inn."

"Sounds reasonable," said Craig.

Mitchell continued, "The one bone of contention among board members is the wish of some to completely renovate the inn to look more like a typical property of the Blaise Group. Both George Hartmann and I are opposed to such a thing,"

"I'm not," said Duncan. "I believe we're losing the flavor of the Blaise Group hotels. I was opposed to the whole idea of a Corona Collection to begin with. Now this."

"If you set up the transition like you did for the Desert Sage Inn, I believe we can make things go smoothly," said Willow.

"Not if a lot of renovation is going to take place," said Mitchell. His gaze pierced her, prompting her to continue speaking.

Willow cleared her throat. "As I mentioned to Mitchell earlier, I believe changing a lot of the décor of the Premio will ruin it's beloved appearance. I've done a little research. Historically, a large portion of the guests are repeat visitors who've made it clear they like the way the inn's furnishings and decorations reflect the true nature of the area."

"But Indian rugs? Tile floors? Adobe fireplaces?" sputtered Duncan. "None of it speaks of the Blaise Group hotels."

"But with a team like Hank and Rose to handle publicity, those are all pluses, not minuses," said Willow. She turned to Mitchell. "I assume they'll be part of the team."

"We haven't decided yet," he said, giving her a look of apology, indicating to her that it was another contentious issue.

"I would suggest taking advantage of the team Alec brought in to help with the Desert Sage Inn," said Craig.

Duncan snorted. "The Desert Flowers as Alec called them?"

"Exactly," said Craig. "My client already knows them, has worked with them. A very advantageous situation for all."

Duncan pounded the table with a fist, turned, and glared at his brother sitting next to him. "They're not on the Blaise Group team! Why are we listening to these people?"

"Excuse me," said Craig. "But Willow Sanchez *is* a member of your team. It's all part of the contract."

"The contract I wasn't privy to," said Duncan.

"Wrong. You and the board members agreed to let me handle the contract. I did so, with input from all who responded to my request for such," said Mitchell.

"But you knew I was away," said Duncan.

Mitchell sighed. "Duncan, the world doesn't revolve around you. You are no more or less important than anyone else."

"Again, I ask why you wanted my client at this meeting," said Craig. "We've heard nothing but bickering between the two of you."

Mitchell's face flushed with color. "You're right. I apologize. The reason we wanted to speak to Willow was to gain her agreement that Brent Armstrong could share her appointment as head of the transition team."

Willow drew a deep breath. She knew if she didn't take a stand now, things would never change, that Brent or Duncan would always be a problem for her.

"Well?" Duncan said.

He thought she'd agree. Thought he could bully her into accepting his inept son on the team. Willow shook her head and took a breath. "No. That would never work. Brent and I have been unable to work well together."

Duncan's complacency was replaced by shock, and then his face flushed with anger.

"May I ask why? I'm sure there's more to the story," Mitchell said, quietly, calmly.

"Now, see here ..." Duncan sputtered.

"I suggest you talk to Brian Walden about it." Willow didn't want to get into a discussion of how Brent had cheated and copied her ideas and tried to present them as her own. There was also the issue of how he mistreated the staff.

Mitchell studied her. "Okay."

"My understanding is that several people working at and for the Desert Sage Inn property have had trouble dealing with Brent," Craig said.

"Lies! All lies! Jealous people!" said Duncan.

"No," Craig said. "I have a client who claims she's been sexually harassed by Brent. In doing my investigation, I've found evidence that he's about to become a serious liability to your company."

Mitchell lowered his head in his hands. "Oh, my God!" When he lifted his face, his eyes blazed with anger. "Thank you, Mr. Kincaid, for sharing that."

Duncan was staring out the window, his eyes unexpectedly moist.

Mitchell got to his feet. "I'm sorry you had to be part of this conversation, Willow. I ask that you be patient and wait to begin your work for the Premio Inn until we're ready to move forward. I expect to be able to do that within the week. In the meantime, you are, of course, welcome to tour the property any time you wish. Four different board members are due to arrive at the Desert Sage Inn this week and will be making their own private inspections of the Premio."

"Is Brian Walden going to oversee the transition team like last time?" Willow asked.

Mitchell smiled. "Yes, though he's been secretly working on the project for us for the past few weeks. It was he who suggested that instead of appointing Brent to the Premio project, we ask you first."

Willow was grateful for Brian's support. She'd need it going forward.

Craig rose and helped her out of her chair. While he and Mitchell shook hands once more, Duncan stormed out of the room.

"I appreciate your honesty, Willow," said Mitchell. "I'm aware it wasn't easy to do with Duncan in the room. Best always to be truthful."

"In my client's contract, there is a clause about how disagreements and intrusions should be handled," said Craig. "We trust that procedure will be followed in the future, should it be necessary."

Mitchell's lips drew into a thin line. When he spoke, it was in a measured tone. "I don't believe that will be necessary. Personal affiliations aside, the Blaise Group cannot afford any personnel issues. I will take care of it."

The two men exchanged meaningful looks, and then Willow followed Craig out of the room.

CHAPTER THIRTY-NINE

WILLOW

Willow and Craig left the hotel and stood outside in the parking lot.

"Thank you for meeting me here," said Willow. "It meant a lot to me to not have to face those two men alone."

"No problem. I think it's only fair for you to have representation until things are settled. Duncan Armstrong would be difficult for you to deal with at best. He's a strange, unhappy individual. I don't know how Mitchell can put up with him. Brother or not, he's a nuisance."

"I wonder if Mitchell will deal with Duncan as he's said. He's had many opportunities to pull him off negotiations, but he hasn't." She looked up at him. "Do you really have a client who's been sexually harassed by Brent?"

Craig gave her a sheepish look. "Not a client, but a friend who sought my advice."

"A non-paying client then?"

"I guess you could say that. But I was being very truthful about Brent being a liability to the company. He hasn't assaulted anyone, but harassment is part of his nature. He's not a good guy."

"I agree," said Willow. "I hope Mitchell will deal with both Brent and his father. Like you say, they're not good for the company."

Craig bobbed his head. "See you later. I have another appointment."

"Yes, see you tomorrow for our game."

He grinned. "Better practice between now and then."

She laughed and took a practice swing.

"Ouch!" He pretended the ball hit him in the head.

Still laughing she headed for her car and phoned Lily, asking if she could stop by.

"Of course," said Lily. "Come for lunch. The kids are just finishing theirs. Izzy will be going down for a nap, and Ollie uses that time as a rest period. So, it'll be a good time to talk."

Pleased to be able to spend time with her, Willow took off.

When Lily opened the front door of her house and smiled at her, Willow's heart filled with pleasure. As they embraced, Willow truly felt as if she and Lily were sisters.

"Hi, Willow!"

Willow looked down at Izzy, who stood holding a stuffed bunny, the one her mother had given her, and knelt to give her a hug. "Hi, Izzy! It's very nice to see you."

Izzy held up the bunny. "Hug, Bun, too."

Holding in a chuckle, Willow hugged the bunny rabbit who looked like he'd already been hugged a lot. She turned as Ollie walked into the front entrance hall. "Hi, Ollie!"

Lily went over to him and wrapped an arm around him. "You remember, Auntie Willow, don't you?"

Ollie nodded solemnly.

"How's Leo?" Willow asked him.

At the mention of his pet Leopard Gecko, a broad smile crossed Ollie's face. "He's great. He's getting a little bigger."

"He's got a very good owner," said Willow. "That proves it."

"Do you want to see him?" Ollie asked.

"Sure," said Willow.

"How about your showing him to Auntie Willow a little later?" said Lily. "We're about to have lunch."

"Okay," he said. "I'll be in my room. I'm building a

spaceship with my Legos."

"I wanna come," said Izzy, starting to follow him.

"No, Izzy. You stay with me," said Lily. "Ollie is working hard on his project and doesn't want anyone to see it until it's done. Right, Ollie?"

"Yes, Mom. It's my secret project for Dad," he announced proudly.

"Okay, then, have fun. Izzy, you lead Auntie Willow to the kitchen."

Willow allowed Izzy to take her hand and lead her down the hallway. She silently mouthed the word "Mom" to Lily, giving her a questioning look. She knew how hard Lily had worked to form a relationship with Ollie.

Tears glistening in her eyes, Lily nodded.

In the kitchen, two places were set at the kitchen table. Willow studied the pretty green placemats, the large white, crumpled paper napkins, and the misplaced silverware.

"Izzy helped me set the table," said Lily, winking at her.

"I see," Willow said, amused. "Very nice."

"Mommy won't let me cook," said Izzy, her lower lip jutting out.

"Not without careful supervision," said Lily calmly. "I've set out a paper and crayons for you right here in the kitchen. Why don't you make Auntie Willow a picture?"

Izzy's expression brightened. "Okay."

Heaving a sigh of relief, Lily said, "Iced tea or lemonade?"

"Unsweetened iced tea for me, please."

Lily poured them each a glass and said, "Why don't we sit outside where I can keep an eye on Izzy through the open sliding door? It's not too hot in the shade. If we need to, I can turn on the misters."

"I'm sure we'll be fine," said Willow, accepting the glass Lily offered her and following her out to the patio.

"Anything for privacy," said Lily, sitting in a chair and facing her on the couch.

"The kids are doing great," Willow said. "Ollie and Izzy both are calling you Mom."

"Yes, things are settling down. Brian's been working on a private project lately, so I've been spending as much time with them as I can." She chuckled. "One reason the house is such a mess."

Willow shrugged. "The kids are happy. That's all that matters. Are you still using Anna?"

"Oh, yes. She's fantastic. I'm still working two days a week at the law office. She's going to help me with the new baby too. What's up with you?"

Willow filled her in on the meeting with Mitchell and Duncan. "I know about Brian's project."

"You do? Great! I've been dying to tell you and Rose, but Brian swore me to secrecy."

"Well, now the secret is out because you, Rose, and I are going to be busy in the weeks ahead."

"Are you saying we, as in The Desert Flowers?" said Lily, grinning.

"Right. The way I see it, with Hank and Rose working on the transition team for the Premio, and Brian involved, I'm going to request you to carry on with your job of sorting through papers, taking notes, and keeping things organized throughout the project."

Lily clasped her hands together. "That would be wonderful! I've missed us being together, working together." She grew serious. "You were brave to speak up about Brent. It's time Mitchell and his father understood what a problem he is."

"Craig was the one who pointed him out as a liability to the company. That seemed to change everything."

"So, Craig to the rescue, huh? He could be my knight in

shining armor anytime," said Lily. She clapped a hand to her mouth. "Oh, my God! I can't believe I said that. You know how much I adore Brian."

Willow laughed. "Of course, I do. We all do. And I have to admit the image of Craig as a knight is becoming more and more suitable to him."

Lily grinned. "I've been waiting for you to see what a great guy he is. He ..."

Willow held up a hand to stop her from continuing. "He and I are just friends. That's the way we both want it. He told me he wasn't interested in wanting more from me or anyone. He just wants to go out and have fun. I get it. Why would I give up my independence? I'm just beginning to enjoy being on my own without having to consult anyone else about anything."

Lily drew in a breath and let it out. "You're both crazy, but if that's how you want to play it, who am I to object?"

"Thanks for not pushing it," said Willow, thinking she couldn't keep up that front for much longer. "I've got a lot on my mind. The transition has to go through well; I have to do a good job as manager even before day one. Did I mention that Duncan and a couple other Blaise Group board members want to completely change the look of the Premio? I can't let that happen."

"Brian mentioned it to me. He's opposed to the idea too."

"Changing it would completely destroy the inn. I can't wait until I can officially talk to Rose about it," said Willow.

"I'm sure she'll let us know as soon as she can if she and Hank are going to work on the project."

"It sounded as if the decision had already been made, but until she tells us, I'm not counting on it."

Izzy walked over to them and handed Willow a piece of paper. "For you!"

Willow looked at the drawing of a dark-haired woman

surrounded by different colored flowers of all shapes. "It's beautiful, Izzy. Truly wonderful. May I keep it?"

Smiling, Izzy nodded. "I'll make one for you too, Mommy."

"Okay, but later. I'm going to tuck you in for a nap."

Willow waited for a cry of protest from Izzy, but the little girl calmly took her mother's hand.

"*We've* been awake since five-thirty this morning," said Lily, rolling her eyes. "And though we don't want to admit it, *we're* exhausted."

Willow laughed as they left the patio. Lily was such a natural mother, very lovely to see.

Willow sat back on the couch wondering what she would be like as a mother. Until recently, she hadn't thought much about it. Perhaps because the men she'd dated in the past weren't thinking about such a thing. Why did things suddenly feel different?

CHAPTER FORTY

WILLOW

Willow had just fixed herself a salad for dinner when her cell chimed. She checked caller ID. *Trace.*

She sighed and picked it up, forcing a cheerfulness to her voice she didn't feel. "Hi, Trace. What's up?"

"I understand you had a tough meeting this morning."

"Yes," she replied unwilling to get into details with him.

"If it's not too late, I thought I'd take you to dinner," he said. "As a friend, of course." A bitterness entered his voice.

"I'm sorry, Trace, but I'm in the middle of dinner now. Maybe another time." She'd already told him she wasn't interested beyond friendship. Would she have to be more direct than that?

"Look, I don't know what's going on, but I thought you and I had an agreement to see where our relationship could go. I introduced you to my parents as someone I was very interested in and received their approval. You're making me look like a loser."

Willow gasped softly. "Is that what this is about? You looking like a loser?"

"Well ... sort of. I mean I don't usually have a problem like this. In fact, I've had to end several relationships over lack of approval from my parents."

"It's nice to know I made the grade with them, but I can assure you that Duncan and Brent and the others might not feel that way." Saying the words, Willow knew them to be true.

She'd never be able to live comfortably in that situation. And she didn't like the idea that Trace was worried about his image more than building a relationship with her.

"They can't stop me from doing what I want ..." Trace began.

"I'm sorry, Trace. Now that I've stepped back, I realize you and I together would never work. It's probably wise to end it now."

"You're ending it? Just like that?" Trace said.

"Yes, I think it's best. I've tried to tell you my feelings, tried to make you respect my boundaries and it isn't working, which makes me believe it never would. As I've said, I want us to be friends. We'll be working for the same company."

"Yeah, that's another thing. You managing the Premio instead of Brent or me? It should've been kept in the family."

"Maybe not." Willow's heart fell to her feet. Beneath his smooth, charming ways, Trace was just as bad as his uncle and cousin. "Sorry, but I have to go. We'll talk another time."

"Maybe not," said Trace, echoing her words before clicking off the call.

Willow set her phone down on the table and sighed. Why couldn't she have a simple date with a friend?

After her light supper, Willow decided to walk off her frustration with Trace. She'd promised Rose to check on the house she and Hank were buying. They'd been told it was a matter of a couple of weeks before they could move in. The idea of having Rose as a neighbor filled Willow with pleasure. Though they'd known each other for only a few months, it seemed like a lifetime. She felt the same way about Lily.

As she walked through the development of upscale homes, she felt her earlier tension leave her body. It was a beautiful evening. The setting sun brought a rosy glow to the western sky. The singing of birds sounded like the beginning of a lullaby.

She glanced at the bikes and strollers at some of the houses and wondered if she might be ready to settle down, after all. Being with Lily, seeing the chaos in her house, she was both intrigued and put off by it. But then, when she'd seen Lily's baby bump, she'd felt a pang and knew she wanted the chance to have a child of her own. Maybe two. At the thought, a smile crossed her face. Her mother would be delirious with joy.

Her thoughts turned to her disappointment with Trace, and then inevitably focused on Craig. There was a connection between her and Craig she couldn't deny. Still, the timing was all wrong. Besides, neither one wanted a serious relationship, and now she wondered if they should even be friends. She couldn't let anything destroy her opportunity to manage the Premio Inn. It was the kind of job she'd worked toward her whole life. With Alec gone and the job at the Desert Sage Inn out of reach, she was being given another chance to do something as close to her wishes as possible. If she did well with the Premio, it might someday lead to becoming general manager at the Desert Sage Inn.

She stopped in front of Rose's house. Rose and Hank had talked about downsizing but had ended up buying a house larger than hers. It was a nice size for a couple but big enough to comfortably house a number of guests, should Hank's girls or friends want to visit.

Seeing the lockbox on the front door, Willow walked around to the back of the house. One of the French doors leading from the house to the patio was unlocked. Glancing around, seeing no one, she stepped inside. It looked and smelled as if the painters had recently left. Drop cloths were still on the floor of the living room. The walls were now a soft gray, and the trim painted a crisp white.

She checked the other rooms, pleased to see that they too appeared to be finished and ready for flooring and carpeting. She sent Rose a text, along with a couple of photographs.

She quickly got a return message. "Thanks! It looks like the Desert Flowers are going to bloom again! Can't wait to get back and talk to you and Lily."

Willow was feeling more comfortable with her decision to focus on work. She liked the idea of the Desert Flowers blooming.

The next morning, Willow awoke and stretched, feeling more rested than she had in weeks. Her life seemed more settled, and the idea of working with Rose and Lily again filled her with a new sense of enthusiasm for life.

She got out of bed and padded to the kitchen for a cup of coffee. Outside, the day was already warm, closing in on hot. The golf game scheduled for the day had successfully been moved to the earlier hour of eight o'clock.

In the kitchen, Willow checked the time and decided she could squeeze in a morning swim. One of the reasons she loved her house was her lap pool and the wide, covered patio beside it.

She took a couple of swallows of coffee and changed into her bathing suit.

Outside, she dove into the pool, loving the feel of her body slicing through the water. After living in Boston, she liked the idea of swimming in her own pool any morning she chose.

She began laps, relishing the exercise. Staying at Alec's, enjoying her mother's cooking, she'd put on a few pounds and was eager to work them off.

Later, dressed for the game, she realized her hair, still damp from the pool, was too wild to do anything with it except to pull it into a ponytail.

She left her house for the inn, ready to face a challenge. She enjoyed these mornings. It was a fun foursome, with each willing to work hard to be the best.

When she arrived at the clubhouse, expecting to find Ken, Ricardo, and Craig waiting for her, she was surprised to see Bennett Williams with Ken and Ricardo.

"Hope you don't mind," Bennett said, helping her with her bag. "I know about the ongoing challenge between you and Craig."

"No, no that's fine," said Willow, her words hollow. She'd looked forward to seeing Craig again, to help her settle her feelings about him.

They headed out onto the course.

The time sped by as Willow played, laughed with the men about the jokes Bennett told, and used the time to improve her game so when Craig joined the group the following week, she'd be ready.

That afternoon, Willow made a spur-of-the-moment decision to go to the Premio Inn. She wanted to prepare a list of reasons the charm of the inn shouldn't be destroyed by the idea that it had to look more like a standard Blaise Group hotel.

As she made her way along the long drive up into the foothills to the inn, Willow went slowly, making mental notes of ideas for improving the entrance without overdoing it. Along the edge of the driveway plants and flowers were unevenly planted, and in some places, left to a natural state that did nothing, in her opinion, to welcome guests.

She came to a stop in front of the main building, got out of the car, handed her car keys to the valet who'd magically appeared, and stood a moment studying the white adobe building. As before, she loved the wide front veranda filled with chairs, inviting guests to sit and admire the view around them.

When she walked inside the inn, she paused to gaze around. The tile floor, colorful rugs, native pottery, artwork, and plants sitting in oversized terra cotta pots gave a stunning Southwestern flair to the atmosphere. To someone else, it might seem too casual. But Willow was well aware of the quality of the rugs, the value of the artwork, and loved the feel of the place she knew sophisticated, well-traveled guests appreciated. This rich, understated style was what she had to convince the Blaise Group to keep. It was one of the things that made the inn special.

As she continued to look around, she noted how polished and clean everything was. Another trademark of the inn was offering immaculate service and attending to detail not only for guests but for the inn itself.

She walked through the lobby out to the pool area. It, too, was beautifully maintained. Off to the right, two tennis courts surrounded by fencing covered with green privacy screens were available to guests. Beyond the pool and tennis courts, several houses of varying sizes sat shaded by palm trees. Lush plantings softened the edges of the tan-painted adobe exteriors, giving the appearance of privacy between them. Willow knew that behind each one, private pools and spas were shielded by carefully planted landscapes.

She went back inside and was about to ask if any of the private guesthouses were free for inspection when an older gentleman approached her. "Willow Sanchez?"

"Yes. May I help you?"

The man held out his hand. "I'm Harold Albright, a board member for the Blaise Group. I'm very pleased to meet you."

"Thank you. I've heard it mentioned that you're a regular guest here at the Premio."

"Yes, my wife, Eleanor, and I have been coming here for years. It's one of our favorite places." He indicated chairs nearby. "May we sit and talk?"

"Certainly," said Willow. She already liked this white-haired man with bright blue eyes who reminded her of a favorite professor at Boston University.

They sat in chairs facing one another.

"May I get you some lemon water?" Harold asked. "They always keep a pitcher of it available to guests."

"Thank you. That would be nice." Willow didn't need the water, but she was curious to know more about this man who had sided with Mitchell on the renovation issue.

Harold rose, went over to the refreshment table, and returned with two glasses of water. He set one down on a table next to her chair and carried one over to his chair. "There," he said, taking his seat again. "One can never have too much water in the desert."

Willow remained quiet. Dehydration could be a problem for an unaware guest.

"I thought we could talk privately here," Harold said. "I've read through your resumé and, more importantly, read several letters of recommendations for both you and your work. Very impressive, I must say. I was more than eager to approve your position here at the inn."

"Thank you," she said. "It means a lot to me. Like the Desert Sage Inn, this hotel, though much smaller, has a character to it that I appreciate."

"Indeed," he said. "I gathered from one of the letters of recommendation Alec Thurston sent to Mitchell Armstrong that you are well trained for managing a place like this, that it's been a dream of yours from childhood."

"Yes. Alec and I had always planned to work together someday. Now, of course, that isn't possible. But I feel very dedicated to this job already because of Alec and all he's done for me."

Harold smiled at her. "You, my dear, are exactly the kind of person I thought you'd be—capable, humble, and grateful. I wish I could say that about every person in the group."

Willow's eyebrows lifted.

"I might as well be honest with you," said Harold. "Now that you're a member of the Blaise Group, you'll discover that the board is often split by loyalties. I've known Mitchell for years. The rivalry between him and his brother goes back a long time. The fact that Mitchell is now the major shareholder of the company rankles Duncan to the point he's become a problem. I understand he's already been an irritant to you and others at the Desert Sage Inn."

Willow nodded but didn't add to his statement.

"I also understand how strongly you feel against the proposal to completely redo the décor of this inn." His blue-eyed gaze settled on her.

This time, Willow couldn't hold back. "It would be a horrible mistake to do anything like that to this lovely, unique property."

"Exactly," said Harold. "I want you to know I support you. Thank you for speaking out for not only keeping the atmosphere here as it is, but also for being honest about Brent Armstrong's actions." He shook his head. "As I mentioned, I've known Mitch for a long time. He and I respect one another. In fact, we rely on each other to be open and forthcoming. I'm on the board to advise him."

"I see," Willow said, her mind racing. "I was about to start a list of reasons for defending my belief about this property. But to be fair, I want to create a list of suggestions about changes that could be made. I understand Hank Bowers and Rose Macklin, working as a team, will be developing a public relations plan much as they did for the Desert Sage Inn."

"Yes," said Harold. "We've talked about that too. George Hartmann, like Alec, doesn't want the flavor of his property to be destroyed. That was very much a part of the agreement made between him and the Blaise Group before the sale could go through."

"That's why I'm suggesting that Lily Walden be brought onto the transition team. With Lily, Rose, and me working together, I believe we can do a good job of making the transition work. I understand Brian Walden is already working for the Blaise Group."

"He is," Harold acknowledged. "So, you, Lily, and Rose ... the Desert Flowers." His eyes twinkled with mischief. "I love the idea."

Willow laughed. "We work very well together." She grew serious. "Going forward, can I count on your support?"

"Absolutely," said Harold. His expression grew somber. "I believe more and more board members are beginning to understand what the real issues are with Duncan and are growing tired of his interference."

"Mitchell, too?"

"Mitchell most of all," said Harold. "However, as far as anyone else is concerned, our conversation never took place. I knew right away from all I'd learned about you I could trust you not to repeat what I say. I feel it best to be honest with you, as you are the person most likely to be caught in the middle of all the changes going forward."

"Thank you." Willow swallowed hard at the thought of the turmoil ahead. Though she knew it wouldn't be easy, she still wanted this job.

CHAPTER FORTY-ONE

WILLOW

At home, Willow went through her notes of her inspection of the Premio she'd written with Harold. He was a keen observer and, together, they'd made a long list of observations, suggestions, and recommendations. Once they'd focused on the hotel and away from personalities within the Blaise Group, Willow felt more comfortable speaking her mind.

Quickly, while things were fresh in her mind, Willow typed up her notes.

She'd just finished and was thinking of pouring herself a glass of wine when her cell chimed. *Craig*. Unsure, she waited until the cell chimed again before clicking on the call.

"Hi, Craig," she said, hating the breathlessness of her voice. Dammit! She'd just spent a grueling afternoon building a case for her leadership with the Blaise Group. She didn't need any emotional entanglements. Especially, not with Craig, and especially after the issue with Trace.

"Hey, there! Sorry I missed the game this morning. Heard you had low score," said Craig, chuckling softly. "Bennett can't wait for a rematch. He's used to winning a few."

Willow smiled. It had felt good to do that well without Craig distracting her.

"I thought I'd take you out to dinner to celebrate."

"Oh, thanks, but ..." Willow began, determined to end the call.

"On second thought," Craig said. "How about I bring a

pizza and cold beer to your house? We'll keep it simple."

Willow checked the time. Six o'clock. She had no desire to fix a meal herself. What harm could come from one evening with him? She'd tell him she had to get to bed early. "Okay, that sounds nice and easy. I've got cheese and crackers and olives. We can have them to start with. A bottle of red wine, too, if you'd rather."

"That sounds great. See you soon."

Willow clicked off the call. She'd changed into shorts and a T-shirt when she'd arrived home earlier. No reason to change for Craig. This definitely wasn't a date.

When Craig arrived with a box of pizza and a six-pack of beer, Willow was pleased to see he was wearing a pair of old shorts and a T-shirt, indicating to her that he didn't think of this as a date either.

"Good to see you. The pizza smells delicious."

"Victor's is the best," he said. "I got half plain and half pepperoni and sausage."

"Perfect. Come on in. I have opened a bottle of red wine and set out the cheese and crackers. Thought we could have that on the patio. We can heat up the pizza later and have it with a cold beer unless you want a beer now."

"The wine sounds great. It's been a busy day and I'm ready to relax."

They set the pizza on the kitchen counter, put the beer in the fridge, poured glasses of wine, and headed outside to the patio. Though she was waiting to add finishing decorative touches to the area, the porch furniture she'd bought was perfect. Made of a durable black wicker, the two comfortable chairs, matching two love seats, and a low coffee table created a lovely outdoor space. The outdoor kitchen was something she hadn't yet used, but she was looking forward to the time when she'd grill dinners. So far, she'd been too tired at the end of the day to think of it.

Craig sat on one of the couches and she took a seat on the other facing him.

"How are things going with the Blaise Group?" Craig asked. "Any more news about when you officially begin your job?"

"It'll be soon. I was inspecting the Premio Inn earlier today and met Harold Albright, a very nice gentleman who happens to be on the Blaise Group board."

"Isn't he the one that was mentioned as a repeat guest at the Premio?" Craig asked.

Surprised he remembered that fact from the meeting with Mitchell and Duncan, she nodded. "He's a supporter of mine and is definitely against changing the décor and ambience of the inn to fit the Blaise Group mold."

"Good. That's important," said Craig.

"He also told me that several of the board members and Mitchell himself are sick and tired of Duncan's behavior. I have a feeling that something is finally going to be done about it."

"I wasn't kidding when I said that Brent could be a liability to the company. Sexual harassment is no longer tolerated."

"It never should've been," said Willow.

"You're right." Craig offered her a cheese and cracker and then took one himself. "I've been working on a big project for a wealthy client, setting up various charitable contributions. We talked about your parents and Juanita's Kitchen, and he was very impressed. In time, I believe you'll have a contributor."

"That's wonderful!" said Willow. "We're still looking for the right place to open up the kitchen. We have plenty of time, because, as you know, the probate of wills in this state takes months. That's why the Desert Flowers will fund the purchase of the right building with proceeds from the sale of the house."

"Sounds like a good plan. The sooner you can get it going, the better. My father can help with the best way to handle the finances. He's already told me that he's been hired to do so."

"It's amazing how all of these friendships have come together to make so many things happen."

"Yeah," Craig grinned. "It's great."

They sat sipping wine and talking about different things going on in the area. When Craig offered to open another bottle of wine, it sounded perfect to Willow. She went inside and pulled a bottle out of the little wine cooler that was included in the kitchen appliance package she'd chosen.

As she lifted it out, she turned and bumped into Craig.

"Steady there," he said as she teetered, trying to catch her balance.

While he opened the bottle of wine, Willow grabbed a can of peanuts out of the cupboard and carried them out to the patio. It was a blissful evening, she thought dreamily. Craig was someone she could talk to about almost anything, and it was fascinating that he knew a lot about many topics.

He came outside with the bottle of wine and poured more into her glass.

She murmured her thanks and took a sip. Leaning back against the cushions, she gazed at him. "What happened with your mother?"

He sighed and looked out at the shimmering pool glowing from the underwater lighting she'd switched on. When he turned back to her his expression was so sad she wanted to go to him and wrap him in her arms.

"My mother suffered from an unusual, fast-growing bone cancer. It was a horrendous time, a difficult death. The thing that was hardest to accept was the change in her behavior as her medication increased and her brain became involved. She was delirious at times, saying the most awful things, acting in a crude way that wasn't normal, belittling the people around her. It took a toll on my father, and he became depressed. I tried to help them both, but it was an endless circle of pain and hurt. She even turned on me." His eyes filled with unshed tears.

Willow's heart went out to him. She rose and sat next to him. "I'm sorry. Very sorry. I can only imagine how much that must have hurt."

"Yeah, it still does. The mother I remembered as sweet, kind, and thoughtful morphed into a person I didn't know or like. Yet I understand how necessary the medication was."

"How old were you when this happened?"

"Twenty-one. Too young to forgive her for all the things she said. Too old to forget. Now, of course, I understand much more about her—where she came from, what kind of person she was, how the changes in behavior could take place. When I think of her now, I go back to the happy days before she became ill."

Seeing the pain on his face, Willow wrapped an arm around his shoulder.

He leaned into her and they stayed that way for a minute before Willow suddenly rose, telling herself to move before the scene turned into something else.

Craig got to his feet and faced her. His green-eyed gaze nailed her to the spot. "Where are you going?"

"To check on the time."

He pointed to the watch on her arm.

"Ah, yes..." She backed up, moving away from him, fumbling for other excuses.

"Careful!" he cried, rushing toward her, pushing her aside before landing in the water off-balance, hitting his head against the edge of the pool.

Willow heard the smack of his body and whirled around to find him floating in the water face down.

"Oh my God! Craig! Craig! Are you all right?" She jumped into the pool and grabbed hold of him.

He found his footing in the shallow end and held a hand to his head where a huge bruise was already forming. "Ow! What happened?"

"You were trying to prevent me from falling into the pool and slipped."

He looked at her. "Guess it didn't work, huh?"

Willow knew from the slurring of his words and the dazed look on his face that he needed to be checked for a possible concussion. She took hold of his arm. "C'mon! We have to get you out of the pool. Someone needs to take a look at your head."She helped him out of the pool. "Sit right here while I call 911."

"I'm not going to a hospital," he said stubbornly.

"No, no. Don't worry about that now. We'll have someone take a look at you here," she said, rushing to get her phone. She watched him steadily while she punched in the number and waited to speak to someone.

Within minutes, she heard a siren in the distance coming closer. "I hear them now," she told the operator. "I'll go meet them at the front door."

Craig was sitting at the edge of the pool holding his head.

"I'll be right back," she told him. "You stay right there."

He didn't respond.

Hearing the sounds of the emergency vehicle out front, she left him and ran to the front door to let the team inside.

A man and a woman in uniforms approached.

Feeling worried sick, Willow waved them inside. "He's out back."

"What happened?" the woman calmly asked.

"He bumped his head hard when he fell into the pool. He's already got a big lump. I'm afraid he has a concussion."

"We'll check that out," said the man carrying an emergency bag.

They walked out onto the patio and found Craig sitting exactly where she'd left him.

The man knelt beside him. "Hey, buddy. I heard you had a fall. You all right?" As he talked, he was checking Craig's pulse and studying his face. "Let's get you up and on a couch where we can get a better look. Okay?"

Silently Craig allowed himself to be led to one of the couches.

The man had a stethoscope and had wrapped a blood pressure cuff around one of Craig's arms. After he'd checked both Craig's heartbeat and his blood pressure, he gave Willow a reassuring smile. "He's strong, and he's got a hard head."

He focused on Craig. "Do you remember what happened?"

"I fell in," said Craig.

The man indicated Willow. "Do you know where you are and who this woman is?"

Craig said, "She's the woman I'm going to marry." He leaned back and closed his eyes.

The EMT shook him gently. "No, sir, we want you to keep awake as best we can. In fact, I think we should take you to the hospital for observation."

Craig's eyes fluttered open. "No! I'm fine. And I'm not going to any hospital!"

The female EMT faced Willow. "All his vital signs are good, but it's important that as he sleeps, he's awakened every few hours and checked. Are you able to stay right with him and keep watch over him?"

Trying not to cry, Willow said, "Yes. It's my fault this happened. I didn't realize I was so close to the edge of the pool.

He tried to save me from falling in."

The woman winked. "Ah, a true gentleman."

The man handed her a list of instructions and told her to call 911 again if she saw any changes in him. "Might want to get him out of those wet clothes."

"Oh, yes. Thanks a lot for your help. I appreciate it."

"You're welcome. Follow our instructions. Ice for the swelling might help."

The woman piped up. "He might complain of a stiff neck because of the way he fell, but other than that, I think he's going to be okay."

"Thank you again." Willow led them to the front door so relieved her knees felt weak.

CHAPTER FORTY-TWO

WILLOW

Willow's mind was still spinning when she walked out to the patio. Craig looked up at her. "Sorry for all the commotion. What exactly happened again?"

She felt the sting of tears. "You fell into the pool while trying to keep me from going in."

"But you're all wet!"

"Jumping in to save you," she said. "Do you remember the EMT's talking to you?"

"I know they were here and asked me questions that I answered. I told them I didn't want to go to the hospital. That's all."

"Oh, okay," said Willow, thinking he must have been delirious when he'd said she was the woman he was going to marry. Probably just as well he forgot it, though her pulse still raced at the thought.

"I'm going to leave to get you a beach towel. I'll bring it back, and then you need to take off your wet clothes. I'll put them in the dryer, and as soon as they're dry, you can put them back on."

He grinned at her. "Unless you want to get naked with me and fool around."

She waved the thought away. "Definitely not. Especially in your state. You're supposed to remain quiet but alert. Those were some of the instructions."

"Yeah? What were some of the other ones?"

She couldn't help smiling at the way he was sitting with his arms crossed in front of him like a petulant child.

"I'm supposed to keep watch over you for at least the next few hours."

"I'm going to stay here?" he said.

"Until morning at least," she said. "We want to make sure you don't have anything wrong with you except a bump on your head."

She left him sitting on the couch and raced inside to get a towel for him.

When she returned, Craig was sitting on the couch completely naked. She tossed the towel at him. "Here. Wrap this around yourself."

He stood and faced her. "Thanks. Sorry to put you through all this." He wrapped the towel around his waist, but Willow would never forget the image of him standing before her. Lily might have thought Craig would be sexy in a kilt, but nothing could be sexier than the man who'd stood in front of her without a stitch of clothing.

Her heart was still fluttering in her chest as she forced herself to pick up his wet clothes. "I'll be back. You stay right here."

"Okay," he said obediently, which made her think she'd have to keep a careful eye on him. He wasn't acting like his normal bold self.

After placing Craig's clothes in the dryer, Willow hurried into her bathroom to remove her wet clothes. The image of Craig standing before her naked sent her emotions reeling. He was one sexy guy! And when he'd revealed to the EMTs that she was the woman he planned to marry, her heart had felt a strange tug, not anger at his being presumptuous. She told herself to chill out. It didn't matter because she didn't think he remembered saying it.

She dressed, put her clothes in the dryer with his, and went out to the patio to check on him. He was dozing. She understood it was going to be a long night, but no way would she step away from her obligation. She owed it to him.

Willow cleared the food and drinks from the patio, realizing how much wine they'd shared over the past several hours. The pizza was still on the counter waiting to be heated. Too tired and upset to eat, she wrapped it up and stuck it in the refrigerator. A slice of cold pizza in the morning was a quirky treat for her.

After she'd made sure everything was in order, she returned to the patio. Craig was stretched out on the couch, the towel half off his body and onto the patio. She went over to him and covered him up. "Craig? Sit up, please. C'mon! We want you to rest but no deep sleep for you."

He blinked. "How about a shallow sleep?"

She tugged on his arm. "I'm serious. Try to stay awake."

Slowly, he came to a sitting position, but when he did, the towel opened up again.

She turned her back to him. "Craig, listen to me. Can you stand and wrap the towel around you?"

"Sure, I guess. Why?"

Feeling like a prude, she faced him. "It just makes things easier. You know?"

He grinned, stood, and rewrapped the towel, exposing himself for mere seconds as he did as she'd requested.

Desire centered in her. Under different circumstances she'd love to see more of his body, but at the moment, he wasn't aware of what he was doing.

Sighing, she went to the laundry room and checked his clothes. Not dry.

She thought of what she could do to keep them both awake and decided on a game of truth or dare, modified so no dare would be required tonight, but could be put off for the future.

It would be a good way to learn more about the man she wanted to know better.

She carried her iPad and a cold icepack out to the patio.

"Okay, Craig. Here's something cold to hold against your head." She handed him the icepack. "Try to keep awake. We're going to talk and get to know each other better. We can ask each other whatever we want as long as the questions are pretty harmless. It's just something to keep us awake. Are you game?"

"Game to play a game? Sure, I guess."

"All right. Let's start with easy questions. Where did you grow up?"

"That's easy. Uh ... let me think. Oh, yeah, a suburb of New York."

"New York City? When did you move here?"

"Right after I started school. Dad wanted to start his own business out here." He pointed a finger at her. "How about you?"

"I grew up here. My parents came here to help Alec after his wife died. Okay, another question," she said. "Did you like being an only child?" His answer was important to her. She needed a man who wanted children.

Craig shook his head and winced. "Ow! And, no, I didn't like being an only child. Too much attention on me. I couldn't get away with a thing. A lot of pressure."

"Do you want a family of your own?" she asked.

"Yes," he said. "Loretta reminds me of that every day at the office."

She'd known *Doña* Loretta through the years as the wife of the golf pro who'd helped her with the game and as someone who attended the same church as she while she was growing up. Loretta was the warm yet commanding type of woman no one wanted to disappoint. It was no wonder Bennett Williams told everyone she was the person in charge of him and his entire office.

"Who was your first girlfriend?" she asked, interested in spite of herself.

"Susie McGregor. Cutest fourth-grade girl around." He frowned. "Look, I'm tired. I just want to go to sleep." He leaned back against the cushions and closed his eyes.

"No! You can't!" she cried, rising and going over to the couch to sit next to him.

"Willow," he touched her hand, "I'm going to be all right. You told me that."

"Yes, but ..."

He closed his eyes.

Willow sat there not knowing what to do. It was getting late, and she was exhausted. Towel still wrapped around him, Craig stretched out on the couch, barely giving her room to sit. Unwilling to let anything happen to him, she stayed put. If she heard him snore, she'd wake him up.

Willow had no idea what time it was when she awoke. But after checking, she realized it was close to dawn. Streaks of light were brightening the dark-gray sky. She glanced at Craig and saw that she was hanging onto the edge of the couch, lying next to him. When she tried to slide off the couch, Craig's arm, draped over her body, kept her in place. Carefully, she lifted his heavy, muscular limb, set it down on his side, and inched her way off the couch onto the floor.

Craig sat up and blinked rapidly. "What happened?" He sat up and touched the lump on the back of his head. "Ow!"

At his movement, his towel opened a crack. He looked down at it. "What am I doing naked?" He grinned at her. "Did we have fun?"

Willow quickly got to her feet. "No, no. It was nothing like that. Don't you remember falling into the pool and hitting your head?"

"Oh, yeah. Now it's coming back. I remember trying to keep you from falling into the pool and later, some silly game we played."

"Nothing else?"

Craig shook his head. "Not really. Where are my clothes?"

"In the dryer. I'll go get them now. Then, I want to check your eyes and your head."

"You can do it now," he said, motioning her closer.

"No way," she said. Her body had already started to hum with interest at the partially opened towel.

She hurried away, gathered his clothes from the dryer, and carried them back to him. "Here. Get dressed and then I'll check on you. In the meantime, I'll make some coffee."

Craig studied her.

She'd just finished pouring coffee into two cups when Craig appeared in the kitchen. "Okay. Here I am."

"Good. Have a seat at the bar, and I'll take a good look at you."

He squinted at her. "I didn't say or do anything stupid, did I?"

"No," she said, but disappointment pricked her. If he didn't recall the words he'd spoken to the EMTs, she was never going to remind him.

She studied his eyes and gingerly felt the back of his head. "Everything seems fine. But remember, if anything changes, you're to go directly to the hospital or call 911."

"I don't think that'll be necessary. As my father is always telling me, I am a hard-headed kind of kid."

Willow returned his smile. She knew now that some of his teasing was to cover the emotional bruises his mother had caused.

"If you don't mind, I think I'll go back to my condo and try to get more rest. I have a busy day at the office."

"Okay," she said, understanding his need to be in his own place. It had been a crazy night. "If you're certain it's safe for you to get behind the wheel. But, Craig, I'd be happy to drive you."

"Thanks, but I'll be fine." He stood, took a breath and patted his pants. "I don't know where my keys are."

"In the kitchen." He'd put them on the counter. "I'll get them for you."

She handed him his keys, walked him out to his car, and stood in her driveway watching him get in and drive off. And just like that, things were back to normal.

Or so she told herself.

CHAPTER FORTY-THREE

ROSE

Rose walked through the house Hank had shared with Leigh in Atlanta, relieved she wouldn't have to live there. She knew from all who spoke about her that Leigh was a sweet, pleasant person, but the idea of living among Hank's memories of her was too burdensome. Besides, their tastes were nothing alike.

The one thing she would miss when leaving Atlanta for Palm Desert was the closeness of his two daughters. Nikki had always been supportive. And what had begun as a rocky relationship with Sam had developed into a rewarding bond with her. Even Hank's friends commented on it.

Hank approached her wearing nothing but pajama bottoms. He pulled her into his arms and nuzzled her neck.

Shivers of pleasure raced through her.

"Good morning," he said. "Happy that we were able to settle things very quickly here?"

"Yes. Doesn't that make it easier for you to leave?"

"*You* make it easy for me. I want to be with you, and desert life suits both of us. Besides, we'll be busy working together there once more."

"I'm very pleased that we'll be able to help with the Premio Inn and most importantly be able to help Willow. She deserves the opportunity she's been given. Especially with her history with Brent and his bullying from their college days."

"When I talked to Mitchell about our new contract with them, he made it clear there would be no interruptions from either Brent or his father," said Hank. "It's about time he understood the damage they were doing to the company. I guess Craig Kincaid made it clear to him."

"Craig? How did that happen?" Rose asked, surprised.

"During a meeting he attended as Willow's legal representative, Craig told about Brent's harassment of a woman he knew. Both Duncan and Mitchell were shocked and embarrassed."

Rose felt her lips curve. Craig and Willow would make a wonderful couple if only they knew it. But then, they both wanted independence, and that was important too.

CHAPTER FORTY-FOUR

WILLOW

Willow walked into a meeting at the Premio Inn and sat at the table in a small conference room, telling herself not to be nervous. Harold Albright, Mitchell Armstrong, and George Hartmann were sitting there with three other men she didn't know. She was relieved that Duncan wasn't present, nor his son. But still, everyone seemed very serious. She fought for control by brushing an imaginary crumb off her skirt as she waited for Mitchell to begin speaking.

"I've called this meeting while four board members of the Blaise Hotel Group are in town. We've been holding back on beginning the ownership transition and your contract while we discuss the matter of how we're going to proceed. I believe we're all in agreement the time has come to move forward."

Harold looked at her and smiled.

Mitchell indicated the other men at the table and introduced them one by one, starting with the three unknown men—an older man named Chuck Ditmar, and two middle-aged men, Richard Hastings and Earl Winthrop. "I believe you know Harold Albright, and you certainly know George."

Willow nodded at them. "I'm very pleased to meet you three gentlemen and to see Harold and George again. It's going to be a terrific project, one that I'm certain will enhance the Corona Collection for the Blaise Group."

"Hold on, Ms. Sanchez," said the older gentleman who'd been introduced as Chuck Ditmar. "I'd like to hear your take on how you intend both to keep the flavor of the Premio and to make it a real part of the Corona Collection."

Willow had already noticed his air of superiority. Small, thin, and wiry, with a pursed mouth and dark, beady eyes that gleamed behind the horn-rimmed glasses perched at the end of his sharp nose, Chuck reminded Willow of a chicken intent on plucking something from the ground. Peck! Peck! Peck!

Willow shook off the horrifying image that had popped into her head, gathered a breath, and began to talk. "The décor issue has been settled and rightly so, but it's more than appearance that makes a small inn like this eligible for the Corona Collection. Anyone can dress up a building and change things around, but the one thing that can't be imitated is the genuine interest and care of the staff. That comes from a different management style, one unlike that of a number of commercial properties catering to people who want ordinary rooms for low rates."

"Wait ..." Mitchell began.

"I'm not talking about Blaise hotels," Willow said, smiling to prevent Mitchell from interfering. He and the others might be a bunch of men used to running their own shows, but she had to grab control of this one from the very beginning. "People who come to a Corona Collection property expect and will receive superior service, sparkling surroundings, and an attentive staff who mean what they say. As you may have experienced if you've stayed at the Premio or the Desert Sage Inn, you would know staff members are trained to believe the inn is theirs to share, and they are not there as someone working only for the paycheck. They take pride in providing quality service. "She gazed at George, who was nodding emphatically, smiling his appreciation.

"I can attest to that," said Harold. "Eleanor and I love this inn."

"But we do a good job and make money at all our properties, always have," protested Chuck.

"There's no reason the same can't be said of a Corona Collection hotel. I've had the opportunity to train at the Desert Sage Inn since I was a young girl first getting a taste of the hospitality business, and I can promise you I know the difference between a Corona hotel and others."

"She's a protégé of Alec Thurston," said George Hartmann. "He was one of the finest hoteliers in the business."

Chuck gave her a thoughtful look. "Okay, I wanted to be sure in my own mind how dedicated you were to the principles behind the idea."

"I understand you're going to head the transition team under Brian Walden. You and the other Desert Flowers will be working on it together. Is that right?" said Harold, grinning.

Willow noted the looks of confusion on the faces of some of the men and said, "Alec Thurston called the three women on the transition team he put together to help with the Desert Sage Inn the Desert Flowers. Sort of an inside story," she explained.

"Hank Bowers and Rose Macklin will be working together on publicity, public relations, and all printed materials for the transition," Mitchell said. "Lily Walden will be working with Willow. All are important to the process because of the work they did for the Desert Sage Inn."

Mitchell said to George, "I think we're ready."

George got to his feet and came to stand beside her. "It is with a great deal of pleasure that I hand you the keys to my office. For the next couple of weeks, I will be here working with you as we go through the transition, but I want you to feel as if the office is yours now that you've been hired as the new manager."

Her cheeks flushed with emotion, Willow got to her feet,

"Thank you, George. I promise to respect all you've done to make this inn such a treasure and to learn everything I can from you about keeping the inn as wonderful as it now is."

"I'm sure you'll find a few things to change," George said, giving her an indulgent look.

Willow laughed. "Well, maybe a few, but only in keeping with what's already here."

George handed her the keys. "Congratulations, Willow. I know Alec would be as happy as I am to have you carry on for me."

"Thank you," Willow said, certain she could say nothing more without her eyes tearing up.

The men all rose and came to her side to shake her hand.

Mitchell was the last to do so. "Welcome to the team. Tomorrow, we'll set up a meeting to introduce you to all the staff. Now, why don't we take these gentlemen to lunch at the Desert Sage Inn so they can get to know you better. Trace might join us."

"Okay," Willow said, wondering if Trace had told his parents she'd ended the budding romance. It didn't sound like it.

As Willow walked into Sage, the gourmet restaurant at the Desert Sage Inn, she admired the stucco walls painted a light shade of green, thinking it balanced the colors of the desert attractively. As always, crisp, white-linen cloths covered the tables, and crystal glasses gleamed near sparkling silverware. She gazed out the windows along the outside wall to where tables had been set up out on the patio. Misters spraying cool water into the dry air were in full use against the heat of the day.

Mitchell led the group to a table for eight, and Willow had the awful feeling Trace was, indeed, planning to join them.

Mitchell directed her to sit beside him, and the others filled the chairs but one, leaving it empty.

Chuck sat on the other side of her. She sighed as he began to drill her with probing questions. Peck! Peck! Peck! She answered them all, trying to remember that any job included working with some people who made it more difficult than others.

They'd just ordered their lunches when Trace came into the room and joined them. Apologizing for being late, he sat opposite Willow, signaled the waitress standing by, and quickly and quietly placed his order.

Smiling, he greeted each of the gentlemen and said to his father, "I thought it would be nice for the board members to meet with me to discuss the latest plans for a charity event we're planning to hold here in the fall."

"Thanks, but I believe most of men have plans to play a round of golf following lunch. We were hoping you'd join us," said his father.

Trace shook his head and said importantly, "Sorry, I'm too busy managing the inn."

Willow remained silent during this exchange, aware of two things. Trace had not acknowledged her, and he was not the manager of the inn; Lou Molina was. He was only the executive assistant manager. Is this how he was going to cope with his disappointment over not getting to manage the Premio?

Trace looked at her. "Perhaps Willow can take my place. I understand she likes to play."

Willow turned to Mitchell. "I have a meeting with Rose and Lily this afternoon, but thanks."

"Well then, not a problem," said Mitchell smoothly. "I see that our management people are busy. That's good."

Throughout their meal, Willow replied to any questions

she was asked, but she otherwise remained quiet, sizing up the people who would have an impact on her job. Harold and she had already clicked. Chuck was someone she'd have to watch. The other two board members seemed amiable. Trace, though he was working at the Desert Sage Inn, wasn't going to be a big supporter even though he'd implied he would be before she'd ended his hopes for a relationship.

George caught her eye and smiled, and she felt better. She both liked and admired him.

After they finished coffee and dessert, Willow prepared to leave. "Thank you all for a lovely lunch. If, at any time, you need to get in touch with me, you have my information. Again, thank you for your support. I appreciate it."

"We appreciate you," said Mitchell, rising and shaking her hand.

She left the room in a hurry, hoping to avoid Trace. But, hearing him call to her, she reluctantly slowed her steps and turned to face him.

"Willow! Wait! I need to talk to you," Trace said, catching up to her.

"Yes?"

"I'm sorry for being rude to you. I'm still angry that you cut things off without giving me a chance."

"As I said earlier, now that we're working together, it's best that we don't pursue it. Besides, I think you already know it wouldn't work." She kept her gaze steady, willing herself to say as little as possible. While he was much more pleasant and easy-going than his cousin, Trace Armstrong had a similar underlying streak of both elitism and entitlement.

"Okay, your loss. See you around, Willow." He turned and walked away.

Willow watched him go, aware that he was considered a big catch for most women. But she wasn't most women. At one time, she'd felt she had to defend her background. Now, she knew better. Any suitor had to be acceptable to her standards as she'd been taught. That included mutual respect. She wasn't going to settle for okay.

At home, she changed her clothes into something comfortable, made her mother's famous lemonade, set out a few snacks, and waited for Rose and Lily to show. They'd purposely set a time when Lily's children would be either napping or resting.

She couldn't wait for the three of them to be together. Her emotions were pretty mixed up, and there was nothing like a good dose of honesty from her friends to set herself straight.

Lily was the first to arrive. "It's good to be here," she said, giving Willow a hug. "Let's see what's new since I was here last."

Willow proudly showed her the new desk chair in her office. "I paid a lot for it, but as the salesman said, it'll be worth it. A sore back can lead to other things."

Lily turned as the doorbell rang.

"Hi, everyone!" called Rose stepping inside as Willow approached her.

"Welcome!" said Willow proudly. They embraced, and then Willow stood aside as Rose and Lily hugged. "Come on into the kitchen. I think it will be comfortable there, and I have lemonade and snacks ready."

"Your mother's lemonade recipe?" Lily asked.

Willow grinned. "Yes. It's too early for wine for Rose and me, and I know you like it."

"Perfect," said Rose. "Especially for this first meeting of the second round of the Desert Flowers."

Willow joined in the laughter that followed. God! She loved these women.

After Willow handed out drinks and snacks, they took seats at the kitchen table that used to be in Alec's home.

Rose immediately began talking about her trip to Atlanta. "I'm very happy I'll be living out here with Hank. It's pretty hard to follow in the footsteps of a sainted woman. I'm sure Leigh was a lovely person, but it's hard to live up to perfection."

"What does Hank think?" asked Lily.

Rose let out a happy chuckle. "He says I'm the best thing ever to happen to him."

"That's so romantic," sighed Willow, unable to think of anyone who would say that about her. She realized Rose and Lily were staring at her. "What?"

"What's going on with you? Why that look?" said Rose.

"What look?" she said, wondering if she should confess about the other night with Craig.

Suddenly realizing these two weren't about to let her get away without explaining, she began talking. "And then when I asked him if he remembered talking to the EMTs, he said he didn't. I haven't heard a word from him since, though I left him a message telling him again how sorry I was that he'd fallen into my pool, and I was hoping he was feeling better."

Rose frowned. "He could've at least answered the message."

Lily shook her head. "That doesn't sound like him. Maybe something's wrong with his phone."

"Go ahead, try calling him," said Willow, stung all over again that Craig hadn't made any effort to get in touch with her.

Lily took her phone out of her purse and called the law office. "Hey, Jonathan. Is Craig around? Oh, I see. Thanks." She clicked off the call and studied Willow. "He hasn't been in the office for a couple of days. Something about an accident."

Willow clapped her hands to her cheeks. "Oh, my God! What if he was badly hurt? I told him if he noticed anything different, he was to call 911 or go to the emergency room."

"Maybe his father knows something," said Rose.

"I'm not calling Ken. If Craig wanted to be in touch, he would," Willow said stubbornly, though she felt both worried and cross at the same time.

Lily patted her hand. "Relax. If something horrible had happened, we'd all know. Craig's been assigned to handle the legal oversight for the transition of the Premio. Brian told me this morning."

"How does it feel to have a friendly team working on the project this time?" Rose said. She leaned closer. "I heard that Brent Armstrong has been taken off any work here in the valley because of sexual harassment. And, if I'm not mistaken, Tiffany, working with Dan at the fitness facility at the Desert Sage Inn, is one of the women involved."

"There was more than one?" Willow asked, appalled.

Rose grimaced and nodded. "He's a creep."

"Just so you know, I've told Trace I am not interested in a romantic relationship with him. He was upset, and when he learned I was to manage the Premio, he became nasty. Beyond having to work for the same company, I want nothing to do with him."

"Do tell," said Rose. "I've been gone less than a week and look at all that's happened."

Lily gave Willow a thoughtful look. "Brian says you have a lot of strong supporters behind you. Mitchell Armstrong is one of the best."

"He's been fair, and I appreciate it. I don't think he realized until today that Trace and I are just friends."

"Either way, it shouldn't affect your job," said Rose. "You earned that spot with your talent."

"Amen," said Lily. "I'm very proud of you."

"Me, too," said Rose. She lifted her glass of lemonade. "Here's to the Desert Flowers! We are talented, we are strong, we are loveable."

"Yes!" cried Lily.

Willow grinned and clicked her glass with theirs.

Talk turned to the job ahead.

Willow told about the difference in opinion, led by Duncan, about changing the décor and atmosphere of the Premio, and how common sense had won out.

"Brian and I went out to the Premio and looked around some time ago before he accepted the job with the Blaise Group," said Lily. "I can't imagine what Duncan was thinking. The Premio is very distinct, so stunning in an understated way, that it would be a shame to change it."

"Hank and I toured it yesterday," said Rose. "I agree with Lily. It's perfect as it is."

"Well, maybe not perfect, but pretty close to it," said Willow. "I met Harold Albright, a board member for the Blaise Group, and he and I agree on a few minor changes. Over time as I gain the confidence of the entire board, I'll be able to do more major changes should they be needed."

"It's perfect for the Corona Collection," said Rose. "A lot of the work Hank and I will be doing for the transition has already been outlined by what we did for the Desert Sage Inn. We'll create a new logo for the hotel and create brochures, ads, and all the other necessary materials. The two hotels are alike in their feel, so it should be fairly easy."

"What are you expecting me to do?" Lily asked Willow.

"The same job you had earlier with Alec's property. The purchase and sale agreement has been signed and the selection of manager complete, but during this transition and due diligence period, we need you to keep all the details straight, to attend meetings when necessary, and keep me up to date on everything."

Lily gave her a happy smile. "I can do that. My last week with the law firm is coming up. The woman I replaced doesn't want to wait any longer before she comes back to work. It's just as well. I don't want to miss out on the kids' activities. I've waited a long time to become a mother."

"And now look at you," said Rose. "From none to almost three."

Lily laughed. "I'm just glad I'm not having twins. Izzy and Ollie are keeping me busy."

"I'm sorry I missed out on having kids, but I intend to be the best auntie ever," said Rose. "And I couldn't be happier to be 'Wosie' for Leah. She's a doll. At least until she's dethroned by a baby brother."

Willow laughed and wondered what it would be like to be a mother. At thirty-one, she had time for babies of her own. An image of Craig standing before her naked caused her to catch the corner of her lip with concern. She'd been very clear with him that she wanted to be just friends, had once told his father how she saw herself as being independent. From the look of things, Craig had taken her words to heart.

CHAPTER FORTY-FIVE

LILY

Lily sipped her lemonade feeling more like herself, talking business with these two women. She couldn't wait to give them the good news.

"Okay, Flowers, I met with the mayor and have some exciting things to discuss with you. With the decision we each made to give a portion of our share of the funds from the sale of Alec's house, I think I may have found the location to set up Juanita's Kitchen. A block away from the law offices of Williams and Kincaid there's a small strip mall that's been mostly empty for some time. It's not on the main drag, so its use for commercial purposes is limited. But it's the perfect place for the kitchen in an area of town that is easy to get to."

"Can we see it?" asked Rose. "And how much are we talking about?"

"Yes, I can take you there. But I must warn you it hasn't been well maintained. We'd have to hire a crew to get the unit I'm thinking of cleaned and repaired in places. But it was once used as a restaurant, and it has plenty of space and the necessary plumbing for a commercial kitchen and room for serving the food and seating for guests."

She handed her phone around. "I've taken several pictures of it. The mayor is very enthusiastic about it and will help with issues if any problems arise."

Willow huddled close to Rose to check the photographs. "It looks like it has a good layout. How many other businesses are there?"

"At the moment, only three, but two other businesses are talking about moving in—a dry cleaning operation and a mailing store. With us, that would complete the strip of storefronts. Another reason the mayor is excited about the plan is she hates to see buildings not being used. They can become an eyesore or an unsavory place."

"I like it," said Willow. "Let's get my parents to come with us when we look at it."

"I've already talked to your mother. She and your father are joining us when we inspect the property."

Willow and Rose glanced at one another. Lily was so organized.

"I can go there most anytime tomorrow," said Rose.

"I have a busy day but will break away whenever you choose. The later, the better. I want to get an early start at the inn tomorrow. George is moving out of his office, and I'm moving in."

"Won't it be nice! A big, fancy office for you!"

Willow laughed. "Not at all, though I hope to dress it up a bit."

Rose laughed. "That sounds right. Hank and I got word on the house. Tomorrow sounds good for checking out the building for Juanita's Kitchen. But, after that, Hank and I will be moving into our new home." She beamed at them. "We're closing on the sale the day after tomorrow. They've moved fast to get us in before Hank's lease is up."

"How exciting!" Lily said. "I'm happy we're all staying here together. The Desert Flowers will be in bloom and together for a long time to come."

"Hear! Hear!" said Rose, raising her glass.

"Amen!" Willow added.

Filled with excitement for the future, Lily returned the bright smiles directed at her.

CHAPTER FORTY-SIX

WILLOW

Willow sat in her kitchen thinking about what to fix for dinner when her doorbell rang. Wondering if her new chair was finally being delivered, she hurried to answer it.

Craig was standing there a pizza box in one hand, a six-pack of beer in the other. "Hi. Thought we could try this over again. I promise I won't fall into the pool." He looked, well ... adorable.

Heartbeat pounding in her ears, images of him naked filled her mind.

He grinned. "Well? May I come in?"

"Oh, yes. Sorry." She opened the door wide enough for him to walk inside with dinner and led him to the kitchen.

"Here, let's put the pizza down on the counter. I'll pre-heat the oven. This time, let's not wait too long to eat."

"Sounds like a plan," said Craig, a smile playing with his lips. He set the pizza on the counter and handed her a can of beer.

She accepted it, telling herself that this was the safest way to play it. She studied him. "How is your head? You never responded to my texts."

He shrugged. "Sorry. I figured I'd let you know after I'd seen my doctor, then time slipped away from me with an important case at work."

She knew it had to be more than that. "And?"

"And I'd said some pretty stupid things and needed time to

regroup." He gave her a sheepish look and glanced out the window. "I know how much you want your independence."

Willow placed her hands on her hips. "Do you remember what you told the EMTs?"

"It took me a couple of days to recall the conversation, but yes." His gaze settled on her. "So, we're back to being friends. Okay?"

Hiding her disappointment, she nodded. He'd told her he didn't want anything more than that. She turned and headed toward the patio to give herself time to deal with her disappointment. He was right. She wanted her independence, especially now that she and George had begun working together at the Premio.

Craig followed her out to the patio. "Ah, the scene of the crime."

She set down her beer on the table between the two couches. "Has your head healed? You mentioned the doctor. What did he say?"

He grinned. "He told me my father was right. I have a hard head. It'll take a while for the hematoma to dissolve, but I'm going to be fine." He reached behind his head and rubbed it gently.

She walked over to him. "Here. Let me see." She pressed up on her toes and felt the lump at the back of his head.

"Ouch!" he cried and turned to her with a teasing grin.

They stood staring at one another.

Desire raced through her with a heat that spread a flush across her cheeks.

Craig's eyes flickered with interest and then he turned away.

Willow eased herself down on the couch, her knees too weak to hold her. Facing Craig, she tried to think of something to say that had nothing to do with memories of that night.

"How are things going with the Premio?" he asked, taking the pressure off her.

"It's very exciting," she said, her comfort level returning. She enthusiastically described what it was like working with George and learning as much as she could about her new role.

"That sounds good," said Craig. "I'm happy for you. I know it's something you've wanted."

"And you've been busy," said Willow. "Are you still working with the client you told me about earlier?"

"Yeah. By the way, how's Juanita's Kitchen coming along?"

"We thought we'd found a location for it at a strip mall not far from your office, but the owner didn't want to sell, so we're still looking around. We'll know the right spot when we find it. With Lily handling the search, I'm sure we'll find something soon."

"She's great," said Craig. "We're sorry to lose her at the firm, but she'll have a job there any time she wants to come back."

"It won't be for a while with a baby on the way," said Willow.

"How do you feel about children?" Craig asked. "Are you one of those women who want a career, not a family?"

Surprised, Willow paused. Apparently, Craig didn't remember her asking him the same question.

"Well?"

"No, I'm not." At one time, her career was what mattered most. But now, though she'd have an excellent job and hopes for a career in the hospitality field, she knew she definitely wanted a family of her own. She gazed at him. "I've been doing a lot of thinking about having children of my own. After seeing how thrilled Brian and Lily are about the new baby, it's made me think about what I really want. How about you?"

He rubbed a hand over the spot at the back of his head.

"With the right woman, the idea is intriguing." He looked at her.

Willow swallowed hard and stood. "I'd better check on the oven."

Craig got to his feet and followed her into the kitchen. "You didn't even turn it on."

She faced him. "You knew that but didn't mention it?"

He shook his head. "Guilty as charged."

"But why?" she asked.

He drew her to him. "I want as much time with you as you'll give me."

She looked up at him. "Oh, but I thought ..."

"Think again," he murmured before pressing his lips to her. His kiss was soft and sweet, an introduction to something more.

She reached up and wrapped her arms around his neck.

His kiss deepened, sending pulses of desire through her, making her yearn for more. She opened her mouth to his tongue and then lost herself in feelings new to her. Maybe it was talk of making a family, but this wasn't an ordinary kiss. It spoke of much more. A soft moan escaped her.

Like a Scottish hero, he lifted her and carried her to the living room sectional couch. With her still in his arms, he settled on the couch, holding her in his lap. He gazed at her steadily. "Is this what you want, Willow? Us like this?"

"I don't want to be just friends anymore," she confessed.

His lips met hers and once more she was lost in the feelings he aroused in her.

When he gently asked, "Want more?"

She whispered, "Please."

Later, in bed next to him, Willow rested her head on his broad chest, listening to the pounding of his heart. Lying on his back, he sighed with satisfaction. She smiled to herself. For such a big, strong man he'd been surprisingly gentle, taking the time to please her at every step. And when he'd cried out, it was her name he spoke.

Craig rolled over and faced her. Willow noticed his eyes brightening with moisture.

"What's this?" she asked softly.

"I just remembered something Alec once told me. He said that when you're with the right woman, your soul will fill."

"You're a romantic like him?" she teased softly.

"I guess so," he said, "because I've never felt like this before. I love you, Willow."

'Me, too." She kissed his lips, and in that moment, she felt so in sync with him she knew Alec's words to be true.

After a while, during which Craig showed her how much he cared, he said, "I'm hungry. How about you?"

Willow started to laugh. "Hope you like your pizza cold because I forgot to turn on the oven."

CHAPTER FORTY-SEVEN

ROSE

Several days later, Rose entered Willow's house anxious to join Willow and Lily to discuss a new building for Juanita's Kitchen. She had some exciting news of her own. She and Hank had set a date for their wedding.

When Rose walked into the kitchen, Lily was talking about a maternity store she'd discovered online. "For the first time in my life, I can't wait to get fat," she said laughing. "Some of the clothes are very cute."

"Talk to me in a couple of months and tell me how you feel then," said Rose, giving her a quick hug before embracing Willow. She faced them with a wide smile. "While we're talking about clothes, you might want to choose something suitable for a casual wedding."

"Really? You and Hank have decided on a date?" said Lily, clasping her hands.

"Does this have anything to do with Hank renting one of the guesthouses at the Premio?" Willow asked, grinning.

Rose settled in a seat at the kitchen table with them. "We've finally decided to go ahead and do something simple. I told Hank I didn't care who attended as long as my desert friends and his daughters were there. That's when we decided to just keep it to that. It's more intimate and simpler all around." She turned to Willow. "Hank rented the house at the Premio for Nikki and Sam and her family. We're going to be married in the small courtyard there, and we're talking to the hotel staff about catering cocktails and dinner after the ceremony."

"That's going to be lovely," said Willow. "The courtyard is perfect. You can dress up the area with fresh flowers or leave it plain."

"Oh, Rose, I'm so happy for you. I wouldn't want to miss it for the world." Lily gazed at them. "Are you two sure you don't mind that Brian and I took off without sharing that day with you?"

Rose reached over and squeezed Lily's hand. "We just wanted you two to be happy."

"So, when is the wedding?" Lily asked.

Rose couldn't stop smiling. "Three weeks from Saturday. We couldn't wait much longer because of Sam's pregnancy and her ability to fly."

"A late summer wedding is perfect," said Lily. "Or anytime." She turned to Willow. "I understand from Loretta that Craig's been singing around the office. What's that all about?"

Rose caught Willow's glance at the refrigerator and studied the flyer for Vincent's Pizzeria taped there. "Does it have anything to do with pizza?"

Willow's cheeks turned a pretty pink. "Should it?"

"I don't know," said Rose. "You tell us."

"Okay. Craig and I are seeing each other," Willow said, her cheeks becoming redder.

"And?" said Rose.

Willow sighed. "And it's very special. I've fallen hard."

"Speaking of falling," said Lily. "Maybe that knock on Craig's head made him come to his senses. The two of you are perfect together."

Willow gave her a shy smile. "Do you think so?"

Rose and Lily exchanged glances.

"Oh, yeah," said Rose chuckling. "We've all been waiting for you two to acknowledge it." She noticed Willow's eyes filling and softened her tone. “What’s wrong, hon?”

Willow let out a shaky sigh. “Thank you both. You’re support makes me happy. I already love Craig in a way I haven’t loved anyone before. He’s already told me he loves me too.”

“Well, then,” said Lily. “I see another wedding coming up.”

Willow’s eyes rounded. “Hold on! Not so fast! We have to get Rose married first.”

“Yes,” said Rose. “Hank has been waiting patiently. I don’t want anything to interfere with our plans.”

“Exactly,” said Lily. “I’m just excited about it all.” She leaned forward. “Okay, I’ve called this meeting because I have more exciting news. I think I’ve found the right building for our project.” She pulled out a piece of paper from her pocket. “I’ve got all the facts here, plus a photo. I’ve also taken pictures on my phone.”

“Leave it up to Lily,” Rose said. She turned to her. “What would we do without you?”

Lily smiled, pleased, and filled them in on what just might be the perfect place for Juanita’s Kitchen—a building in Cathedral City, convenient to all who might benefit.

CHAPTER FORTY-EIGHT

WILLOW

Willow said goodbye to Rose and Lily and went back to the kitchen to clean up. She studied the flyer on the refrigerator. Pizza was definitely part of the story. From the night they'd finally been able to share it, Craig and Willow could hardly stand to be apart. Though they were both busy with their careers, it wasn't unusual to exchange text messages a couple of times a day.

Thinking of Rose and Lily's reaction to the news of Craig and her being together, Willow called her mother and asked her to come for coffee early the next morning.

Juanita arrived at Willow's house with coffee cake and a hug. "Thank you for inviting me to coffee. It seems strange, yet wonderful to be here in a house of your own." Her mother took a seat at the kitchen table and patted it. "Alec would be pleased to see this here. He knew how often we women sat around it for our morning chats."

Willow set the coffee cake on the table and handed her mother a cup of coffee. "*Mami*, there is something I want to talk to you about." She couldn't hold back a smile. "It's about Craig Kincaid and me."

Her mother's twinkling gaze settled on hers. "Have the two of you discovered one another at last?"

"What?" Willow said, taken aback. "Why would you say that?"

"Because your father, Alec, and I all believed he would be a good choice for you. Everyone, including Craig's father, thinks so. We just had to wait for the two of you to realize it."

"But you never told me," said Willow.

Her mother squeezed her shoulder. "Oh, I wanted to, but I couldn't, of course. It's your decision and his."

"But you're happy with the idea?"

"Oh, yes. It's something we were hoping for. Rose and Lily made it easy, falling for Hank and Brian. But you and Craig? Not so much." Her mother laughed. "Loretta kept us informed from her end. Craig fell for you some time ago. It's a good thing the accident made him think about what he wanted and made you realize how much you cared."

Deflated, Willow sank back in her chair. "Wow! Everyone knew but us."

"Just about," said her mother, chuckling softly as she planted a kiss on her cheek.

Willow grinned. "Let's not mention it to Craig. I want him to think being with me was his very own idea."

Her mother patted her hand. "Good thinking."

They chatted about Rose's wedding and the building Lily had found for Juanita's Kitchen, then Willow rose. "I'm sorry to cut our visit short, but I have to get to work."

"How's the job going?" her mother asked, rising and putting her coffee cup in the sink.

Willow let out a sigh of happiness. "I love it."

"Good. Craig doesn't have a problem with you working as much? I know about the hospitality business and long hours."

Willow shook her head. "He understands and supports my commitment to it." They'd talked about that and everything else since the night they spent together.

When Willow walked into the inn, staff greeted her with smiles. As Mitchell had promised, he and George had introduced her both at a staff meeting and then individually.

With over 250 employees, it had taken several days for her to meet them all, but the effort was well worth it. She knew every job because she'd worked most of them at one time or another, and she respected the work they were doing. In return, perhaps because of that, the staff easily related to her.

Waving to the clerks behind the front desk, she headed for her new office behind the reception area eager to begin another day's work. Though George had removed his personal belongings from it, she was waiting for the training period with him as well as Rose's wedding to be over before putting in personal items of her own.

She was sitting at her desk checking bookings on her computer when George walked in. "Good morning, Willow! I understand one of your friends is having the kitchen cater her wedding in a couple of weeks. Let's talk about that."

He took a seat beside her desk, and they discussed arrangements in the past and how they'd handled catered affairs. "Even though our restaurant is small, we keep staff available for those guests who have special requests throughout the day and evening. In the case of your friend's wedding and reception, because the number is small, we could get by adding only a bartender and two servers."

"Yes, that should be fine. I'll be around to see things are set up the way Rose wants them. Do you have special teams for this kind of thing?"

"Yes," said George. They went over the list of people who volunteered for extra shifts and made a decision.

"I'm going to go over to the guesthouse and check it out. I want to be able to visualize how everything will work," said Willow.

As she'd been trained, Willow automatically searched the area for housekeeping and maintenance issues as she walked from the main building to the house Rose and Hank had rented for their wedding. In a corner of the property, the large, one-story adobe structure sat in the shade of palm trees and was surrounded by lush landscaping that both softened the lines of the building and lent privacy to the area around it. Tasteful and adaptable, the house and the setting were often used for small weddings and private celebrations.

She unlocked and opened the carved-wooden front door and stepped inside to a tiled entryway. From there, she faced a living room with a dining room to her right and a family room to her left. Through sliding-glass doors on the far wall of the living room, she viewed the central courtyard surrounded by what she knew were bedrooms and along the right side, the modern, commercial kitchen. Beyond the rooms in the back were the pool and large patio perfect for outdoor entertaining.

In the silence of the empty house, she walked through the dining room into the kitchen and out to the courtyard. Standing there, she observed the water fountain bubbling in a corner, the stone bench under a willow tree, and the flowering plants carefully arranged to give color in the natural setting. She couldn't wait to talk to Rose about the flowers she was going to use for the ceremony. The courtyard was the perfect place to add any color she wanted.

Satisfied the house was perfect for the use Rose wanted and that the addition of three staff members would be adequate, Willow locked up and left the house.

When Willow drove up to her house after work, she was delighted to see Craig's car in the driveway. She drove past it into the garage and got out. Craig emerged through a door from the pool area.

"Hope you don't mind. I've been sitting on your patio waiting for you to get home. At the last minute, I thought maybe you'd like to go to Tico's for some Mexican food."

She accepted a quick kiss from him. "That sounds great. Let me change my clothes and I'll be ready to go."

"Deal." Craig followed her inside. "I want to celebrate."

She turned and faced him. "What's going on?"

He grinned. "I've just come from a meeting with your parents about the Juanita's Kitchen project. If you Flowers go ahead and purchase the building Lily found, the project can get started sooner than they thought. My client, the one I told you about, has agreed to donate money to cover the start-up costs."

Willow broke into a broad smile. "Really? That's terrific!"

"Yeah, I'm pretty pleased about it. Your parents are thrilled. They'll set up a meeting with you Flowers, me, and some other people they've have been talking to. With luck, we can have things up and running in a couple of months."

Willow hurried to him and threw her arms around his neck. "You're wonderful. Have I told you lately?"

He bent down to kiss her. "No, but you can show me later."

She met his lips eagerly. This was much better than words.

When they finally pulled apart, Willow let out a happy sigh and smiled up at him. "I really love you."

"Yeah? The feeling's mutual."

She stepped away and shook her head. "My friends are pleased we're together."

Craig gave her a sheepish look. "Loretta told me it was just a matter of time for us to realize it was right."

"I wasn't going to mention it, but according to the Flowers and my mother, we're the last to know. They were all rooting for us to get together. Even Alec!" said Willow.

Craig's look of surprise was comical. "Huh. We were the last to know."

Willow couldn't help laughing.

He drew her into his arms and they laughed together, hugging each other tight.

After a delicious meal at Tico's of her favorite chicken *molé* and plenty of cold beer, Willow returned to her house with Craig.

"Are you coming in? It's still early." They sat in front of her house in Craig's car.

Craig shook his head. "Not tonight. I just realized there's something I have to do."

Puzzled, she studied him. "Is everything all right?"

"Yes. But like I said, I have to take care of something."

"Okay. You'd let me know if you needed help with anything, wouldn't you?"

"Of course." He leaned over and kissed her, lightly at first, then deepening it until they both were ready for more.

Craig pulled away and sighed. "You'd better get inside before I change my mind."

Still puzzled, she climbed out of the car. "Will I see you tomorrow?"

"Definitely," he said.

She watched him take off, wondering what he was up to.

Later that evening, Willow was in her pajama bottoms and tank top when she heard the sound of her doorbell. She crept to the door and peeked out. Her father was standing there.

She flung open the door. "*Papi!* Is everything okay? Where's Mom?"

"Everything's fine. May I come in?"

"Yes, of course." She stepped back to allow her father to pass by and then closed the door and gave him a worried look. Her father and she were close, but they didn't often get together like this.

"May I get you something? Water? Coffee? Beer?" she asked, anxiously.

"Water would be nice," he said. "Though it's almost sundown, it's still hot."

Willow went over to the refrigerator and dispensed ice and water into a glass. "Here. Would you like to sit down?"

"Yes. We can talk right here in the kitchen if you wish." He sat down in a chair at the kitchen table and she followed suit.

"What is it? You have me worried," she said. "Is this something to do with Juanita's Kitchen?" Her father wasn't a talkative man, but she always listened carefully to what he had to say.

He took a sip of his water and studied her. "Are you happy, *Cariña*?"

"Yes, I love my new job." She couldn't help smiling. "It's a dream come true to be able to manage the Premio."

"Ah, yes," he said. "And otherwise?" His dark gaze settled on her.

She felt like a schoolgirl but refused to squirm in her chair. "Are you talking about Craig and me?"

"Yes. I understand you and he ..."

"We're together, *Papi*," she interjected, needing to be open about it. "I know we were the last to realize it, but it's a perfect match."

"Well, I think you ought to know that a certain gentleman came to see me earlier." Her father gave her a self-satisfied look.

"Craig?"

He nodded. "He wanted to speak to me about you. We had quite a nice conversation and I've given him my permission to court you."

"Court me? Isn't this something out of the dark ages?" She

couldn't decide if she was flattered or angry.

"Your mother and I are very pleased he extended this courtesy, old-fashioned or not. It shows he respects you and us." Her father kept his gaze on her. "We give him and you our blessing. That's all I came to say." He got to his feet.

Willow jumped up. "Wait! Don't you want to stay?"

Her father's grin was impish. "No. I believe he plans on stopping by to tell you himself. But I knew you'd want to hear it directly from me. He's a good man."

Willow wrapped her arm around the quiet, dependable man who was her father. Unshed tears blurred her vision. She loved him so much. "Thank you."

She walked him to the front door and watched as he got into his car and drove away, surprised by what Craig had done.

Knowing Craig was going to return, Willow went into her bedroom. This was not a night for pajamas. She needed to put on something better.

When Willow received a text from Craig asking if he could come over, she wasn't surprised. Her father had given her a warning, and she was ready, dressed in a new silk lounging robe. Underneath, she wore lacy pink panties and a matching bra. Smiling, she still couldn't get over the fact that Craig had actually asked her father for permission to court her. It was such a romantic move.

She heard the sound of Craig's car pulling into the driveway and drew a deep breath. More than ever she was ready for a sexy evening.

The doorbell rang, and she moved forward to answer it, awash in emotions. Smiling, she opened the door. "Hi, Craig."

"Hi," His gaze wandered up and down her, and a frown creased his forehead. "Hey, do me a favor and change your clothes. I want to take you somewhere."

Willow's sexual fantasy exploded inside her head. "What?"

"Please go get dressed. I've made plans to go out."

She studied him. He was still wearing the khaki pants and polo shirt he'd worn earlier. And now that she thought about it, he looked a little frazzled.

"Okay," she said. "Wait here."

He checked his watch. "Hurry. We don't have much time."

She stopped and turned around. "What do you mean?"

"Just trust me, okay?" he replied, waving her on her way.

She ran back into the bedroom, threw her silky robe on the bed, gave it a regretful look, and pulled on a denim skirt and a knit top. She didn't know what all the rush was about, but she figured she'd better do as he asked and simply trust him.

He hurried her to his car, got in, and drove away.

"Where are we going?" she asked. He was hunkered over the wheel like a racing car driver. He turned to her for a moment, grinned, and turned back to driving. "You'll see."

He pulled into a parking lot behind a group of stores on El Paseo Drive and got out. By the time she opened her door, he was already there, helping her out.

Taking her hand, he hurried her out of the lot and down the street, stopping in front of her favorite jewelry store.

"Craig, is this ..." she began.

"Just wait," he said, knocking on the door as the lights inside dimmed.

Smiling, an older man approached, unlocked the door and welcomed them inside. "I'll give you two some privacy."

"Thanks, Mr. Jenkins. I really appreciate it."

Mr. Jenkins bobbed his head. "My pleasure, Craig. I was very glad to hear from you." He left them and disappeared in the back.

Willow turned to Craig. "What are you doing?"

Craig lowered himself on bended knee and gazed up at her.

"I know this is a little bit rushed, but when you told me we were the last to know how right we were for one another, I figured I had to move fast if you were going to be the first to know I actually wanted to propose."

Grinning, holding in a laugh, she covered her cheeks with her hands. "You mean it?"

"I also wanted you to be the first to see the ring I want to give you by picking it out yourself. Mr. Jenkins is going to help us."

He took hold of her hands and gazed up at her adoringly. "Willow, I fell in love with you the first time I saw you sitting with your friends. I knew then I'd have to work hard to prove to you I was different from the man you thought I was. I understand you want your independence, and I promise not to stand in your way but be a help to you. The last weeks with you have opened my heart to loving you. I know now I could never live without you. As corny as it sounds, I want to love you always, just like marriage vows say. Willow Sanchez, will you do me the honor of marrying me?"

Willow pressed her lips together to keep from sobbing. It was a dream she hadn't shared with anyone. He rose and drew her into his arms. She clung to him, knowing she'd found the right person for her, just as everyone had promised.

"Willow, you didn't answer…" he prompted.

She laughed. "Yes, oh yes! I'll marry you Craig Kincaid. I love you too!"

As if on cue, Mr. Jenkins appeared. "Are we ready to select the ring?"

Willow glanced at Craig and grinned. "Yes, I want to be the first to see it."

Later, when Willow left the store with a large diamond on her left ring finger, she sighed. The ring, a symbol of their love, fit perfectly.

CHAPTER FORTY-NINE

WILLOW

Willow awoke and sighed happily at the sight of the big, brawny man lying asleep next to her. They'd made love with abandon after toasting the purchase of the ring with a bottle of champagne Willow just happened to find in her refrigerator. A gift from her parents.

She quietly got out of bed and tiptoed into the kitchen to make coffee. She thought about calling her friends. Lily would, no doubt, be up. Rose, maybe not.

As the coffee was dripping into the pot, Willow lifted her cell. Before she could punch in a number, her cell chimed. *Rose.*

Smiling, Willow clicked on the call. "Hi, Rose! You're up early."

"Yes, Hank and I are about to do a final inspection on our house. I saw the lights on in your house and wondered if I could stop by for a cup of coffee later."

"Absolutely. I have a meeting midmorning but am available until then because I'll be working late."

"Okay, I should be there no later than nine o'clock."

"Perfect." She clicked off the call and punched in Lily's number.

"Good morning. What's up?" Lily said.

Not wanting to give anything away, Willow said, "I'm inviting you to coffee. Rose will be here around nine o'clock."

"Sounds perfect. Anna will be here with the kids so I can go to the doctor's later. I'll see you then."

Craig padded into the kitchen, wearing his rumpled clothes. "Good morning. I have to get back to my condo and get ready for work. I have a meeting at eight-thirty." He kissed her. "M-m-m, almost wife. Can't wait until this is all legal."

"In time, it will be. Before then, we have Rose's wedding and a couple of things to take care of first." She smiled happily at him as he moved in for another kiss.

After he left, she took a shower. She wanted to be sure she looked perfect for her big announcement to her friends.

She was still filing her nails when she heard someone at the front door. She hurried to answer it.

Lily stood outside, beaming at her. "May I see it?"

"See it?"

"The ring. Loretta called me with the news."

"*Doña* Loretta from Craig's office?" Willow knew she sounded dimwitted but she was shocked by how quickly news had traveled.

Willow stood back to allow Lily to enter.

Lily took hold of her hand and squealed, "It's gorgeous!" She hugged her. "Oh, Willow, I'm so happy for you! According to Loretta, Craig can't stop smiling."

Rose hurried up the front walk and joined them at the front door. "Let me see it!"

"Wait! You already knew?" said Willow.

Rose nodded. "Lily told me."

Willow began to laugh. "I guess there are no secrets in this group. That's why Craig proposed quickly. He was afraid everyone would know before me."

The three of them laughed together.

"No matter what it took to make him move, it was a good decision," said Rose, hugging her.

As Willow waved them into the kitchen, she observed the sparkle on her left hand and sighed with happiness. She didn't care who knew it now.

During coffee they discussed the building they were going to buy for Juanita's Kitchen. Plans were coming together quickly.

"Craig's client contributing to start-up costs is a real blessing," said Lily. "Juanita and Pedro are anxious to get to work on the project."

"Best to keep them busy," said Willow. "Otherwise, my mother will want to begin planning a wedding. I talked to my parents last night, and needless to say, they're thrilled. They knew about it, of course, and slipped a bottle of champagne into my refrigerator while Craig was proposing."

"Tell me every detail," said Lily. "I want to hear it all, and then we're going to talk about Rose's wedding. I can't wait."

Rose's smile lit her face. "Just a week or so, and I'll officially be Mrs. Hank Bowers."

CHAPTER FIFTY

ROSE

Rose awoke early, her body humming with anticipation. Though she'd been married before, it soon became apparent that marriage was a big mistake. This one, she knew, was not.

This time, her desert friends, along with Hank's family, were sharing in the joy she'd found in him.

She walked into the kitchen and stopped to gaze around. She already loved her new house. It was perfect for when Nikki or Sam and their families visited. Her thoughts turned to his daughters. It had been a surprise to both Hank and her to meet Nikki's guest for the wedding, a sweet woman named Kari, who was a nurse at the hospital where Nikki worked. After talking to them both for quite a while, it seemed a good pairing.

As she'd told Hank, any loving parent wishes for their children to be happy. Samantha, Nikki's sister, had already met Kari and liked her. Leah, at almost four, was happy to add Kari to her list of admirers.

Rose smiled at the thought of Leah, her first grandchild. Full of self-confidence, bright, and caring, she was an adorable little girl who loved pink and sparkly things. In keeping with the color theme of the wedding, Leah had told everyone she was wearing a ballerina costume and a tiara. No one could convince the little girl that even real princesses went without a tiara from time to time.

She fixed herself a cup of coffee and carried it out to the

patio. Today of all days she needed some private moments. So much had happened to her in the last several months that she sometimes found it hard to believe. The pure happiness of making new, close friends, more like sisters, and becoming part of a real family in which those included in it were truly loved was a welcome change in her life.

She was still lost in thought when Hank opened the sliding door behind her and stepped out onto the patio.

"Good morning, love," he said, bending to kiss her.

"Good morning. This is the day we've been waiting for, and it couldn't be more perfect." She indicated the blue sky above her.

He sat beside her on the couch and clasped her hand. "Any idea how happy you've made me?"

She turned. Seeing the emotion on his face, she leaned over and kissed him on the lips. It was still hard to believe this wonderful man was all hers. She looked forward to making a life with him.

After sitting quietly together, Rose got to her feet. "Guess we'd better get a move on. I've got to check on things at the house, and then the brunch the girls are giving me will happen before we know it. You're meeting the guys for a morning game of golf?"

Hank grinned. "To work my jitters off," he teased.

She laughed and went inside.

When Rose went to the guesthouse later, Leah and the rest of the family were out back in the swimming pool. Rose greeted them with a wave and went to talk to the florist about decorating the center courtyard. As Willow had once mentioned, the courtyard was attractive as it was, but Rose loved the idea of softening the look with plenty of flowers.

She stood next to Marley, the owner of Floral Accents, and

watched as Marley's assistant strung ropes of pink flowers, like leis, above the end of the courtyard where a small, altar-like table had been set up. Baskets of all kinds of pink flowers would be placed on either side of the table, and each of the cloth-covered chairs in the semicircle would have a little nosegay attached to the back. These would then be used as a live, pink centerpiece for the dining room table set for dinner.

"It's going to be stunning," said Marley. "I'm glad you decided to dress up the area. The contrast between rock, stone, and native plants with the pink flowers is wonderful."

"I think so too."

"You said everyone is wearing pink?"

"I've suggested that each woman wear a pink dress in whatever style they wish, but it's not a requirement."

"Lovely," said Marley. "If there's anything else you need me to do, please let me know. It's been such a pleasure working with you, Rose."

"And for me," said Rose. "I'm going to feature the courtyard and your flower shop on my blog, 'You Deserve This.'"

"That would be wonderful," Marley exclaimed. "The flower business is very competitive. I've talked to Willow Sanchez about doing work here."

"Willow is one of my best friends. I'll put in a good word for you," said Rose, chuckling when Marley gave her an enthusiastic hug.

Waving goodbye, Rose went to join the others at the pool.

When Leah saw her, she climbed out of the pool and ran over to her. "Hi, Wosie! Want to see me swim?"

"Yes, I do," said Rose, remembering the horror of Leah falling into the pool when Rose had been babysitting her. Since that time, everyone had made a fuss over Leah's swimming ability, encouraging her to become better.

With deep affection for the little girl, Rose watched Leah jump into the pool and then swim to her mother, kicking furiously. When Leah surfaced, she grinned at Rose.

"Very good, Leah! I'm proud of you!"

"I know," Leah said, and splashed away.

Rose winked at Sam. "Guess I'd better get ready for the brunch. See you at the Sage Restaurant. Can't wait."

Wrapping a towel around her waist, Nikki walked over to her. "I just wanted to thank you for being kind to Kari. It means a lot." Her lips trembled. "My mother wouldn't have been so gracious."

Rose hugged her. "Nikki, your father and I just want you happy."

Nikki sighed. "I'm glad he found you. I know it's been difficult for you to be around Mom and Dad's old friends and hearing all about my mother, but he's as happy as I've ever seen him."

"He's an incredible man," said Rose.

"And you're a very special woman," Nikki said, giving her a quick hug.

As Rose turned to go, she blinked away tears.

That evening, at five o'clock, Rose glanced at the people she loved sitting in chairs ready for her and Hank to appear. The minister who'd performed the memorial service for Alec had agreed to marry them. He stood by the makeshift altar waiting for them.

"Shall we do this?" Rose asked Hank.

He squeezed her hand. "You look beautiful, Rose." He took her in his arms and kissed her, careful not to wrinkle the white silk dress she wore.

"I think you're supposed to do that after we say our vows, not before," quipped Rose in an effort not to show her nerves.

They left the room together and walked into the courtyard, turned into a magical garden with the scent and sight of many flowers. Everyone swiveled in their chairs to get a good look at them.

Leah left her chair and raced toward them, the skirt of her ballerina outfit bouncing with every step. "Hi, Wosie. I love you!"

Amid the chuckles that followed, someone started to clap and then all joined in.

Rose's vision blurred. Standing here beside the man she loved, hearing the sounds of approval, she knew she'd never forget this special day.

CHAPTER FIFTY-ONE

WILLOW

Watching Rose and Hank exchange vows, listening to their words, Willow was very conscious of the man beside her. Every so often, Craig would give her hand a squeeze, telling her in his own way what those words meant to him.

She turned and smiled at him. Their love, which had been difficult to acknowledge, had blossomed into a steady, loving relationship that brought a new discovery every day. She glanced at the diamond on her hand and couldn't wait until a wedding band joined it. Now that everyone, probably everyone in the valley, knew about the engagement, they were all waiting anxiously for them to get married. Willow didn't mind the pressure. No matter what, in many ways, she and Craig had already made their vows.

A week later, Willow felt a pang of sorrow at what the day would bring, then reminded herself this was what Alec had wanted all along—to be with his beloved wife and daughter. She walked over to the sliding-glass door leading to her patio and looked up at the mountains in the distance, their peaks glowing in the early morning light. They stood like sentinels watching over the valley. Observing their majesty, sensing their strength, Willow drew a deep breath and let it out slowly thinking of Alec, who, like the mountains, had watched over her as she grew up, helping to guide her with a quiet strength.

She flicked away the tears that escaped her eyes with her fingers. He'd wanted today to be one of celebration. She owed it to him to try.

As Willow headed to the kitchen, she paused to take a look at her new surroundings. She loved her home. It was already filled with touches from Alec's house and gifts from her parents, Rose, and Lily, making it seem less a brand-new house and more like a well-loved home. Without the promise of financial support from Alec, she might not have jumped as quickly on purchasing a house of her own. But Ken Kincaid had agreed with her that it made sense. Back then, a couple of months ago, she'd been very certain that she'd be living here alone for years. But now, she looked forward to sharing it with the man she loved. Seeing him in her mind, the way his caramel-colored hair swept his wide brow, how his green eyes shone with love, and the way it felt to be in his arms, she sighed happily. Theirs was already a strong, deep relationship.

As if her thoughts had conjured him up, Craig walked into the kitchen, his hair wet from the shower, a towel wrapped around his body. Gazing at him, she couldn't help the smile that crossed her face and made his lips curve. After Lily had been first introduced to him, she'd told Rose and her that she'd envisioned Craig wearing a kilt like the hero on the cover of a Scottish romance book. Admiring him now, she thought a towel was just as good as a kilt, hiding a portion of his body she loved, baring the rest for her to appreciate. His broad shoulders, trim waist, and muscled torso provided an excellent view. More importantly, they hid the gentle, sweet nature inside him that meant so much to her.

He walked over to her and wrapped an arm around her, drawing her close.

She gazed up at him, seeing his concern.

"How are you doing?" he asked, studying her, thumbing a

tear from her cheek.

She shrugged. "It's both a sad and happy day."

He lowered his lips to hers, giving her a gentle kiss before pulling away. "Let's make it a happy one. Alec would want that."

Willow nodded, knowing he was right.

She fixed herself a cup of coffee and took it to her bathroom. A refreshing shower is what she needed to start the day. She wanted to look and feel her best.

As promised, she and Craig met the others outside Alec's house. It had been sold to the Blaise Group, bringing a healthy financial reward to Willow and the other two Desert Flowers.

Still, a tug of sadness pulled at Willow as she got out of Craig's car. She'd loved coming home to Palm Desert and living in this house with the two women who'd become her best friends. Now it was someone else's turn to stay there.

Her parents were standing in the driveway talking to Rose and Hank. Seeing them, Willow joined them.

"Good morning!" Rose called cheerfully. She and Willow embraced, while Hank and Craig shook hands.

Willow turned to her parents and watched as Craig greeted them both. Dressed for the occasion, they looked as if they, too, were struggling with emotions. Though they'd worked for Alec for years, they were actually family—something he'd always appreciated after they'd helped him through depression following the death of Conchita, her mother's cousin.

Willow hugged them both, loving them for being the down-to-earth, wonderful people they were.

"Where's Lily? And Brian?" Willow asked.

"They're on their way. They had to wait for the babysitter to arrive," said Rose.

At the mention of babysitter, Willow caught Craig's eye and chuckled softly at the way he was cocking his eyebrows at her. They'd spent hours discussing the number of children they wanted someday. She'd talked him down from having four or five to maybe three or four. He'd told her no matter what, they'd practice for ten.

When she looked away from him, she was aware of the smile crossing Rose's face.

Rose shook her head. "You've got it bad, girl."

Willow couldn't help her silly grin. No use arguing about it. Still, she was glad when Lily showed up with Brian looking quite pregnant, diverting Rose's attention.

"You look wonderful," Willow said, embracing her.

Lily stroked her round belly, and took hold of Brian's hand. "Announcement, everybody! We decided to find out the sex of the baby, after all. It's a boy due in early January!" Her lips trembled. "Brian and I have talked about it, and with your blessing, we're going to call him Alec. Alec Thurston Walden."

Willow clasped her hands. "How exciting! This is the perfect day to tell us." As one life was being put to rest, another was soon to be born. No one could ever replace Alec, but the little baby inside Lily was bound to have a good life if he was anything like his namesake.

Rose hugged Lily and gave Brian a bright smile. "Congratulations, you two! I love it. A touching tribute to Alec."

Lily and Brian grinned at one another. "We thought so too."

Willow watched her mother embrace both Lily and Brian. She'd grown up an only child, but now, standing here with everyone, it felt right to have this new family. Another gift from Alec.

"Are we ready?" asked Willow's father. "I'll lead the way.

There are enough golf carts on loan from the hotel for everyone."

When she'd lived at Alec's house, traveling through the hotel property on a cart was the easiest, fastest way to get around. And then when she'd used one to try to outdo Craig, it was even better.

Craig looked at her. "Why don't you drive? It seems appropriate."

"Thanks." After battling it out on the golf course, they'd grown more comfortable about not trying to outdo one another. Ken, Craig's father, had confided he'd never known Craig to be this happy. He'd told her that she'd given Craig a chance to create his own happiness with her after finding it difficult to deal with his mother's horrible death.

Sitting beside Craig in the golf cart, Willow followed her father and the others forming a procession making their way toward Alec's chosen destination.

In the quiet of the early morning, she was aware of the beauty of her surroundings and knew she'd miss living on the luxurious hotel property. It had taken Alec years to build the Desert Sage Inn into the lovely resort it now was. While sections of the land were perfectly landscaped and groomed, other parts of it were allowed to remain natural with sand, stone, cacti, and other local plants that kept the hummingbirds, snakes, small rodents, and other desert creatures happy.

As she continued to follow the line of carts in front of her, Willow realized she'd been to Alec's special spot just once before, when she was a teenager trying to deal with bullying at school. He'd brought her there, and they'd sat together looking out over the valley, saying little for a long time until she was ready to talk. Becoming emotional at the memory, Willow pressed her lips together. Alec had been very good to her. She'd well understood children could be cruel, but after spending time with Alec, talking about many things with him, she understood the problem wasn't hers, but with the bullies. They were the ones who needed to feel better about themselves by tormenting others. He'd helped her realize how special she was and what she wanted for her future.

They left the paved path that encircled the golf course and headed up a dirt road at the very corner of the property, bypassing the private sign posted there. Willow was reminded that the sale of the inn excluded this small part of the landscape and knew from the reading of Alec's will that her father or someone appointed by him would maintain perpetual care of this small plot.

As they rose higher and higher into the foothills, tension grew inside Willow. She remembered the pain on Alec's face whenever he talked about Conchita. Today, the ceremony he'd planned was supposed to take that pain away forever.

Ahead of her, her father pulled off the narrow road and stopped his cart. Willow parked hers beside the others and sat a moment.

"Ready?" Craig asked her softly.

As ready as I'll ever be," she said sadly.

As she got out of the cart, she felt as if she were stepping onto hallowed ground. In a way, it was exactly that. Inside a large rectangle encircled by stone, which Willow knew from her earlier visit was the outline of the house where Alec had lost his wife and daughter, was a lovely desert garden. In the center was a desert willow tree. Assorted flowers and cacti filled the rest of the area. Among the flowers Willow noted a desert lily and an old desert rose, whose twisted trunk was the base of a beautiful flowering plant. A stone bench sat beneath the willow tree whose drooping branches seemed like arms ready to comfort. Noticing the stone statue of a woman holding a baby, tears stung Willow's eyes. Alec was a true romantic. No wonder he'd wanted his ashes scattered here. Conchita and their baby were waiting for him.

Rose walked over to her and held her hand. Lily joined them and the three of them continued to hold hands, brought together by their love and admiration of and gratitude to the man who'd summoned them. As if the others knew how important this moment was to the three of them, they stayed back allowing them this time.

Then her father moved forward and placed the urn containing Alec's ashes next to the statue of mother and child.

"Before we begin, Alec wanted me to say a few words. As some of you may know, one of his favorite books was *The Prophet* by Kahlil Gibran. He asked me to read a couple of passages from it to you." He cleared his throat and began:

"And a woman spoke, saying, "Tell us of Pain."

And he said: Your pain is the breaking of the shell that encloses your understanding.

Even as the stone of the fruit must break, that its heart may stand in the sun, so must you know pain.

And could you keep your heart in wonder at the daily miracles of your life, your pain would not seem less wondrous than your joy;

And you would accept the seasons of your heart, even as you have always accepted the seasons that pass over your fields.

And you would watch with serenity through the winters of your grief.

Much of your pain is self-chosen.

It is the bitter potion by which the physician within you heals your sick self.

Therefore trust the physician, and drink his remedy in silence and tranquility:

For his hand, though heavy and hard, is guided by the tender hand of the Unseen,

And the cup he brings, though it burn your lips, has been fashioned of the clay which the Potter has moistened with His own sacred tears."

Willow listened to her father speak slowly, his words accented by the speech of his homeland. They were sweeter because of it.

"And one more passage," said her father. He paused, took a deep breath, and began to read.

"The timeless in you is aware of life's timelessness. And knows that yesterday is but today's memory and tomorrow is today's dream."

Her father drew a deep breath and let out a long sigh. "Alec Thurston, you will be missed. I loved you like a brother." He dabbed at his eyes with a tissue he pulled from his pants pocket.

Willow's mother went to him, took his hand, and gazed at him sadly. "Alec loved you, too, like he loved all of us here." She faced the group. "Now it's time to leave him with those he loved most of all."

She bent over and lifted the urn from beside the statue.

Her father opened it.

Carefully, her mother scattered some of the ashes around the statue of mother and child, then knelt and patted them into the soft earth surrounding it. Rising, she handed the urn to Rose.

Rose, more vulnerable than she usually allowed herself to show, tearfully scattered more ashes by the statue and spread some around the desert rose tree. When she was through, she handed the urn to Lily.

Lily, quietly sobbing, did her part, leaving ashes by the

figurine and sprinkling a few near the desert lily plant before handing the urn to Willow.

Willow closed her eyes, whispered a prayer of thanks to Alec and scattered ashes by the silent figure of mother and child and spread some more beneath the willow tree. Blinded by tears, she handed the urn to her father, who set it on the ground before walking to his cart and withdrawing a small shovel from the back of it.

Willow watched with the others as her father dug a hole in the ground near the bench. It was only then that she noticed the words formed on the edge of the seat: *A place to sit while waiting for you.*

What a lovely, devoted man he was, Willow thought, remembering him acting as host at the hotel and realizing how lonely he'd been no matter who was with him.

She glanced at Craig and her heart filled with love. She didn't know what the future held, but she promised herself to take a chance on finding the kind of devotion Alec had shown for Conchita. She gazed at Rose standing with Hank and then looked over to Lily and Brian talking quietly together. She wondered if, as Rose had always thought, Alec had brought them together with the men he'd chosen for them. Had he meant for her to be with Craig? The idea brought a smile to her lips.

Craig wrapped an arm around her and drew her close. She lay a head against his chest and heard the strong, steady beat of his heart and felt her breathing slow to match his.

Once her father had covered the urn with the dirt he'd dug up, he set down his shovel and held out his hand to her mother. She stood beside him and signaled the others to join them. They formed a circle around the spot of freshly turned earth and stood silently, each with his or her own thoughts.

Looking up at the blue sky, Willow saw two hawks circling

above them and knew that life would go on for all of them, and that Alec would always be a part of it.

"And so be it," her father said into the silence, as if it was an ending to her prayer.

After the group broke apart, Willow went to Rose and Lily and they embraced one another.

"We did our best for Alec," said Rose quietly. "We should be proud of that."

"And we still have much more to do," Lily said.

"Long live the Desert Flowers," said Willow, smiling at Rose and Lily through her tears.

They returned her smile, sisters of the heart.

Willow turned to Craig.

Staring steadily into her eyes, he whispered, "I love you" and kissed her. Here in this place full of love, she kissed him back. Then, content with the ceremony they'd shared for a man they'd all loved, she accepted the hand Craig offered her, and they walked together into the future.

# # #

Thank you for reading *The Desert Flowers – Willow*. If you enjoyed this book, please help other readers discover it by leaving a review on Amazon, Goodreads, BookBub, or your favorite site. It's such a nice thing to do.

Enjoy an excerpt from my book, *The Desert Flowers – Mistletoe and Holly*, – Book 4 in The Desert Sage Inn Series:

CHAPTER ONE

JUANITA

Filled with excitement on this October day, Juanita Sanchez climbed out of her car and went to greet the three women whom Alec Thurston had named the Desert Flowers—her daughter, Willow, and Rose Macklin Bowers and Lily Weaver Walden. They were standing in front of a building Lily had found for the Juanita's Kitchen project. Now, it awaited her approval.

As she walked toward them, she thought the three Flowers were as pretty as their names. Smart too. As Alec was dying of cancer, he'd requested each of them to come to Palm Desert and use their business skills to help him with the ownership transition of his resort, the Desert Sage Inn, to another hotel company.

"We think this is the one," said Rose, waving her over. The oldest of the Flowers at fifty-two, Rose was the tallest and most flamboyant with her red hair and green eyes.

"I hope you like it," said petite, blonde Lily. "We've pretty much run out of places to look at if we want to get the food kitchen up and running before the holidays."

"I'll know if this feels right," said Juanita. She stared at the sturdy, brown-stone building they were thinking of purchasing. Twice, they'd thought they'd found the right place, had received the mayor's approval for one of them, and then backed out after an owner decided not to sell in one case and after pre-sale inspections were made in another.

Her daughter, Willow, a dark-haired beauty about to get married, looped an arm around her. "We're pretty excited about this one, but if you feel the building isn't right, we won't go ahead with it."

Juanita smiled at her. "If it's right, I'll feel Alec's approval." It was through their inheritances from him that they were able to move forward with this charitable idea—something they knew would please him.

Juanita studied the exterior of the building. It was in fairly good shape and would require just a little dressing up. Attention to the parking lot and landscaping would make a big difference, but could easily be done. Her husband, Pedro, had worked for Alec as a landscaper for years while she'd worked in his kitchen. Rose opened the door and held it for her as Juanita made her way inside.

"I know it's a mess," said Lily behind her, "but I believe the bones of the building are good. Follow me."

Lily led her down a hallway into the back where a kitchen filled with grubby pans and dirty countertops displayed evidence of a previous owner.

"We'll have someone come take a look at expanding the kitchen and tearing down some of the walls out front," said Rose.

"Upstairs, like we talked about for the other places, we'll put an office and a couple of ensuite bedrooms in case staff members need to stay there from time to time," said Willow.

Lily gave her a hopeful smile. "I think this one can work, Juanita."

Juanita walked back to the open front door. Turning and

facing inside, she stood in a ray of sunshine that entered the building in a lemony wash of warmth. Closing her eyes, she let the image of what the Flowers described take shape in her mind. She imagined she could hear the sounds of people working in the kitchen, others coming through the door to get a hot, noonday meal they couldn't afford otherwise.

She opened her eyes and smiled. "This has a good feeling. Let's take a look around."

"Wonderful!" cried Lily, her brown eyes alight with excitement.

"I've already called an inspection company," said Rose. "They'll meet with us this afternoon, if it's agreeable with everyone. I know we want to move quickly on this."

Juanita laughed. It was so like Rose to be ahead of everyone else. "Okay, let's do it."

A couple of months later, Juanita walked into the large front room of the building they were using as a kitchen and dining room and gazed at the fresh, cream-colored paint on the walls. Workmen were busily putting in kitchen appliances, and others were working on building out the service area. The sound of their work was magical. What had started as a dream was coming to fruition.

Interviews for the six-member staff were taking place in a private office at Juanita's church. Several of the candidates had been referred from that source. Their plan was to offer work to those who might not easily find work elsewhere.

Juanita left the building and hurried over to the church. Rose would meet her there. Together they hoped to recommend six people as staff members to Willow and Lily. Then, they'd all decide what they could do to help those individuals.

Outside the office a number of people were sitting in chairs lined up against the wall, including a young woman with a boy.

Rose met her at the door to the private office. "A lot of people have shown up. It looks like we might have a good selection."

"Great." Juanita was counting on Rose to be her usual sensible self because she knew she'd want to hire them all.

Rose opened the door and called off the name of the first person.

Seated in one of the two chairs facing them, the woman answered their questions, fidgeting nervously.

One face became two, then three, then four.

The young woman she'd seen with a boy came into the office with him in tow. Juanita studied his sweet face, his shining eyes. When he looked right at her and grinned, her heart filled.

They quickly learned his mother, Ivy Barrett, was in her early twenties, and her son, Benjy, was seven. She'd left her home in the South at eighteen and had worked in resorts since that time and was now studying for her Associates Degree in the Culinary Management program at the College of the Desert.

As they chatted, Juanita understood that Ivy's background was a painful one. When questioned, Ivy made it plain she had no plans ever to return to the South, that her family didn't want them. She also said they were living in temporary quarters in an apartment that wasn't in a good area, and she was looking for something better for her son. She also explained she had no babysitter which is why she'd brought him to the interview.

During this conversation, Benjy sat with a book, leafing through the pages as if he'd heard this conversation before.

Juanita and Rose probed for more information about Ivy's

ability to handle pressure in a kitchen, oversee staff, and what her thoughts were about the idea behind Juanita's Kitchen.

"I think it's a wonderful program, a much-needed one. From a staffer's point of view, I see no difference between feeding someone in a high-end resort and a crowd in Juanita's Kitchen. I know what it's like to be on the receiving end."

Rose and Juanita exchanged glances of approval.

"We'd very much like you to meet our other two partners. Are you available tomorrow?"

"Yes, I'd like that a lot," said Ivy. "Thank you."

"And feel free to bring Benjy. He's been so good," said Juanita smiling at him.

After phone numbers were exchanged and times agreed upon, Ivy stood. "Come, Benjy. Time to go."

Benjy gave them a little wave. "See y'all tomorrow."

Juanita chuckled. Such a bright little boy. He hadn't missed a word of their conversation.

The next day, Juanita and Rose presented their choice of six candidates to Willow and Lily, and the four of them all agreed they were perfect. Only one man, Isaac Newman, was selected to be part of the staff. The rest were women of varying ages.

As another part of their plan, Juanita and the Flowers spent considerable time to help get three of the women into apartments of their own. Only two didn't require that kind of assistance. Isaac lived with his sister, and Summer Hunter lived with her boyfriend. It was decided that Ivy and Benjy would live in the rooms above the kitchen, and in exchange for keeping watch over the property, Ivy would be given a small bonus.

With growing anticipation, the days crept closer to the grand opening ...

About the Author

A ***USA Today* Best Selling Author**, Judith Keim is a hybrid author who both has a publisher and self-publishes. Ms. Keim writes heart-warming novels about women who face unexpected challenges, meet them with strength, and find love and happiness along the way. Her best-selling books are based, in part, on many of the places she's lived or visited and on the interesting people she's met, creating believable characters and realistic settings her many loyal readers love. Ms. Keim loves to hear from her readers and appreciates their enthusiasm for her stories.

Ms. Keim enjoyed her childhood and young-adult years in Elmira, New York, and now makes her home in Boise, Idaho, with her husband, Peter, and their lovable miniature Dachshund, Wally, and other members of her family.

While growing up, she was drawn to the idea of writing stories from a young age. Books were always present, being read, ready to go back to the library, or about to be discovered. All in her family shared information from the books in general conversation, giving them a wealth of knowledge and vivid imaginations.

"I hope you've enjoyed this book. If you have, please help other readers discover it by leaving a review on Amazon, Bookbub, Goodreads, or the site of your choice. And please check out my other books:

The Hartwell Women Series
The Beach House Hotel Series
The Fat Fridays Group
The Salty Key Inn Series
Seashell Cottage Books
The Chandler Hill Inn Series
The Desert Sage Inn Series
Soul Sisters at Cedar Mountain Lodge
The Sanderling Cove Inn Series
The Lilac Lake Inn Series

"ALL THE BOOKS ARE NOW AVAILABLE IN AUDIO on Audible, iTunes, Findaway, Kobo and Google Play! So fun to have these characters come alive!"

Ms. Keim can be reached at **www.judithkeim.com**

And to like her author page on Facebook and keep up with the news, go to: **https://bit.ly/3acs5Qc**

To receive notices about new books, follow her on Book Bub: **http://bit.ly/2pZBDXq**

And here's a link to where you can sign up for her periodic newsletter! **http://bit.ly/2OQsb7s**

She is also on Twitter @judithkeim, LinkedIn, and Goodreads. Come say hello!

Acknowledgments

It takes a team to make a book. I couldn't do it without my editors, Peter and Lynn, my book cover designer, Lou Harper, my narrator, Angela Dawe, and the support of my writing friends, and most of all, my readers! I'd also like to thank a special member of my Review Team, Cindy Bonner, for her most valuable contribution and comments. Thank you so much for believing I can do this every time!

www.ingramcontent.com/pod-product-compliance
Lightning Source LLC
Chambersburg PA
CBHW061559190726
48288CB00007B/2096

* 9 7 8 1 9 6 2 4 5 2 2 3 6 *